WOMEN IN THE EIGHTEENTH CENTURY

During the eighteenth century the status of 'the sex' was a much debated issue. Definitions of 'women' and 'femininity' played a crucial part in a wider redefinition of social categories and social roles.

The five sections of this anthology represent significant areas within this debate: conduct, sexuality, education, writing, and feminism. The passages are taken from various kinds of texts – instruction manuals, medical literature, works of political and educational theory, literary criticism – which have in common an interest in women specifically, or in gender and sexuality more generally. They demonstrate the construction of a powerful dominant ideology of femininity and explore its effects on ideas of sexuality, women's education, and women's writing. More important still, they illustrate the oppositional voices of early feminists.

By making this material more widely available, *Women in the Eighteenth Century* complements the current upsurge in feminist writing on eighteenth-century literary history. And it extends that revisionary process by offering readers the opportunity to make their own rereadings – of 'literary' texts, of the texts included here, and, through them, of the period as a whole.

WORLD AND WORD SERIES
Edited by Professor Isobel Armstrong, Birkbeck College, University of London

The Victorian Novelist: Social Problems and Social Change
Edited by Kate Flint

Reform and Intellectual Debate in Victorian England
Edited by Barbara Dennis and David Skilton

The Victorian Poet: Poetics and Persona
Edited by Joseph Bristow

Poetry and Ireland Since 1800: A Source Book
Edited by Mark Storey

The Feminist Critique of Language: A Reader
Edited by Deborah Cameron

WOMEN IN THE EIGHTEENTH CENTURY

Constructions of femininity

Edited by
Vivien Jones

London and New York

First published 1990
by Routledge
11 New Fetter Lane, London EC4P 4EE
29 West 35th Street, New York, NY 10001

Reprinted in 1991, 1994

Typeset in 10/12 Baskerville by Saxon Typesetting, Derby
Printed in England by Clays Ltd, St Ives plc.

British Library Cataloguing in Publication Data

Women in the eighteenth century: constructions of
    femininity - (World and Word)
    1. Society Role of Women
    I. Jones, Vivien II. Series
    305.4'2

Library of Congress Cataloging in Publication Data

Also available

ISBN 0-415-03488-4
      0-415-03489-2

GENERAL EDITOR'S PREFACE

The *World and Word* series, as its title implies, is based on the assumption that literary texts cannot be studied in isolation. The series presents to students, mainly of English literature, documents and materials which will enable them to have first-hand experience of some of the writing which forms the context of the literature they read. The aim is to put students in possession of material to which they cannot normally gain access so that they may arrive at an independent understanding of the interrelationships of literary texts with other writing.

There are to be twelve volumes, covering topics from the Middle Ages to the twentieth century. Each volume concentrates on a specific area of thought in a particular period, selecting from religious, philosophical, or scientific works, literary theory or political or social material, according to its chosen topic. The extracts included are substantial in order to enable students themselves to arrive at an understanding of the significance of the material they read and to make responsible historical connections with some precision and independence. The task of compilation itself, of course, predetermines to a great extent the kind of connections and relationships which can be made in a particular period. We all bring our own categories to the work of interpretation. However, each compiler makes clear the grounds on which the choice of material is made, and thus the series encourages the valuable understanding that there can be no single, authoritative account of the relationships between world and word.

Each volume is annotated and indexed and includes a short bibliography and suggestions for further reading. The *World and*

Word series can be used in different teaching contexts, in the students' independent work, in seminar discussion, and on lecture courses.

Isobel Armstrong
Birkbeck College
University of London

CONTENTS

CONTENTS

CONTENTS

CONTENTS

ACKNOWLEDGEMENTS

Various friends and colleagues have contributed to this project in all sorts of direct and indirect ways. I want to thank Lesley Johnson, Rick Jones, Susan Matthews, Mike Rossington, Sally Shuttleworth, and John Whale for their invaluable help and support. I am also grateful to David Fairer, Paul Hammond and Alistair Stead who helped me identify several references, and to the staff of the Brotherton Library, Leeds, particularly Peter Morrish and Malcolm Davies of Special Collections, Chris Sheppard of the Brotherton Collection, and Oliver Pickering who helped me run an ESTC search in the early stages. The anthology developed out of my course at Leeds, 'Eighteenth Century Fiction: A Feminist Perspective', and I want finally to thank the students who have taken the course over the past few years and who helped to make my work on this material so enjoyable.

School of English
University of Leeds
September 1988

INTRODUCTION

In January 1794, this notice of death appeared in the *Morning Chronicle:*

Early on Thursday morning, at Clapham Terrace, after a short illness, Mrs. Barclay, wife of Mr. Robert Barclay, in Southwark. To those who enjoyed the happiness of an intercourse with the numerous and well-ordered family over which she presided, with equal elegance and decorum, it cannot be necessary to describe the excellencies which distinguished her character as a wife, a mother, a mistress, and a friend, amiable, affectionate, upright, and humane. Born to affluence, and endeared to her nearest connections early in life, by an uncommon sweetness of disposition, and a person singularly lovely; instead of launching into the common amusements and dissipation of the age, her mind was early imbued with sentiments that regarded the serious and important duties of life; her conduct, regulated by these sentiments, gave a distinction to her character, as well in the sedulous care and education of her children, twelve of whom survive her, as in the discharge of the social and domestic duties, which were marked with acts of tenderness and benevolence. Such excellence departs not without tears of friendship; what then must be the feelings of her tender, but mournful offspring, of an affectionate, but afflicted husband! to whom the deceased was endeared by every consideration that a constant attachment, and a continued scene of domestic felicity can suggest.[1]

1

How do we read this short and apparently straightforward text? At first glance, it is simply a loving memorial to a particular, and particularly virtuous, woman, an individual example which gives us a glimpse into the life lived by women of her class at the end of the eighteenth century. But the account is strangely generalized. Mrs Barclay's family and friends remember 'the excellencies which distinguished her character' in terms which actually depict her as a characterless paragon, a representative of her sex. Apart from the daunting detail of her twelve or more children, the portrait could have come from a book of moral instruction or a work of didactic fiction, so exactly does it conform to a dominant eighteenth-century ideal of femininity. The apparently idiosyncratic detail of her preference for 'the serious and important duties of life' over 'the common amusements and dissipation of the age', for example, is a commonplace of didactic literature: Mrs Barclay is subsumed by 'Mrs Barclay', a character in a conventional moral narrative constructed for public consumption. In other words, what we are faced with here is not a factual account, but a representation; not actuality but ideology, a distinction which has important implications for the way we use texts which, like this obituary and many of the texts in this anthology, appear to give us accurate documentary evidence about a historical period.

To read the obituary in this way is not to accuse the writer of conscious falsification – far from it. The 'truth' or otherwise of the account is unverifiable and irrelevant, not simply because Mrs Barclay survives for modern readers only through her obituary, but because the admiration of Mrs Barclay's relatives, however sincerely felt, would necessarily be experienced and articulated in terms of the established images and expectations of middle-class womanhood available in the culture of the time. Putting Mrs Barclay beside a very different kind of text might help to clarify the point. The following passage, from Edmund Burke's *Philosophical Enquiry into the Origin of our Ideas of the Sublime and the Beautiful* (1757), is from the section on 'How far the idea of BEAUTY may be applied to the qualities of the MIND':

Those virtues which cause admiration, and are of the sublimer kind, produce terror rather than love. Such as fortitude, justice, wisdom, and the like. Never was any man amiable by force of these qualities. Those which engage our hearts, which impress us with a sense of loveliness, are the softer virtues; easiness of temper, compassion, kindness and liberality; though certainly those latter are of less immediate and momentous concern to society, and of less dignity. But it is for that reason that they are so amiable. The great virtues turn principally on dangers, punishments, and troubles, and are exercised rather in preventing the worst mischiefs, than in dispensing favours; and are therefore not lovely, though highly venerable. The subordinate turn on reliefs, gratifications, and indulgences; and are therefore more lovely, though inferior in dignity. Those persons who creep into the hearts of most people, who are chosen as the companions of their softer hours, and their reliefs from care and anxiety, are never persons of shining qualities, nor strong virtues. . . . To draw things closer to our first and most natural feelings, I will add a remark made upon reading this section by an ingenious friend. The authority of a father, so useful to our well-being, and so justly venerable upon all accounts, hinders us from having that entire love for him that we have for our mothers, where the parental authority is almost melted down into the mother's fondness and indulgence. But we generally have a great love for our grandfathers, in whom this authority is removed a degree from us, and where the weakness of age mellows it into something of a feminine partiality.[2]

Burke's *Enquiry*, an influential work on aesthetic theory, is not overtly about women at all, but cultural assumptions about gender difference operate here as clearly as in Mrs Barclay's obituary. His categorization of mental attributes in terms of a comparison between the 'softer virtues' and those of the 'sublimer kind' depends on a distinction between 'feminine' and 'masculine' qualities. Softness is opposed to strength, amiability to dignity, nurture to authority, and so on, and it comes as no surprise when the implicit gendering of these oppositions is made explicit in the comparison between 'the mother's fondness and indulgence' and the 'authority of a father', and in the reference to the grandfather's 'feminine partiality'.

Burke's view of the feminine/female role is strikingly similar to that in the obituary: Mrs Barclay conforms exactly to Burke's maternal 'softer virtues'. But what Burke's text makes abundantly clear are the social and moral inequalities implicit in his apparently complementary oppositions. The 'softer virtues' become the 'subordinate virtues'; complementarity gives way to hierarchy. In a version of the familiar sexual division of labour, for example, the softer virtues are associated with domesticity, or more generally with the private sphere, and are 'of less immediate and momentous concern to society' than the 'highly venerable' public virtues; and implicit throughout is a moral evaluation of masculine discipline and responsibility over feminine 'gratifications and indulgences'. Perhaps the most telling image is that of the 'persons who creep into the hearts of most people, who are chosen as the companions of their softer hours'. It is very difficult to avoid the conclusion that the 'persons' who insinuate themselves, to be indulged at moments of leisure, are women; as women, they are implicitly excluded as subjects from Burke's text: 'most people' are in fact men.

One of the effects of this male exclusivity is actually to complicate sexual stereotypes by describing the possibility of acceptable 'feminine' behaviour for men (I shall be discussing this phenomenon of 'feminization' later). But this more radical suggestion constantly collapses back into an idea of natural sexual difference which extends from biological function through social roles to mental qualities, an idea to which Mrs Barclay – perhaps literally, certainly textually – was made to conform. In revealing the actual sexual inequalities masked by images of a 'natural' complementarity of gender, and in the implicit conflict between an emergent idea of male femininity and standard binary oppositions, Burke's text makes it clear that, once again, we are dealing not with nature or actuality but with ideology. What it also suggests is the pervasiveness of that ideology: as I pointed out earlier, Burke is not overtly concerned with women or gender, yet his basic categories of sublimity and beauty ultimately reproduce dominant cultural representations of sexual difference. The discourse of femininity in this high cultural text is continuous with that in the humble newspaper obituary – and in many of the passages on women's conduct and education included in the anthology.

In the final text I want to look at here, Mary Wollstonecraft challenges women's subjection to this model of femininity in a passage from her *Vindication of the Rights of Woman* (1792):

> In the middle rank of life . . . men, in their youth, are prepared for professions, and marriage is not considered as the grand feature in their lives; whilst women, on the contrary, have no other scheme to sharpen their faculties. It is not business, extensive plans, or any of the excursive flights of ambition, that engross their attention; no, their thoughts are not employed in rearing such noble structures. . . . In fact, from the education, which they receive from society, the love of pleasure may be said to govern them all; but does this prove that there is a sex in souls? It would be just as rational to declare that the courtiers in France, when a destructive system of despotism had formed their character, were not men, because liberty, virtue, and humanity, were sacrificed to pleasure and vanity. . . .
>
> The same love of pleasure, fostered by the whole tendency of their education, gives a trifling turn to the conduct of women in most circumstances; for instance, they are ever anxious about secondary things; and on the watch for adventures instead of being occupied by duties.

And she goes on to describe women's 'over-exercised sensibility' which means that 'all their thoughts turn on things calculated to excite emotion and feeling, when they should reason'.[3]

Wollstonecraft is very much aware that the characteristics ascribed to women are not natural but constructed, the result of limited education and expectations. According to her argument, to restrict women's social role to marriage is to restrict their minds, to force them into 'over-exercised sensibility' rather than allowing them to exercise their reason. Her position is the opposite of the standard view according to which women's 'softer' mental qualities were of a piece with their function as wives and mothers, evidence of their natural suitability for a domestic role. Wollstonecraft challenges two of the most basic elements in what I have identified as the dominant eighteenth-century ideology of femininity: the natural association between women and the private sphere, domesticity and leisure (Burke's 'softer hours');

and the identification of women with feeling and sensibility rather than reason (Burke's 'softer virtues' and Mrs Barclay's 'uncommon sweetness of disposition').

But the relationship between Wollstonecraft's text and the other two is not just one of straightforward opposition. In some ways, Mrs Barclay's obituary could be read as a refutation of the kinds of libertarian claims being made in the post-revolutionary 1790s by writers like Wollstonecraft – its promotion of a conservative female ideal implicates it in those debates. But at some points the two texts are unexpectedly close: Mrs Barclay's exemplary rejection of 'the common amusements and dissipation of the age' for 'the serious and important duties of life' actually echoes Wollstonecraft's criticism of women's pursuit of pleasure, her concern that women are 'on the watch for adventures instead of being occupied by duties'. Both texts, like Burke, are involved in an implicit argument against luxury, both moral (Burke's 'gratifications and indulgences') and material. For Burke, the threat of undisciplined indulgence is closely identified with the feminine principle; in the obituary, the ideal domestic woman represents a defence against that identification; Wollstonecraft demystifies the ideology which identifies women with dissipation, but in doing so she almost inevitably, it seems, invokes the obituary's morally acceptable, but equally restricting, version of femininity.

I want now to put my readings of these three texts into the context of the anthology as a whole. 'Women in the Eighteenth Century' is an impossibly general title (a similar anthology on 'Men in the Eighteenth Century' would be self-evidently absurd), so I should make a few methodological points about the scope of this collection and ways in which the texts included might be used. The anthology does not, and clearly could not, claim to be in any way comprehensive; nor does it claim to provide a documentary account of women's 'real experience' in the period.[4] Apart from the obvious impossibility of ever fully knowing 'women' in any period, its subject is written culture, and its concern, as I hope my readings have already suggested, is with representation, with 'women' as a culturally defined category which women had to negotiate and to suffer. Given eighteenth-century literacy levels, the focus is therefore predominantly on middle-class discourses of femininity, discourses which restricted middle-class women to the role of domestic consumers and subjected working-class women to a double repression, erasing them culturally and economically by projecting leisured domesticity as universal.

During the eighteenth century, the status of 'the sex' was a much-debated issue. Pope's (in)famous commonplaces in his 'Epistle to a Lady' - 'Most Women have no Characters at all'; 'A Woman's seen in Private life alone'; 'ev'ry Woman is at heart a Rake'[5] – draw from and feed back into a generalizing tradition which extends far beyond satiric discourse. In a period of major political and economic change, definitions of 'women' and 'femininity' played a crucial part in a wider redefinition of social categories and social roles, and the anthology's five sections represent significant areas within this debate about women's nature and status. The passages are taken from all kinds of texts – instruction manuals, medical literature, works of political and educational theory, literary criticism – which have in common an interest in women specifically, or more generally in gender and sexuality. With one or two exceptions (verse satires, and a poem about the lives of rural working-class women), I have not included strictly 'literary' texts since the emphasis is on the discursive context within which literary texts were produced – but at various points the passages included suggest how fluid the boundaries were, particularly in narrative fiction, between what we would describe as 'literary' and other kinds of texts. The five divisions are necessarily somewhat arbitrary: discussions about women's education are often organized in terms of pro and anti-feminist arguments, for example[6]; much conduct literature is centrally concerned with sexuality; and so on. And all the sections of the anthology, like the three texts I have just looked at, provide direct or indirect evidence of the dominant ideology of middle-class femininity which, in its essential features, remains fairly constant throughout the period.

This is not to say, of course, that this ideology was not open to challenge, as Wollstonecraft's rationalist analysis of social conditioning, and all the texts in the final section of the anthology, demonstrate in a very obvious way. Less overtly, like all ideologies, it is internally contradictory: Burke's text, for example, conflated complementarity and hierarchy and, implicitly, women as nurture and comfort and women as (sexual) indulgence. And both the discourse of femininity itself, and those which challenge it, are in constant contention with other discourses of class, politics, religious affiliation, and so on, which produce unexpected alliances and contradictions. Out of this discursive process comes change – both the possibility of challenge and intervention in a dominant ideology, but also of shifts within that ideology which contain those challenges. One of the questions I shall be raising again in specific contexts in the introductions to individual sections is that of how, and to what extent, women were enabled to transgress the constraints of acceptable femininity.

The three texts we have just looked at illustrate something of what I mean. As we saw, Mrs Barclay's orthodox obituary and Wollstonecraft's feminist radicalism had a surprisingly similar emphasis on 'duty', a coincidence of view that can be partly explained in terms of a common class, and very probably religious, position. All three texts at least implicitly involved an opposition between luxury and responsibility, a discourse of moral respectability through which an emergent middle class defined itself against the supposed indulgences of an aristocratic lifestyle, and this common economic/moral vocabulary cuts across and destabilizes the more obvious differences between them.[7] On the other hand, Burke's gender position, his almost unconscious association of women with indulgence, differentiates him again from the other two texts' identification of women with morality.

I explore these kinds of alliances and contradictions in more detail in my introductions to individual sections. Here I want to make a more general methodological point about ways of reading. My analysis of these three short texts has, I hope, offered some suggestions as to how the material collected in the anthology might be approached and used. What I have tried briefly to demonstrate is the way in which detailed comparative analysis of language can give a sense of the dynamic discursive relationships within and between texts, of the various, sometimes contradictory, positions and presuppositions operating in a particular text or at a particular historical moment. In other words, I am suggesting that a reading process already familiar from the study of more purely 'literary' works can be applied to all kinds of texts as an important means of gaining access to the complexities of ideology: in this case, to the ways in which discourses of femininity are constructed across a wide range of writing. The

8

passages included here are *continuous* with the literary texts you read alongside them and should be read in similar ways; they are not, as is sometimes assumed with anthologies of this kind, static 'background', a supply of historical facts to be pillaged in support of 'authentic' readings of literary works.

The passages are arranged chronologically in each section so that change (or lack of it) within particular debates is apparent, and in teaching situations individual sections might be used as the basis of discussion on a particular topic. But the arbitrary juxtapositions of strict chronology can again reveal unexpected ideological alignments and differences. This kind of juxtaposition will of course work across as well as within individual sections, and an alternative basis for discussion would be to compare a selection of passages of similar date from different sections, perhaps using the cross-references suggested in the short introductions as a starting-point.

To read and use the anthology in the way I have just outlined makes it impossible for 'women' to operate as a fixed and knowable category. As I pointed out earlier, 'Men in the Eighteenth Century' would be an absurd title, and though it is strategically important to focus on women in the period, it is equally important not to repeat the asymmetry which defines men in terms of variety and difference and women as a unified object of knowledge. A methodology which pays constant attention to the construction of 'women' in discourse – as well as to the women which that term erases – is crucial if feminism is to avoid simply reproducing, from the opposite perspective, the power relations represented, for example, by Pope's influential generalizations. So though I want to avoid any sense of history or ideology as static, I want also to stress the importance of context – both the historical context governing a text's ideological effects and the modern context in which texts are reappropriated as part of particular historical narratives.

Of course, given this kind of approach, 'the eighteenth century' also ceases to be a static term. Indeed, the viability of anthologies like this one is evidence that it has begun to change, and feminist historians and critics have played a prominent part in recent attempts to construct a 'new eighteenth century'.[8] In traditional social and literary histories, women, like other repressed groups, have been invisible or at best marginal; by reading self-consciously from a different perspective, by privileging different kinds of documents, a new narrative emerges and a different account of power relations and social change in the period can be given. I want to spend the final part of my introduction looking at what this means by focusing briefly on three versions of the eighteenth century, each of which is implicit in this anthology.

The first of these is the familiar socio-economic account of the period covered, punctuated by the revolutions of 1688 and 1789. The 'Glorious Revolution' of 1688 is generally taken to symbolize the ascendancy of Protestant, mercantile interests and a commitment to some form of representational government; at the end of the century, the French Revolution signals the beginning of a different era, epitomizing the debates which threatened the relative economic and political stability established after 1688. This was the period during which England's economy completed the change from a predominantly feudal organization to pre-industrial capitalism, political power shifted correspondingly from an aristocratic base to an alliance between landed and mercantile wealth, and a rapidly expanding middle class gained cultural ascendancy. Crude though this short version of events is, it suggests a framework within which the texts in the anthology can usefully be read.

But what happens to this familiar socio-economic account of eighteenth-century history when women are inserted into it? A different version of the period emerges when we explore the effects of reading, say, the conduct literature addressed to women which proliferated during the eighteenth century. Attention to this kind of evidence suggests that for much of the period, middle-class women were confidently identified as a group in a way that men, differentiated by their public, professional status, were not. In a developing consumer economy to have, or to become, a 'leisured' wife was a measure of social success, underwriting the dependence of that economy on the isolated unit of the nuclear family, serviced by an invisible working class. According to one view, women's role within this model is passively functional. They are the objects of exchange on which male social mobility depends, and conduct literature is similarly reflective, a means of reconciling women to a domestic, deferential position. Recently, a more complex reading of the role of conduct literature has been put forward, and one which is potentially much more enabling for women. In various accounts which correct an earlier emphasis on the public sphere, it has been argued that this dominant ideal of femininity, with its emphasis on morality and feeling (the 'softer virtues' again), was one of the most powerful factors not only in establishing a sense of middle-class identity, but in bringing about a general 'feminization' of culture.[9] The eighteenth-century new man, it is argued, had to win his mistress through a matching display of refined sensibility. In Richardson's *Pamela*, for example, Pamela finally succeeds not simply in capturing but in 'civilizing' Mr B., and the hero of Richardson's final novel, *Sir Charles Grandison*, is an obvious example of a new standard of sensitive masculinity.

The full development of this argument involves women not only as increasingly significant consumers of literature, but women as writers, especially of novels, and a third account of the eighteenth century identifies it as the period during which women began to write in significant numbers. Repeatedly in the texts which follow, women's supposed special capacity for sympathy and feeling is assumed to make them peculiarly fitted for literary pursuits. Their influence on fiction particularly, both as readers and writers, has been seen as a major factor in the novel's emphasis on private experience generally, and, more specifically, in the development of the cult of sensibility which dominated fiction in the later part of the century and which plays a significant part in the emergence of Romanticism.[10]

This kind of revisionary reading is important in its concern not simply to make issues of gender central to historical study but to give women an active role in cultural change. But there are dangers. An eagerness to celebrate women can sometimes, paradoxically, result in a playing down of the power relations which have kept women invisible. Sensibility is a case in point. In stressing the enabling effects of a discourse which privileged 'feminine' qualities, it is easy to forget the surrounding discourses which continued to subordinate fiction to other literary genres and feeling to virtues of, in Burke's terms, 'the sublimer kind'. The history of the reception of women's writing in the period (see Section 4) makes depressing reading as a record of continuing marginalization and containment. The generic uncertainty of Mary Wollstonecraft's *Maria: or, The Wrongs of Woman* (1798), or the shift in Fanny Burney's *Evelina* (1778) from heroine as

independent social satirist to heroine as submissive feminine ideal
are just two examples of women's texts which bear the scars of a
struggle to negotiate dominant ideologies of gender and literary
value. But for women, to write and publish at all was by definition
a transgressive and potentially liberating act, a penetration of the
forbidden public sphere, and the virulence with which fiction was
attacked as a corrupting 'female' genre is telling evidence of its
disruptive potential. Writing women into eighteenth-century
literary history involves scrupulous attention to the details of this
ambivalent position.

This brief survey of some of the issues currently being debated
draws on various important feminist studies which over the past
few years have begun an exciting rewriting of eighteenth-century
literary history.[11] This anthology complements those accounts by
making the kinds of documents they use more widely available.
And in doing so it extends the revisionary process by offering you
the opportunity to make your own rereadings – of 'literary' texts,
of the texts included here, and of the histories through which
they were constructed and, in their turn, help(ed) construct.

Notes

1 *Morning Chronicle*, 6 January 1794.
2 Edmund Burke, *A Philosophical Enquiry into the Origin of our Ideas of the
  Sublime and the Beautiful*, 1757, ed. J.T. Boulton (London: Routledge
  & Kegan Paul, 1958), pp. 110-11.
3 Mary Wollstonecraft, *A Vindication of the Rights of Woman* 1792, ed.
  Miriam Brody Kramnick (Harmondsworth: Penguin, 1975), pp.
  150-2.
4 In that sense, it complements Bridget Hill's very useful collection
  Eighteenth Century Women: An Anthology (London: Allen & Unwin,
  1984) which is socio-historical in method.
5 Pope, 'Epistle to a Lady' (1735), ll. 2, 200, 216.
6 For a discussion of the problems of using the term 'feminist' in an
  eighteenth-century context, see my introduction to Section 5.
7 For a full discussion of anti-luxury discourses, see Stephen Copley's
  volume in this series, *Literature and the Social Order in Eighteenth-
  Century England* (London: Croom Helm, 1984).
8 See Laura Brown and Felicity Nussbaum (eds), *The New Eighteenth
  Century: Theory Politics English Literature* (New York and London:
  Methuen, 1987). The collection brings feminist, Marxist, and new
  historicist methods to bear on eighteenth-century literature.
9 On women's position within a consumer economy, see Terry Lovell,
  Consuming Fiction (London: Verso, 1987). On conduct literature and

the 'feminization' of culture, see: Nancy Armstrong, 'The rise of the domestic woman' in Nancy Armstrong and Leonard Tennenhouse (eds), *The Ideology of Conduct: Essays on Literature and the History of Sexuality* (London and New York: Methuen, 1987); Nancy Armstrong, *Desire and Domestic Fiction: A Political History of the Novel* (Oxford: Oxford University Press, 1987); Sylvana Tomaselli, 'The Enlightenment debate on women', *History Workshop Journal* 19 (1985), pp. 101–24.

10 See Janet Todd, *Sensibility: An Introduction* (London and New York: Methuen, 1986).

11 See, particularly, Ruth Perry, *Women, Letters, and the Novel* (New York: AMS Press, 1980); Mary Poovey, *The Proper Lady and the Woman Writer: Ideology as Style in the Works of Mary Wollstonecraft, Mary Shelley, and Jane Austen* (Chicago: University of Chicago Press, 1984); Jane Spencer, *The Rise of the Woman Novelist* (Oxford: Blackwell, 1986); Terry Castle, *Masquerade and Civilization: The Carnivalesque in Eighteenth-Century English Culture and Fiction* (London: Methuen, 1986). Examples of studies which offer useful but disappointingly descriptive surveys of eighteenth-century women's writing are Katharine Rogers, *Feminism in Eighteenth-Century England* (Brighton: Harvester, 1982); Dale Spender, *Mothers of the Novel* (London: Routledge & Kegan Paul, 1986); Alice Browne, *The Eighteenth Century Feminist Mind* (Brighton: Harvester, 1987).

Textual note

I have preserved eighteenth-century spelling, punctuation, and capitalization throughout. Notes which are part of the original texts are numbered (a), (b), etc.; my own notes are numbered 1, 2, etc. or are included with original notes in square brackets. Line numbers in verse extracts refer to the full text.

1

CONDUCT

The concern of all eighteenth-century 'conduct' manuals for women is how women might create themselves as objects of male desire, but in terms which will contain that desire within the publicly sanctioned form of marriage. They form a significant sub-genre among the hundreds of books and periodicals (the most famous of which is Addison and Steele's *Spectator*) which offered instruction in all areas of social, domestic, and professional behaviour to a rapidly growing readership. Highly popular, they were powerfully instrumental in defining an ideological identity for the emergent middle class. Fictionalized forms of advice literature were also popular, and in this section three examples of these moral narratives (1.2, 1.4, 1.5) are juxtaposed with extracts from more straightforwardly instructional conduct manuals (1.1, 1.2, 1.6). The final extract (1.7) is from a conduct book by Mary Wollstonecraft. Her *Thoughts on the Education of Daughters* (see also 3.4) is an early work, published in 1788, and its inclusion here demonstrates the common ground that frequently exists between moral instruction, educational literature and 'feminist' texts (cf. Sections 3 and 5).

The extracts from conduct manuals span the whole period and are taken from three of the best-known examples of the genre. The first passage (1.1) is from George Savile, Marquis of Halifax's *Advice to a Daughter*, first published in 1688 and reprinted at least fourteen times throughout the eighteenth century. It was eventually superseded, in 1774, by John Gregory's *A Father's Legacy to his Daughters* (1.6) which Mary Wollstonecraft attacks in her *Vindication of the Rights of Woman*. Halifax, Gregory, and Wilkes's

Letter of Genteel and Moral Advice (1.3) have in common the standard eighteenth-century image of the socially desirable woman. In these texts, young women are taught 'natural' femininity in terms of negation and repression – silence, submission, '*abstinence* or *continence*' (Wilkes) – and are offered an illusion of power based on sublimation and passive virtue. The emphases within the three texts vary, however, as their particular ideological context modifies the basic paradigm.

For Halifax, an aristocrat, a Whig, and one of the architects of the Protestant Settlement of 1688, marriage is 'an Establishment, upon which the Order of Humane Society doth so much depend'. The 'rational subjection' demanded of members of the state by a just ruler is extended, by a familiar patriarchal analogy, to women within marriage. (For a feminist appropriation of this political position, see passage 5.2.) Public interest is privileged over individual desire and women are regrettably but inevitably denied any choice of marriage partner. Wilkes and Gregory are later texts, recognizable as part of an emerging middle-class morality which identifies the aristocracy with indulgence and excess. Their ultimate object is still social stability based on the subjection of women within marriage, but the language of affective individualism masks actual power relations by offering women the promise of romantic attachment and personal choice. In Wilkes, the main threat to social stability comes from 'the passions': implicitly sexuality itself, both male and female; explicitly male sexuality in the figure of the (aristocratic) 'licentious rake' who must be subjected to a feminized, virtuous, 'heroic passion' by female chastity. (For two rather different contemporary accounts of sexuality which indicate its importance as a subtext in conduct literature, see 2.6 and 2.7; and for other texts stressing a heroic romantic ideal, see 2.5, 4.13.) In Gregory, we can see a later stage of this process of 'feminization', though the effect is still to deny women any choice of partner. Here, sexuality is figured almost entirely through the language of sensibility: men and women are differentiated by their capacities for feeling, but it is now men rather than women who are capable of forming powerful emotional attachments. Women's unequal role in the marriage market can thus be depicted as the natural consequence of female sensibility, conceived in terms of a capacity for passive

15

rather than active affection. (For comparable accounts of female mental qualities, see 3.7, 3.9.)

The vocabularies and views of female sensibility in Gregory and Wollstonecraft have a lot in common, but Wollstonecraft reads like a pragmatic lament for the standard conduct-book idealization of marriage. In her account, sensibility is a vital source of strength for women suffering the inequalities of the 'married state'.

The fictional texts explore some of the consequences of transgressing the rules of conduct literature. They have obvious points in common with the other texts: the sublimation of sexual desire into spiritual reward in Rowe, Wilkes, and Wollstonecraft; the problem of choice of marriage partner in Richardson, Halifax, and Gregory; the fascination with the rake figure in Rowe, Wilkes, and Haywood. But in the fictionalized accounts moral judgement becomes more overtly problematic. Even Rowe's static letters offer possibilities for fantasy and their unfinished narrative structure invites speculation about the permanence of the writers' moral resolve. In Richardson, the multiple voices which were to develop into *Pamela* and, supremely, *Clarissa* undermine the possibility of a fixed moral message. And in Haywood, the classic narrative of sexual vulnerability (cf. 2.3, 2.9, 4.7) overtly questions the heroine's assumption of guilt and, at a more troubling level, disrupts the asexual ideology of the family through the rake/brother identification.

The generic and ideological boundaries between narrative fiction and various forms of conduct literature were very fluid, particularly at the beginning of the period. There is a clear continuity between the literature of moral instruction written in letter form included here, the more explicitly fictional letters of Rowe and Richardson, and eighteenth century novels. In spite of the mistrust of novels which abounds in conduct manuals (see Wilkes, Gregory and Wollstonecraft, and cf. 3.1, 4.13), to suggest a rigid distinction between their moral clarity and the ambiguities of fiction is too simple. The warnings against romantic fiction in Wilkes and Gregory are oddly redundant given their own implicit narratives of triumphant female virtue; and their fears that novels over-excite women's imaginations sit strangely beside their own depictions of courtship as a state of high sexual tension. Such depictions stimulate and empower the desire they seek to deny. A product of the same ideological moment, conduct literature enacts the same potentially liberating contradictions as the novels against which it is so often seen as static 'background'.

1.1 George Savile, Marquis of Halifax, from *The Lady's New Year's Gift: or, Advice to a Daughter*, 1688

'Introduction'

Dear Daughter,

I Find, that even our most pleasing Thoughts *will* be unquiet; they *will* be in motion; and the *Mind* can have no rest whilst it is possess'd by a darling Passion. *You* are at present the chief Object of my *Care*, as well as of my *Kindness*, which sometimes throweth me into *Visions* of your being happy in the World, that are better suited to my partial *Wishes*, than to my reasonable *Hopes* for you. At other times, when my *Fears* prevail, I shrink as if I was struck, at the Prospect of *Danger*, to which a young Woman must be expos'd. But how much the more *Lively*, so much the more *Liable* you are to be hurt; as the finest Plants are the soonest nipped by the *Frost*. Whilst you are playing full of Innocence, the spitefull World will bite, except you are guarded by your *Caution*. Want of *Care* therefore, my dear Child, is never to be excus'd; since, as to *this* World, it hath the same effect as want of *Vertue*. Such an early sprouting Wit requireth so much the more to be sheltred by some *Rules*, like something strew'd on tender Flowers to preserve them from being blasted. You must take it well to be prun'd by so kind a Hand as that of a *Father*. There may be some bitterness in meer Obedience: The natural Love of *Liberty* may help to make the Commands of a Parent harder to go down: Some inward resistance there will be, where *Power* and not *Choice* maketh us move. But when a *Father* layeth aside his Authority, and persuadeth only by his Kindness, you will never answer it to Good Nature, if it hath not weight with you.

'Husband'

It is one of the *Disadvantages* belonging to your *Sex*, that young Women are seldom permitted to make their own *Choice;* their

Friends Care and Experience are thought safer Guides to them, than their own *Fancies;* and their *Modesty* often forbiddeth them to refuse when their Parents recommend, though their *inward Consent* may not entirely go along with it. In this case there remaineth nothing for them to do, but to endeavour to make that easie which falleth to their *Lot*, and by a wise use of every thing they may dislike in a *Husband*, turn that by degrees to be very supportable, which, if neglected, might in time beget an *Aversion*.

You must lay it down for a Foundation in general, That there is *Inequality* in the *Sexes*, and that for the better Oeconomy of the World, the *Men*, who were to be the Lawgivers, had the larger share of *Reason* bestow'd upon them; by which means your Sex is the better prepar'd for the *Compliance* that is necessary for the better performance of those *Duties* which seem to be most properly assigned to it. This looks a little uncourtly at the first appearance; but upon Examination it will be found, that *Nature* is so far from being unjust to you, that she is partial on your side. She hath made you such large *Amends* by other Advantages, for the seeming *Injustice* of the first Distribution, that the Right of Complaining is come over to our Sex. You have it in your power not only to free your selves, but to subdue your Masters, and without violence throw both their *Natural* and *Legal Authority* at your Feet. We are made of differing *Tempers*, that our *Defects* may the better be mutually supplied: Your *Sex* wanteth our *Reason* for your *Conduct*, and our *Strength* for your *Protection: Ours* wanteth your *Gentleness* to soften, and to entertain us. The first part of our Life is a good deal subjected to you in the *Nursery*, where you Reign without Competition, and by that means have the advantage of giving the first *Impressions*. Afterwards you have stronger Influences, which, well manag'd, have more force in your behalf, than all our *Privileges* and *Jurisdictions* can pretend to have against you. You have more strength in your *Looks*, than we have in our *Laws*, and more power by your *Tears*, than we have by our *Arguments*.

It is true, that the *Laws* of *Marriage*, run in harsher stile towards your *Sex*. *Obey* is an ungenteel word, and less easie to be digested, by making such an unkind distinction in the Words of the Contract, and so very unsuitable to the excess of *Good Manners*, which generally goes before it. Besides, the *universality* of the Rule seemeth to be a *Grievance*, and it appeareth reasonable, that there might be an *Exemption* for extraordinary Women, from ordinary Rules, to take away the just Exception that lieth against the false measure of *general Equality*.

It may be alledged by the *Counsel* retained by your Sex, that as there is in all other Laws, an Appeal from the *Letter* to the *Equity*, in Cases that require it, it is as reasonable, that some *Court* of a larger *Jurisdiction* might be erected, where some *Wives* might resort and plead *specially*. And in such instances where Nature is so kind, as to raise them above the *level* of their own *Sex*, they might have *Relief*, and obtain a *Mitigation* in their own particular, of a *Sentence* which was given generally against *Woman kind*. The causes of *Separation* are now so very coarse, that few are confident enough to buy their *Liberty* at the price of having their Modesty so exposed. And for *disparity of Minds*, which above all other things requireth a *Remedy*, the *Laws* have made no *provision;* so little refin'd are numbers of Men, by whom they are compil'd. This and a great deal more might be said to give a colour to the Complaint.

But the Answer to it, in short is, That the *Institution* of *Marriage* is too sacred to admit a *Liberty* of *objecting* to it; That the supposition of yours being the weaker *Sex*, having without all doubt a good Foundation, maketh it reasonable to subject it to the *Masculine Dominion;* That no *Rule* can be so *perfect*, as not to admit some *Exceptions;* But the Law presumeth there would be so few found in this Case, who would have a sufficient Right to such a Privilege, that it is safer some *Injustice* should be *conniv'd* at in a very few Instances, than to break into an Establishment, upon which the Order of Humane Society doth so much depend.

You are therefore to make the best of what is *settled* by *Law* and *Custom*, and not vainly imagine, that it will be *changed* for your sake. But that you may not be discouraged, as if you lay under the weight of an *incurable Grievance*, you are to know, that by a *wise* and *dexterous* Conduct, it will be in your power to *relieve* your self from any thing that looketh like a disadvantage in it. For your better direction, I will give a hint of the most ordinary *Causes* of *Dissatisfaction* between Man and Wife, that you may be able by such a *Warning* to live so upon your *Guard*, that when you shall be married, you may know how to *cure* your Husband's *Mistakes*, and to *prevent* your own.

First then, you are to consider, you live in a time which hath rendred some kind of Frailties so habitual, that they lay claim to large *Grains* of *Allowance*. The World in this is somewhat unequal, and our Sex seemeth to play the *Tyrant* in distinguishing *partially* for our selves, by making that in the utmost degree *Criminal* in the *Woman*, which in a Man passeth under a much *gentler Censure*. The Root and the Excuse of this Injustice is the *Preservation* of Families from any *Mixture* which may bring a Blemish to them: And whilst the *Point* of *Honour* continues to be so plac'd, it seems unavoidable to give your *Sex*, the greater share of the Penalty. But if in this it lieth under any *Disadvantage*, you are more than recompens'd, by having the *Honour* of *Families* in your keeping. The Consideration so great a Trust must give you, maketh full amends; and this Power the World hath lodged in you, can hardly fail to restrain the Severity of an *ill* Husband, and to improve the Kindness and Esteem of a *good* one. This being so, remember, That next to the danger of *committing* the Fault your self, the greatest is that of *seeing* it in your *Husband*. Do not seem to look or hear that way: If he is a Man of Sense, he will reclaim himself; the Folly of it, is of it self sufficient to cure him: if he is not so, he will be provok'd, but not reform'd. To expostulate in these Cases, looketh like declaring War, and preparing Reprisals; which to a *thinking Husband* would be a dangerous Reflexion. Besides, it is so coarse a Reason which will be assign'd for a Lady's too great Warmth upon such an occasion, that Modesty no less than Prudence ought to restrain her; since such an undecent Complaint makes a Wife much more ridiculous, than the Injury that provoketh her to it. But it is yet worse, and more unskilful, to *blaze it* in the World, expecting it should rise up in Arms to take her part: Whereas she will find, it can have no other Effect, than that she will be served up in all to be the common Entertainment, till she is rescu'd by some *newer Folly* that cometh upon the Stage, and driveth her away from it. The Impertinence of such Methods is so plain, that it doth not deserve the pains of being laid open. Be assur'd, that in these Cases your *Discretion* and *Silence* will be the most *prevailing Reproof*. An *affected Ignorance*, which is seldom a *Vertue*, is a great one here: And when your *Husband* seeth how unwilling you are to be uneasie, there is no stronger Argument to perswade him not to be unjust to you. Besides, it will naturally make him more *yielding* in other things: And whether it be to *cover* or redeem his *Office*, you may have the most reasonable Ground that can be, of presuming, such a Behaviour will at last entirely convert him. There is nothing so glorious to a *Wife*, as a Victory so gain'd: A Man so reclaim'd is for ever after subjected to her *Vertue;* and her *bearing* for a time, is more than rewarded by a Triumph that will continue as long as her Life. . . .

With all this, that which you are to pray for, is a *Wise Husband*, one that by knowing how to be a *Master*, for that very reason will not let you feel the weight of it; one whose Authority is so soften'd by his Kindness, that it giveth you ease without abridging your *Liberty;* one that will return so much tenderness for your *Just Esteem* of him, that you will never want *power*, though you will seldom care to use it. Such a *Husband* is as much above all the other Kinds of them, as a *rational subjection* to a Prince, great in himself, is to be preferr'd before the disquiet and uneasiness of *Unlimited Liberty*.

'House, Family, and Children'

You must lay before you, *My Dear*, there are degrees of Care to recommend your self to the World in the several parts of your Life. In many things, though the doing them well may raise your *Credit* and *Esteem*, yet the ommission of them would draw no immediate reproach upon you: In others, where your duty is more particularly applyed, the *neglect* of them is amongst those Faults which are not forgiven, and will bring you under a *Censure*, which will be a much heavier thing than the trouble you would avoid. Of this kind is the *Government* of your *House, Family*, and *Children*, which since it is the Province allotted to your Sex, and that the *discharging it well*, will for that reason be expected from you, if you either desert it out of *Laziness*, or manage it ill for *want of skill*, instead of a *Help* you will be an *Incumbrance* to the *Family* where you are placed. . . .

In such a Case, when a *Husband* seeth an empty airy thing sail up and down the House to no kind of purpose, and look as if she came thither only to make a Visit; when he findeth that after her *Emptiness* hath been extreme busie about some very senseless thing, she eats her Breakfast half an hour before Dinner, to be at greater liberty to afflict the *Company* with her *Discourse;* then calleth for her Coach, that she may trouble her Acquaintance, who are already cloy'd with her: And having some *proper Dialogues* ready to display her *Foolish Eloquence* at the top of the Stairs, she setteth out like a Ship out of the Harbour, laden with trifles and cometh back with them: at her return she repeateth to her faithful waiting-Woman, the *Triumphs* of that day's *Impertinence;* then wrap'd up in Flattery and clean Linen, goeth to Bed so satisfied, that it throweth her into pleasant Dreams of her own Felicity. Such a one is seldom serious but with her *Taylor;* her *Children* and Family may now and then have a random thought, but she never taketh aim but at something very Impertinent. I say, when a *Husband,* whose Province is without Doors, and to whom the Oeconomy of the House would be in some degree Indecent, findeth no *Order* nor *Quiet* in his *Family,* meeteth with *Complaints* of all kinds springing from this Root; The *Mistaken Lady,* who thinketh to make *amends* for all this, by having a well-chosen *Petty-Coat,* will at last be convinced of her *Error,* and with grief be forced to undergo the Penalties that belong to those who are wilfully *Insignificant.*

1.2 [Elizabeth Singer Rowe], from *Letters Moral and Entertaining, in Prose and Verse,* 1728; 3rd edn 1735

'To BELINDA, from SILVIA, to inform her of the reasons of her sudden retreat into the country.'

My dear Belinda,
I am indeed got back again
> *To harmless plainwork, and to croaking rooks,*
> *Old fashion'd halls, dull aunts, and godly books.* Mr. POPE[1]
to a view of nature in that simplicity which you rally so agreeably: but 'tis here I have recover'd my peace, and am again grown a reasonable creature; to which those godly books that you seem to have such a notion of, have very much contributed, particularly bishop *Tillotson.*[2]

I see you smile, not in malice, but good nature, at the sober confession, and want of delicacy in the choice of my reading: it diverts you, I know, that I should let *Dryden* and *Otway*[3] lie stupidly by me, and impertinently spend an hour in reading a sermon; that when I am so well at ease in this world, it should ever enter into my head to think of another; and, that in the bloom of eighteen, I should have such a gloomy disposition, as to think myself mortal: and, if you will forgive me, I will own, that I sometimes read the bible, in contempt of all modern refinements, and hope to form my life on that antiquated scheme. These are, I confess, my dear *Belinda*, a very unfashionable set of thoughts, and have nothing in them modish or polite.

I believe you will be very inquisitive to find what has put these odd, these strange unaccountable whimsies into my brain.

'Tis love, (you start – you pity – you pray for me) but 'tis love, a tender hopeless passion, that has had this surprizing effect! 'Tis an absolute despair of being happy in this world, that has put me on endeavours to secure the happiness of the next: Could I have possest the idol of my soul, I had been at rest, and had lost the relish of superior joys.

But mine, with confusion I own it, was a criminal affection forbid by earth and heaven; my bliss was prohibited by laws human and divine. This confession will surprize you, but could you know the severity of my conduct, you would excuse me. I have torn my self from the sight of the lovely youth for ever, though I could have lost the light of the sun with less reluctance. My hasty retreat into the country was free and voluntary; and not, as was thought, the effect of my father's command. I was sincere, heaven is my witness, in my desire to free myself from the criminal passion, and I thought the most certain way to conquest, was by flight.

You know the tour my brother made to *Paris*, brought him acquainted with *Monsieur le Comte de R--*, and when he came into *England*, my brother return'd with his family: I was in town, and waited on *Madame la Comtesse*, who did me the honour to detain me for some time with her.

Monsieur le Comte was one of the handsomest and best bred men in the world, and had as much of the *English* gravity as was agreeable to my own temper, which made me find his conversation very grateful and entertaining; nor had I the least suspicion that there was any hazard in such a harmless satisfaction. I had convers'd in town with as much freedom as a virtuous education allow'd, and kept an equal indifference, without the least inclination to love, or even pretending to hate any mortal man.

The *Comte* was perfectly well-bred, and my vanity made me interpret every little turn of gallantry, as the mark of some peculiar value and innocent friendship he had for me: any other thought would have shock'd my delicacy, and put me on my guard, against the guilty passion I found kindling in my own breast, which, instead of opposing, I indulged as gratitude, and a just sense of merit.

But I was soon sensible of the delusion, and how easily vice betrays an unguarded mind, under the specious disguise of virtue. I found this freedom of conversation would prove fatal to all the peace and innocence of my mind, which had now lost its native calmness, and I began to experience all the fantastick effects of spleen, vapours, caprice; in short, an uneasiness with myself, and every thing else in the world, the charming *Comtesse* herself not excepted.

But this set my guilt before me in its full aggravation. Envy and deceit had till now been strangers to my breast, which made me start at the monstrous forms: every new favour from *Madame la Comtesse* reproach'd me with violating the trust and confidence she had in my truth and virtue, and for having a wish that she had been less beautiful and deserving. The affection and intimacy with which she treated me, gave me an horror for my self, and I was again generous and sincere, and, as I thought, perfectly confirm'd in virtue, 'till the charming *Comte* appear'd, when I found myself jealous, unjust, and perverted to vice in a moment.

However, I disguis'd my folly, from a secret delicacy in point of reputation, and an unaffected sense of honour. I am asham'd to tell you I had a thought that needed a disguise, tho' 'twas tell you I had a thought that needed a disguise, tho' 'twas involuntary and unallow'd: but I was an ill dissembler, and have some reason to believe the real disposition of my heart was perceiv'd by the *Comte*, who, one evening, surpriz'd me reclined on the side of a fountain, repeating these lines.

> *Come blest religion, with thy angel's face,*
> *Dispel this gloom and brighten all the place!*
> *Drive this destructive passion from my breast,*
> *Compose my sorrows, and restore my rest!*
> *Shew me the path the sainted-virgins trod,*
> *Wean me from earth, and raise my soul to God!*
> *No more let guilty love my heart inflame!*

The *Comte* understood *English* perfectly well; but I recover'd myself with as good a grace as I could, and put on more gaiety and assurance than was indeed natural to my disposition; and to conceal my disorder, left him with precipitancy, and return'd to the *Comtesse*, who was in her apartment, reading the story of *Rhetea* in the life of *Cyrus;*[4] she ask'd me, *How I liked it?* The question I am persuaded was accidental, but I answer'd *That I thought it well told.* However, it awaken'd my remorse, and gave me an exquisite sense of the injustice of my secret inclinations.

From this moment I resolved to go back into the country, to conceal and conquer my folly. The tenderness and unaffected concern the *Comtesse* express'd in parting with me, confirm'd my virtue, and gave me a secret confusion for the injustice of having wish'd her less happy. The calmness and sanctity of my soul seem'd to be restor'd, and I had left the place a conqueror, if the *Comte* had not led me to the coach, and by an accidental sight, and a sort of serious air in his face, given my mind a softer turn, and convinc'd me of the vanity of human confidence, and that I had triumph'd without a victory.

But the retirement of the country, and serious reflection, soon freed me from the tumultuous effects of a guilty passion: the scene alter'd with infinite advantage, and all grew peaceful and serene. I am now reconcil'd to my self, and find an ineffable satisfaction in the silent approbation of my own conduct; a satisfaction superior to all the empty applause of the crowd. I reflect with pleasure on the happy change. My soul seems now in its proper situation, and conscious of its dignity, looks above this world for its rest and happiness: I am almost in a state of insensibility, with regard to mortal things, and have fix'd my views on those infinite delights, which will be the certain rewards of virtue.

> *What is there here to fill these vast desires?*
> *Should fancy all her dazling scenes display,*
> *Our wishes unconfin'd would wander still*
> *Beyond the limits of these narrow skies,*
> *In search of boundless and immortal joys.*

Adieu, my dear *Belinda:* As long as I leave you to the quiet possession of the dear town and its dear joys, you will not envy me all that a gay imagination can form of future pleasures. – I have trusted you with the inmost secrets of my soul, and know I can depend upon your fidelity.

I am,

Your unalterable Friend,

SILVIA.

'From HERMINIUS to his Sister, acquainting her with the happy effects of his passion for CLEORA.'

My dear SISTER,

It is with great pleasure I obey your command, in letting you know the disposition of my heart to the charming CLEORA. To one whose thoughts were less refin'd than yours, my discourse would be incredible; but you are a sort of platonick, and may perhaps approve the effects of a generous passion, and give credit to the reformation it has made in my life.

You will forgive me, madam, for being once in the right, when I have dissented from you, since 'tis the only instance I have to boast of: Had I been govern'd by your advice, and fled the fair CLEORA, instead of conversing with her, I might have been an unreform'd libertine: But she set virtue in my view with its most charming advantages, I saw an angel in her form, and heard celestial musick in her voice; she was the messenger of the skies to convert me, I own'd the credentials, and yielded to the heavenly inspiration.

You know, my dear sister, that her dawning beauty had made an impression on my heart before I went to travel.

> *I watch'd the early glories of her eyes,*
> *As men for day-break watch the eastern skies.*

DRYDEN[5]

I left *England* with the flattering hopes of finding her free on my return, and with a full intention to make my addresses to her. While I stay'd at *Rome*, that imperial seat of vice, the only loose amour I had, was with a beautiful *Italian*, who something resembled the matchless CLEORA, who was still the mistress of my reasonable affections.

But how great was the anguish of my soul, when after all my gay expectations, the first news that surpriz'd me at my return was,

26

that she was just married to *Philaret?* the man that of all the world
I would not have hated or injur'd: A man that had every amiable
quality, and was the pride and joy of all his acquaintance: Nor
could I forget some former obligations his popular interest had
laid on me. In this exigence I resolv'd to dispense with the
ceremony of paying my compliments to him, that I might avoid
the sight of his lovely bride; nor did I frequent any publick place
where I was likely to meet her.

But at last the fatal interview came, and in the drawing-room,
sparkling as an angel, I saw the lovely creature. From this
moment I became an apostate to virtue, and secretly renouncing
all the ties of truth and honour, resolv'd with great deliberation to
be a villain. This noble design was the subject of my retir'd
contemplations. With what wild, what impious soliloquies, have I
whisper'd to the groves and streams! wishing the laws of heaven
cancell'd, and the state of nature, in the fiction of a golden age,
real. . . . Such were my secret extravagancies, the entertainments
of my solitary walks: but in the height of my folly heaven did not
entirely abandon me.

I took all handsome opportunities to follow and converse with
the fair CLEORA, a favour she never refused me, if she had, I
should have entertain'd more hopes, than from the manner in
which she treated me. I attended her coach, her chair, haunted
her at publick places, ogled, star'd, sigh'd, and practis'd all the
modern fopperies of love, which she never thought it worth her
while to observe; and to my great mortification, I found I neither
pleas'd, nor molested her. All my dumb eloquence and mute
address was lost on her; she minded it no more, nor, perhaps, so
much, as she would the frolicks of a monkey. I might give myself
what postures and airs I thought most becoming, and act the
indolent, or languishing lover, without interruption; she look'd as
if she had no manner of apprehension what I was doing, or what I
intended. My breath had been as well employ'd, in talking of darts
and flames, to the plants and trees; the jargon was so perfectly
unintelligible to her, that she either answer'd nothing to the
purpose, or turn'd the discourse to some grave moral subject.

And as she had the finest turn of wit, and the most graceful
manner of speaking in the world, every thing she said made an
impression on my soul: every vice on which she set a mark of

infamy, though ever so modish, lost its credit with me; and every virtue, tho' ever so severe, seem'd practicable with her applause.

The manner in which she treated my passion, set me in a very ridiculous light to myself. The vanity appear'd unpardonable, that inspir'd me with the hopes of rivalling the happy man, to whom, in the light of heaven, with her vows she had sincerely given her esteem and tenderest affections. Whatever regard was due to such distinguishing merit as *Philaret's*, she gave him: Nothing could be more soft and engaging than her whole behaviour to him. Her modesty was unaffected, truth and justice appear'd in all her actions: In the gayest bloom of youth, and triumph of beauty, she practis'd the strictest rules of piety. This, join'd to the most gentle disposition, and a genius turn'd to every thing that was beautiful and polite, makes her one of the brightest characters of the age.

A thousand times blest be the heavenly power that kept me back from the ruin I courted, and by the example and conversation of this lovely woman, made me a proselyte to virtue, and guided me to a rational and lasting happiness!

But, my dear sister, this fortunate event shall not encourage me to contemn your advice on any future occasion; and in this instance I know you will forgive,

> *Madam,*
>
> *Your most obedient humble Servant,*
> HERMINIUS.

Notes

1 Slightly misquoted from Pope's 'Epistle to Miss Blount, on her leaving Town, after the Coronation'.
2 John Tillotson (1630–94), latitudinarian Archbishop of Canterbury whose lucid sermons were very popular.
3 Thomas Otway (1652–85), tragedian. Dryden is also identified here primarily as a writer of heroic plays about the conflict between love and duty.
4 One of the idealized female characters in Madeleine de Scudéry's popular heroic romance *Artamène, ou Le Grand Cyrus* (1649–53). Cf. 5.1, note 4.
5 From Dryden's heroic tragedy, *The Indian Emperour* (1667), I.ii.145–6.

1.3   Wetenhall Wilkes, from *A Letter of Genteel and Moral Advice to a Young Lady*, 1740; 8th edn 1766

'A Dissertation on Chastity'

Chastity is the next virtue, that is to fall under your consideration; no charm can supply its place; without it beauty is unlovely, wit is mean and wanton; quality contemptible, and good-breeding worthless. She, who forfeits her chastity, withers by degrees into scorn and contrition; but she, who lives up to its rules, ever flourishes, like a rose in *June*, with all her virgin graces about her – sweet to the sense, and lovely to the eye. Chastity heightens all the virtues, which it accompanies; and sets off every great talent, that human nature can be possessed of. It is not only an ornament, but also a guard to virtue. This is the great point of female honour, and the least slip in a woman's honour, is never to be recovered. This, more than any other virtue, places your sex in the esteem of ours; and invites even those to admire it, who have the baseness to profane it[a]. I therefore recommend it to your approbation, in the minutest circumstances. Chastity is a kind of quick and delicate feeling in the soul, which makes her shrink, and withdraw herself, from every thing that is wanton, or has danger in it. This makes it so great a check to loose thoughts, that I prescribe to you the practice of it in your greatest solitudes, as if the best judges were to see and censure all you do: however, I caution you against an affected modesty; which, instead of exalting your character, would raise a fresh attention of the public, to observe and censure your conduct. The part of virtue may be over-acted. Not daring to laugh at a facetious, innocent jest, is a ridiculous affectation; and hypocrisy, or ill-nature, is often discovered under the disguise. Honest pleasures are not inconsistent with true modesty; but an affected air of coyness and gravity is always suspected. When a young lady is praised for her merit, good mien or beauty, she should not reject such commendations, with an angry look, or a scornful disdain; but receive it with ease and civility, if it be obligingly offered. Rather modestly bear being praised, if you have any right to it, than refuse compliments with a mysterious, scrupulous affectation; and then you will escape the censure of preciseness, or morose virtue; either of which, is the poison of life, and scourge of civil society. Modesty does not prescribe roughness and severity against all, who tell you soft things; who unbosom a violent passion for you; or take any other little freedoms that are not rude. It always acts evenly, and without formality; nor has it any thing wild, or austere in it. It will preserve you against insolent attacks and pathetic addresses; and keep your conscience always clear and calm.

Chastity is a suppression of all irregular desires, voluntary pollutions, sinful concupiscence, and of an immoderate use of all sensual, or carnal pleasures. Its purity consists in *abstinence* or *continence*. The first is properly attributed to virgins and widows, the other to married women. It is the proper office of this virtue, to resist all impure and unclean thoughts; to mortify all unchaste longings, and to avoid all alluring objects. This is a sublime virtue. If wanton dreams be remembered with pleasure, that, which before was involuntary, and therefore innocent, becomes a voluntary and sinful transgression of this virtue. Chastity is so essential and natural to your sex, that every declination from it is a proportionable receding from womanhood. An immodest woman is a kind of monster, distorted from its proper form. Shame is the eldest daughter of a defiled female. The appetites of lust are full of care, and the fruition is folly and repentance. 'The way of the adulterer is hedged with thorns.' 'Know ye not (says St. Paul) that your body is the temple of the Holy Ghost?' This makes the defiling of it the more dangerous; but, as to the actual breach of this lovely virtue, forbid in the seventh commandment, it is, in its own nature, so vile, and throughout the whole book of life, represented in such dreadful lights; threatn'd with such terrible vengeance; punished with such heavy and miraculous judgments; that I shall not take up your time, with a dissertation on a vice, so opposite to your temper, and so much below your thoughts. My present design is to caution you against all levities of dress, carriage, or conversation, that may taint or blemish the purity of the mind. . . . That girl, who endeavours, by the artifice of dress, to attract the admiration, to stir up languishing desires, and to provoke the wanton wishes of her gay beholders, is as guilty of breaking the seventh commandment, as the woman in the *Gospel*, that was taken in the fact. Therefore be not industrious to set out the beauty of your person; but, as I said before, let your dress always resemble the plainness and simplicity of your heart.

'Advice in the Time of Courtship'

As love-addresses are either expected by, or imposed upon all your sex, a few cautions to be used in the time of courtship, may deserve a place among my other precepts. Give me leave upon this occasion to recollect some remarks which I have met with in discourse, and to compare them with what falls under my own observation.

I have heard a lady of nice discernment say, that 'nothing is more dangerous to a female, than the vanity of conquests; and that it is as safe to play with fire, as to dally with gallantry'. That this lady collected the phrase from experience, it would be ungenerous to suspect; but hence it may be inferred, that a young lady conspires against her own safety and honour, who is over free of temper, forward in talking, or fond of being thought witty, in the presence of her admirer. Except wit be tempered with discretion, and ripened by experience; improved by reading, and guarded by judgement; it is the most dangerous companion that can lurk in a female bosom. It softens her sentiments; makes her fond of being politely addressed; curious of her fine speeches; impatient of praise; and exposes her to all the temptations of flattery and deceit. Ladies have great reason to be cautious and watch over themselves; for even to listen to compliments, and gay addresses, may betray them into weakness and indiscretion.

If it be agreeable to see craft repelled by cunning: it must be much more so, to behold the snares of a seducer defeated by the management of innocence. It is as much the province of a licentious rake, to betray the young, the rich, the beautiful, or gay female; as it is the quality of a fox to prey upon poultry: wherefore, if one of these sparks were about drawing her into a compliance with his destructive measures, by pretended civilities, and extraordinary concern for her interest; she ought to consider his proposals in their true light - as a bait, artfully placed to conceal the fatal hook which was designed to lead her into ruin. An honest man, with a moderate share of good sense, may as easily convince a lady of his designs being honourable, and intended for her welfare, as the best master of address and rhetoric, if destitute of sincerity - though he had a head turned for calculation, equal to Sir *Isaac Newton's*, and a tongue as eloquent as that of *Cicero*, or *Demosthenes*. The truth is – great speechers to the fair, in points of so great importance, are either knaves, fops, or very silly fellows. How disappointed is the amorous youth, who, endeavouring to plunder an outside of bloom and beauty, finds a treasure of impenetrable virtue concealed within!

Be careful how you give way to what many ladies call 'an innocent liberty'; for her civility may be taken for an invitation. The double temptation of vanity, and desire, is so prevalent in our sex, that we are apt to interpret every obliging look, gesture, smile, or sentence, of a female we like, to the hopeful side. Therefore, let your deportment forbid without rudeness, and oblige without invitation. We look upon a woman's eyes to be the interpreters of her heart; and we often gather more encouragement from a pleasing glance, than from her softest words. The language of the eyes is very significant.

. . . Opportunities should be avoided as much as possible. Great is the danger, that a female incurs, let her imagine her simplicity and innocence to be ever so invincible, by too much familiarity with a male companion. She that wonders, what people mean by temptations, and thinks herself secure against all attacks, and defies mankind to do their worst; depends too much on her own sufficiency, and may be surprized into weakness and deceit. Whoever is made of flesh and blood, is subject to human frailties; wherefore, it must be much safer to fly from, than to fight with, what the world calls *opportunities*, and religion, *temptations*. Thousands of your sex have been gradually betrayed from innocent freedoms to ruin and infamy; and thousands of our sex, have begun with flatteries, protestations, and endearments; but ended with reproaches, perjury, and perfidiousness. She that considers this, will shun, like death, such baits of guilt and misery, and be very cautious to whom she listens. When a man talks of honourable love, you may with an honest pleasure hear his story; but, if he flies into rapture, calls you an angel, or a goddess; vows to stab himself, like a hero; or to die at your feet, like a slave; he no more than dissembles: or, if you cannot help believing him, only recollect the old phrase 'violent things can never last'.

Tenderness, friendship, and constancy, dressed in a simplicity of expression, recommend themselves by a more native elegance, than violent raptures, extravagant praises, and slavish adoration;

all which perhaps may be no more than a repetition of the same things, said to a hundred of the sex before.

The motions of an honest passion, are regular and lasting; its elegance consists in purity, and its transports are the result of virtue and reason. It never sinks a man into imaginary wretchedness, nor transports him out of himself; nor is there a greater difference between any two things in nature, than between true love, and that romantic passion which pretends to ape it.

Criminal love is not a subject for my present design; but, as curiosity is one of the strongest, and most lasting appetites implanted in us; and, since admiration is one of our most pleasing passions, what a perpetual succession of joy must flow from the springs of untainted love! all the pleasing motions of the soul, rise in the pursuit of this heroic passion, when the party beloved is kind, with discretion and virtue.

'A Comparison drawn between Virginity and Marriage'

The observations I have made upon the constitution, frame, and design of human nature, and upon the different tempers and dispositions inherent to it, have produced the following speculation, upon virginity and marriage.

Virginity, as it is a state, in many respects, free from worldly cares and troubles, furnishes means and opportunities of high advancements in a devout life. I now suppose you are at years of discretion, and fully prepared to be informed, that the very name of *virgin* imports a critical niceness, with respect to virtue, innocence, modesty and decent behaviour: every improper curiosity defiles the character. She that listens, with pleasure, to wanton discourse, defiles her ears; she that speaks it, defiles her tongue; and immodest glances pollute the eyes. As nothing is more clean and spotless, than pure virginity, so the least recession from it is the more discernable. Curiosity, even in paradise, betrayed virtue; but it was gratified at great expence. I join with all persons, in opinion, that she, who lives to be an old maid, against her will, is unfortunate, and therefore not without reason peevish; but, if such of the sex would learn to suppress their desires, the original of their misfortunes would be removed; superannuated virginity, occasioned by necessity or restraint from marriage, is an affliction too severe for any of the fair sex, because in these kingdoms it is a kind of imputed scandal: but where this state results from a free choice – from a pre-engagement to the spiritual bridegroom – from a devotion of heart to heaven – from an humble desire of resisting all human love, then it may properly be called a life of angels. But, as the God of nature has, for wise ends, added desires to the constitution of both sexes; where those desires prevail, it is but convenient, the design of them should be answered in chaste marriage, which is an honourable state, attended with many blessings.

If we take a view of conjugal love in all its native beauties and attractions, we must be persuaded, that the pleasures and advantages of it are preferable to a single state; and that whatever is delightful in human life, is to be enjoyed in greater perfection, in the married condition. If it were not so, the wisest and best of all ages and nations, have consented in an error. This institution was calculated for a constant scene of delight, as much as our being is capable of it; and this state, with the affection suitable to it, is the completest image of heaven we can receive in this life: the greatest pleasures we can enjoy on earth, are the freedoms of conversation with a bosom friend; who, in occasion of joy, will congratulate, and in occurrences of distress or danger will mingle his concern; one, who will divide our cares, and double all our joys. When two have chosen each other, out of all the species, with a design to be each other's mutual comfort and entertainment; while they perform the vows they have made, all the satisfactions of the one must be doubled, because the other partakes of them – all the sorrows of one must be lighten'd, because the other is (as to person) exempt from them[b]. How must the hearts of those rejoice, who see a beautiful and numerous offspring of their own, playing about them, and endeavouring to excel one another, in little innocent sports, to please their parents! What an exalted delight must it be to well-disposed persons – what a comfort must it be to them in their old age, to see a number of reasonable creatures, which they themselves have produced, enjoying the fruits of a virtuous education! What unspeakable pleasure must a virtuous female take, in loving and conversing with the worthy object of her utmost affection; who is faithful and just to all, constant and affectionate to her, with whom she is to tread the paths of life, in a pleasing constant course of love and virtue; to be a partner of whose kindness, and under whose protection she has put herself, till death dissolves their union!

'The Duties of a Married Female'

. . . There is great discretion required, to keep love alive after marriage; and the conversation of a married couple, cannot be agreeable for years together, without an earnest endeavour to please on both sides. If the love of a wife be tempered with a tolerable share of good sense, she will be sure never to have any private views of her own; nor do any thing of consequence, which her husband may possibly dislike, without consulting him. To behave with an obliging air of friendship, and courtesy, towards his relations, and friends, engages the affection of a husband greatly.

The duties of a wife to her husband, in every degree and state of life, can be no less than love, fidelity, and obedience to all his lawful desires, and prudent counsels; so that, according as she is disposed, in herself, to perform these duties, every circumstance of life is to give her pleasure or pain.

The utmost happiness we can hope for in this world, is contentment; and, if we aim at any thing higher, we shall meet with nothing but grief and disappointments. Hence, it reasonably follows, that a wife must direct all her studies, and endeavours, to the attainment of this virtue; before her thoughts can attend to all the softnesses, and endearments, of refined love in the married state. Without this disposition, if she were possessed of all the happiness that is dispersed through the whole world, her life would be uneasy – her pleasures all insipid.

Notes

(a) *Spec.* No. 99. [Addison and Steele, *Spectator*, 99: 'The great Point of Honour in Men is Courage, and in Women Chastity'.]
(b) See *Spectator*, No. 500. [In which a supposed correspondent, 'Philogamus', endorses the *Spectator*'s praise of marriage and cites 'Power or Dominion' and 'having a Multitude of Children' as the two main pleasures it has given to him.]

1.4   Samuel Richardson, from *Familiar Letters on Important Occasions*, 1741

'To a Daughter in a Country Town, who encourages the Address of a Subaltern (a Case too frequent in Country Places)'

Dear Betsy,

I have been under the deepest affliction ever since I heard of your encouraging the addresses of a soldier, whether Serjeant or Corporal, I know not; who happens to quarter next door to your uncle.

What, my dear child, can you propose by such a match? Is his pay sufficient to maintain himself? If it be, will it be sufficient for the support of a family?

Consider, there will be no opportunity for *you* to increase his poor income, but by such means as will be very grating for you to submit to: Will your hands be capable of enduring the fatigues of a washtub, for your maintenance? Or, will following a camp suit your inclinations? Think well of the certain misery that must attend your making such a choice.

Look round at the wives of all his fellow-soldiers, and mark their appearance at their homes, and in public. Is *their* abject condition to be coveted? Do you see any thing desirable in poverty and rags? And, as to the man for whom you must endure all this, he may possibly indeed be possessed of honesty, and a desire to do his best for you, at least you may think so; but is it probable he will? For if he be wise and industrious, how came he to prefer a life so mean and contemptible? If he was bred to any trade, why did he desert it?

Be cautious of pushing yourself into ruin; and, as I am not able to maintain you, and a young family, do not throw yourself upon the uncertain charity of *well-disposed* people; who are already vastly incumbered by the miserable. I hope you will not thus rashly increase the unhappy number of such, but will give due attention to what I have said; for I can have no view but that of discharging the duty of

Your loving Father

'From a Daughter to her Father, pleading for her Sister, who had married without his Consent'

Honour'd Sir,

The kind indulgence you have always shewn to your children, makes me presume to become an advocate for my *sister,* 'tho not for her *fault.* She is very sensible of *that,* and sorry she has offended you; but has great hopes, that Mr. Robinson will prove such a careful and loving husband to her, as may atone for his past wildness, and engage your forgiveness. For all your children are sensible of your paternal kindness, and that you wish their good more for *their* sakes, than *your own.*

This makes it the more wicked to offend so good a father: But, dear sir, be pleased to consider that it now cannot be helped, and that she may be made by your displeasure very miserable in her own choice; and as his faults are owing to the inconsideration of youth, or otherwise it would not have been a very discreditable match, had it had your approbation, I could humbly hope, for my poor sister's sake, that you will be pleased rather to encourage his present good resolutions by your kind favour, than make him despair of a reconciliation, and so perhaps treat her with a negligence, which hitherto she is not apprehensive of: For he is really very fond of her, and I hope will continue so. Yet is she dejected for her fault to you, and wishes, yet dreads, to have your leave to throw herself at your feet, to beg your forgiveness and blessing, which would make the poor dear offender quite happy.

Pardon, sir, my interposing in her favour, in which my husband also joins. She is *my* sister. She is *your* daughter; tho' she has not done so worthily as I wish, to become that character. Be pleased, sir, to forgive her, however; and also forgive me, pleading for her: Who am,

Your ever dutiful Daughter.

'The Father's Answer'

My dear Nanny,

You must believe, that your sister's unadvised marriage, which she must know would be disagreeable to me, gives me no small concern; and yet, I will assure you, that it arises more from my affection for her, than any other consideration. In her education I took all the pains and care my circumstances would admit, and often flattered myself with the hope, that the happy fruits of it would be made [to] appear in her prudent conduct. What she has now done is not *vicious,* but *indiscreet;* for, you must remember, that I have often declared in her hearing, that the wild assertion, of a rake making a good husband, was the most dangerous opinion a young woman could imbibe.

I will not, however, in pity to her, point out the many ills I am afraid will attend her rashness, because *it is done,* and cannot be *helped;* but wish she may be happier than I ever saw a woman who leap'd so fatal a precipice.

Her husband has this morning been with me for her fortune; and it was with much temper I told him, That as all she could hope for was wholly at my disposal, I should disburse it in such a manner as I thought would most contribute to her advantage; and that, as he was a stranger to me, I should choose to know he *deserved* it, before he had power over what I intended to do for her. He bit his lip, and with a hasty step was my humble servant.

Tell the rash girl, that I would not have her to be afflicted by this behaviour in me; for I know it will contribute to her advantage one way or other: If he married her for *her own sake,* she will find no alteration of behaviour from this disappointment: But if he married her only for her *money,* she will soon be glad to find it in my possession rather than his.

Your interposition in her behalf is very *sisterly:* And you see I have not the resentment she might expect. But would to God she had acted with your prudence! For her own sake I wish it. I am
Your loving Father.

1.5   [Eliza Haywood], from *The Female Spectator*, Vol. I, Book I, 1744

But of all who ever suffer'd by their Curiosity or Attachment to this dangerous Diversion [masquerades], the Case of the Innocent *Erminia* was most truly pityable.

This young Lady, and her Brother, were the only Issue of a very happy Marriage, and both shar'd equally the Tenderness of their indulgent Parents. – They were educated in the strictest Rudiments of Piety and Virtue, and had something so innately good in their Dispositions, as made the Practice of those Duties, which to others seem most severe, to them a Pleasure. – The

Family lived in the Country, and came not to *London* but once in two or three Years, and then stay'd but a short Time, 'till the young Gentleman having finish'd his Studies at *Cambridge*, it was thought proper he should see more of the World, than he could possibly do in that retir'd Part. But, fearing he should fall into the Vices of the Age, in case he were left too much to himself, they resolv'd on removing to Town, in order to have him still under their own Eye.

Accordingly a House was taken in a certain Square, and the whole Family came up, and, not to seem particular, were oblig'd to live after the Manner People do in Town: *Erminia* was not now above Sixteen, and (as all new Faces are, if tolerably handsome) was extremely taken Notice of, yet was not her young Heart puff'd up with the least Pride or Vanity; and tho' she had all that Chearfulness which is the inseparable Companion of Innocence and Good-nature, yet did it never transport her so far as to take, or permit, any of those Liberties, which she saw some of her new Acquaintance make no Scruple of.

Soon after their Arrival Winter came on, and wherever either she or her Brother went, nothing was talk'd on but the Masquerade; neither of them had ever seen one, and the Eagerness they observed in others, excited a Curiosity in them. – Their Parents would not oppose the Inclination they express'd, and consented they should go together, but gave their Son a strict Charge to be watchful over his Sister, and never to quit Sight of her 'till he brought her home to them again. – Tho' this was an Entertainment unknown in *England* in their gay Time of Life, and, consequently, they were Strangers to the Methods practised at it, yet having heard somewhat of the Dangers, they repeated over and over the same Injunction to the young Gentleman, who assured them, he would take the same Care as if themselves were present.

Alas! he little knew how impracticable it was to keep his Promise; they were no sooner enter'd, than both were bewilder'd amidst the promiscuous Assembly, – the strange Habits, – the Hurry, – the Confusion quite distracted their Attention. – They kept close to each other, indeed, for some Time, but were soon separated by a Crowd that came rushing between them, some accosting the Brother, others the Sister. – Those who talk'd to them easily found they were Strangers to the Conversation of the

Place, and whispering it about, our young Country Gentry serv'd as Butts for the Company to level all the Arrows of their Wit against.

Erminia had lost her Brother for a considerable Time, and was encompass'd by Persons of both Sexes, whose Mode of Speech was neither pleasing to her, nor did she know how to answer; at last, the Sight of a *Blue Domine*, which was the Habit he went in, revived her, and she ran to the Person who wore it, and catching fast hold of him, – *Dear Brother*, (cry'd she) *let us go home, I have been frighted to Death by those noisy People yonder. – I wonder what Pleasure any body can take in being here*.

The Person she accosted made no Reply; but taking her under the Arm, conducted her out as she had desired, and went with her into a Hackney Coach. Little suspecting the Accident that had befallen her, she attended not to what Orders he gave the Coachman, and, glad to find herself out of a Place which for her had so few Charms, entertain'd her suppos'd Brother with a Repetition of what had been said to her, 'till the Coach stop'd at the Door of a great House: As it was not yet light, she distinguish'd it not from their own, and innocently jump'd out, and was within the Entry before she discover'd her Mistake; but as soon as she did, *Bless me*, (cry'd she) *where have you brought me, Brother?* She follow'd him, however, up Stairs, where he, pulling off his Vizard, discover'd a Face she had never seen before.

Never was Surprize and Terror greater than that which now seiz'd the Heart of this unfortunate young Lady: – She wept, she pray'd, she conjur'd him by every thing that is call'd sacred or worthy of Veneration, to suffer her to depart; but he was one, to whom had she been less Beautiful, her Innocence was a sufficient Charm. – The more averse and shock'd she seem'd at the rude Behaviour with which he immediately began to treat her, the more were his Desires inflam'd, and having her in his Power, and in a House where all her Shrieks and Cries were as unavailing, as her Tears and Entreaties, he satiated, by the most barbarous Force, his base Inclinations, and for a Moment's Joy to himself, was the eternal Ruin of a poor Creature, whose Ignorance of the World, and the Artifices of Mankind, alone had betray'd to him.

The cruel Conquest gain'd, he was at a Loss how to dispose of his Prey; a thousand times she begg'd he would compleat the Villany he had begun, and kill the Wretch he had made; but this was what neither his Safety, nor perhaps his Principle, wicked as he was, would permit him to do. – He easily found she was a Girl of Condition, and doubted not but she had Friends who would revenge the Injury had been done her, could they, by any Means, discover the Author; he therefore, after having in vain endeavour'd to pacify her, and prevail on her to comply with his Desires of holding a secret Correspondence with him, compell'd her to let him bind a Handkerchief over her Eyes, that she might not be able to describe either the House, or Street where she had been abused; then put her into a Hackney Coach, which he order'd to drive into an obscure, dirty Lane, in the *Strand*, near the Water Side, where he made her be set down, and immediately drove away with all the Speed the Horses could make.

She no sooner found herself at Liberty, than she pluck'd the Bandage from her Eyes, – she cast a disconsolate Look about, – she knew not where she was; but the Sight of the Water at some little Distance from her, tempted her more than once, as she has since confess'd, to throw herself into it. – The Precepts of Religion, however, restrain'd her, and she wander'd backwards and forwards for some Time, uncertain what to do; at length she came to a more populous Place, and seeing a Chair, made herself be carried home, tho' with what Agonies of Shame and Grief is easier to imagine than describe.

The young Gentleman, her Brother, had all this Time been in the utmost Distraction; he no sooner miss'd, than he went in search of her round and round the Room, and through all the little Avenues that led to it, describ'd her Habit to the Servants, and ask'd if they had seen such a Lady; but all his Endeavours being fruitless, he ran home, flattering himself, that missing him, she was gone before. – Not finding her there, he flew back again to the *Haymarket*, – made a second Search, a second Enquiry, and that being ineffectual as the first, his Grief and his Despair was beyond all Bounds. – He truly lov'd his Sister, and doubted not but some very unhappy Accident had befallen her; but what involved him yet in greater Horrors, was how he should answer to his Parents his so ill acquitting himself of the Charge they laid on him concerning her. – Dreading their Reproaches, and even yet more the Agonies they would feel at seeing him return without her, he flew about the Streets like one totally depriv'd of Reason, 'till Day being far advanc'd, and every body he met staring at him as a Person whom Drink or Madness had render'd an Object of Derision, Shame, at last, got the better of his Vexations, and he ventur'd to encounter what was more dreadful to him than Death itself.

The anxious Parents could not think of going to their Repose 'till their dear Children were return'd in Safety; they had Apprehensions which they could not account for, none having dared to inform them, that *Erminia* was missing, or that her Brother, many Hours before, had call'd at the Door to ask if she was come, but when they now saw him enter with that confus'd and dejected Air, and found their Daughter was not with him, they both at once cry'd out, in a Transport of mingled Rage and Grief, – *Where is your Sister? – What is become of* Erminia? – *Dare you approach us without her?*

The Condition this poor Youth was in, would be very difficult to express, – he trembled, – hung down his Head, and his flowing Eyes let fall a Shower of Tears upon his Breast, but had not Power to speak, 'till his Father, impatient of knowing even the worst that could befal, commanded him either to repeat what had happen'd, or that Instant leave his Sight for ever. *O Sir,* (then cry'd he) *what can I say, – My Sister is gone, – all my Care in obeying your Commands was vain, and I am wholly ignorant how this Misfortune happen'd.*

Scarce had he spoke these Words, when the ruin'd Maid appear'd. – Father, Mother, Brother, all ran at once to catch her in their Arms, but the Shock of returning to them as she now was render'd, work'd too powerfully on the Weakness of her Spirits, to leave her in a Condition to receive their Embraces, and she fell into a Swoon, in which she continu'd a long Time, tho' they immediately undress'd, put her to Bed, and used all possible Means for her Recovery.

On the return of her Senses, she fell into the most lamentable Complaints, but could not be prevail'd upon, while her Father and Brother were in the Room, to reveal any thing of the Occasion. Her Mother observing their Presence was a Restraint, desir'd them to withdraw, after which, partly by Commands, and partly by Intreaties, but more by mentioning all the Evils that her Imagination could suggest, at last the whole sad Secret was reveal'd.

Never was so disconsolate a Family, and the more so, as they could by no means discover the brutal Author of their Misfortune; the Precautions he had taken render'd all their Search in vain, and when some Days after they prevail'd on *Erminia* to go with them in a Coach almost throughout all *London*, yet could she not point out either the House or Street where her Ravisher had carried her.

To fill the Measure of her Woes, a young Gentleman arriv'd in Town, who long had lov'd, and had the Approbation of her Friends, and for whom she also felt all of that Passion that can inspire a virtuous Mind; he had by some Business been prevented from accompanying the Family in their Removal, but was now come full of the Hopes of having his Desires compleated, by a happy Marriage with the sweet *Erminia*.

Melancholly Reverse of Fate! instead of being receiv'd with open Arms, and that chearful Welcome he had been accustom'd to, and had Reason to expect, the most heavy Gloom appear'd on all the Faces of those he was permitted to see; but *Erminia* no sooner heard of his Arrival, than she shut herself up in her Chamber, and would, by no means, be prevail'd upon to appear before him. – To excuse her Absence, they told him she was indispos'd; but this seem'd all Pretence, because the Freedom with which they had always liv'd together, might very well have allow'd him the Privilege of visiting her in her Chamber. – He complain'd of this Alteration in their Behaviour, and doubted not, at first, but it was occasion'd by the Preference they gave to some new Rival. – The true Reason, however, could not be kept so much a Secret, but that it was whisper'd about, and he soon got a Hint of it. – How sensible a Shock it must give him may easily be conceived; but he got the better of it, and after a very little Reflection, went to her Father, told him the afflicting News he had heard, but withal assur'd him, that as his Love for *Erminia* was chiefly founded on her Virtue, an Act of Force could not be esteem'd any Breach of it, and was still ready to marry her, if she would consent.

This Generosity charm'd the whole Family, but *Erminia* could not think of accepting the Offer; – the more she found him worthy of her Affections in her State of Innocence, the less could she support the Shame of being his, in the Condition she now was. – She told her Parents, that she had taken a firm Resolution never to marry, and begg'd their Permission to retire to an Aunt, who was married to an old Clergyman, and lived in one of the most remote Counties in *England*. Dear as her Presence was, they found something so truly noble in her way of Thinking, that they would not oppose it; and even her Lover, in spite of himself, could not forbear applauding what gave a thousand Daggers to his Heart.

Erminia in a short Time departed for her Country Residence; nothing was ever more mournful than the Leave she took of her Parents and Brother; but not all the Entreaties of her Lover, by Messages and Letters, could gain so far upon her Modesty, as to prevail on her to see him; she sent him, however, a Letter, full of the most tender Acknowledgments of his Love and Generosity, and with this he was oblig'd to be content.

It is not every Woman would have resented such an Injury in the same Manner with *Erminia;* and it must be confess'd, that her Notions of Honour and Virtue had somewhat superlatively delicate in them. – What a Loss then to the World to be depriv'd of so amiable an Example, as she would have doubtless prov'd, of conjugal Truth, Tenderness, and a strict Observance to every Duty the Men so much desire to find in her they make a Partner for Life. How can her brutal Ravisher reflect, as it is impossible but he sometimes must, on the Mischiefs he has occasion'd without Horrors, such as must render Life a Burthen! – Tho' he yet is hid in Darkness, and left no Traces by which the Publick may point the Villain out, and treat him with the Abhorrence he deserves, his own Thoughts must surely be the Avengers of his Crime, and make him more truly wretched than any exterior Punishment could do.

1.6   John Gregory, from *A Father's Legacy to his Daughters*, 1774

'Introduction'

. . . You will all remember your father's fondness, when perhaps every other circumstance relating to him is forgotten. This remembrance, I hope, will induce you to give a serious attention to the advices I am now going to leave with you. – I can request this attention with the greater confidence, as my sentiments on the most interesting points that regard life and manners, were entirely correspondent to your mother's, whose judgment and taste I trusted much more than my own.

You must expect that the advices which I shall give you will be very imperfect, as there are many nameless delicacies, in female manners, of which none but a woman can judge. – You will have one advantage by attending to what I am going to leave with you; you will hear, at least for once in your lives, the genuine sentiments of a man who has no interest in flattering or deceiving you. – I shall throw my reflections together without any studied order, and shall only, to avoid confusion, range them under a few general heads.

You will see, in a little Treatise of mine just published,[1] in what an honourable point of view I have considered your sex; not as domestic drudges, or the slaves of our pleasures, but as our companions and equals; as designed to soften our hearts and polish our manners; and as Thomson finely says,

To raise the virtues, animate the bliss,
And sweeten all the toils of human life.[2]

I shall not repeat what I have there said on this subject, and shall only observe, that from the view I have given of your natural character and place in society, there arises a certain propriety of conduct peculiar to your sex. It is this peculiar propriety of female manners of which I intend to give you my sentiments, without touching on those general rules of conduct by which men and women are equally bound.

While I explain to you that system of conduct which I think will tend most to your honour and happiness, I shall, at the same time, endeavour to point out those virtues and accomplishments which render you most respectable and most amiable in the eyes of my own sex.

'Conduct and Behaviour'

One of the chief beauties in a female character, is that modest reserve, that retiring delicacy, which avoids the public eye, and is disconcerted even at the gaze of admiration. – I do not wish you to be insensible to applause. If you were, you must become, if not worse, at least less amiable women. But you may be dazzled by that admiration, which yet rejoices your hearts.

When a girl ceases to blush, she has lost the most powerful charm of beauty. That extreme sensibility which it indicates, may be a weakness and incumbrance in our sex, as I have too often felt; but in yours it is peculiarly engaging. Pedants, who think themselves philosophers, ask why a woman should blush when she is conscious of no crime. It is a sufficient answer, that Nature has made you to blush when you are guilty of no fault, and has forced us to love you because you do so. – Blushing is so far from being necessarily an attendant on guilt, that it is the usual companion of innocence.

This modesty, which I think so essential to your sex, will naturally dispose you to be rather silent in company, especially in a large one. – People of sense and discernment will never mistake such silence for dullness. One may take a share in conversation without uttering a syllable. The expression in the countenance shews it, and this never escapes an observing eye. . . .

Be even cautious in displaying your good sense. It will be thought you assume a superiority over the rest of the company. – But if you happen to have any learning, keep it a profound secret, especially from the men, who generally look with a jealous and malignant eye on a woman of great parts, and a cultivated understanding.

A man of real genius and candour is far superior to this meanness. But such a one will seldom fall in your way; and if by accident he should, do not be anxious to shew the full extent of your knowledge. If he has any opportunities of seeing you, he will soon discover it himself; and if you have any advantages of person or manner, and keep your own secret, he will probably give you credit for a great deal more than you possess. – The art of pleasing in conversation consists in making the company pleased with themselves. You will more readily hear than talk yourselves into their good graces.

Beware of detraction, especially where your own sex are concerned. You are generally accused of being particularly addicted to this vice. – I think unjustly. – Men are fully as guilty of it when their interests interfere. – As your interests more frequently clash, and as your feelings are quicker than ours, your temptations to it are more frequent. For this reason, be particularly tender of the reputation of your own sex, especially when they happen to rival you in our regards. We look on this as the strongest proof of dignity and true greatness of mind.

Shew a compassionate sympathy to unfortunate women, especially to those who are rendered so by the villainy of men. Indulge a secret pleasure, I may say pride, in being the friends and refuge of the unhappy, but without the vanity of shewing it.

Consider every species of indelicacy in conversation, as shameful in itself, and as highly disgusting to us. All double entendre is of this sort. – The dissoluteness of men's education allows them to be diverted with a kind of wit, which yet they have delicacy enough to be shocked at, when it comes from your mouths, or even when you hear it without pain and contempt. – Virgin purity is of that delicate nature, that it cannot hear certain things without contamination. It is always in your power to avoid these. No man, but a brute or a fool, will insult a woman with conversation which he sees gives her pain; nor will he dare to do it, if she resent the injury with a becoming spirit. – There is a dignity in conscious virtue which is able to awe the most shameless and abandoned of men.

You will be reproached perhaps with prudery. By prudery is usually meant an affectation of delicacy. Now I do not wish you to affect delicacy; I wish you to possess it. At any rate, it is better to run the risk of being thought ridiculous than disgusting.

The men will complain of your reserve. They will assure you that a franker behaviour would make you more amiable. But trust me, they are not sincere when they tell you so. – I acknowledge, that on some occasions it might render you more agreeable as companions, but it would make you less amiable as women: An important distinction, which many of your sex are not aware of. – After all, I wish you to have great ease and opennness in your conversation. I only point out some considerations which ought to regulate your behaviour in that respect.

'Amusements'

Dress is an important article in female life. The love of dress is natural to you, and therefore it is proper and reasonable. Good sense will regulate your expence in it, and good taste will direct you to dress in such a way as to conceal any blemishes, and set off your beauties, if you have any, to the greatest advantage. But much delicacy and judgment are required in the application of this rule. A fine woman shews her charms to most advantage, when she seems most to conceal them. The finest bloom in nature is not so fine as what imagination forms. The most perfect elegance of dress appears always the most easy, and the least studied.

Do not confine your attention to your public appearances. Accustom yourselves to an habitual neatness, so that in the most careless undress, in your most unguarded hours, you may have no reason to be ashamed of your appearance. – You will not easily believe how much we consider your dress expressive of your characters. Vanity, levity, slovenliness, folly appear through it. An elegant simplicity is an equal proof of taste and delicacy.

In dancing, the principal points you are to attend to are ease and grace. I would have you dance with spirit; but never allow yourselves to be so far transported with mirth, as to forget the delicacy of your sex. – Many a girl dancing in the gaiety and innocence of her heart, is thought to discover a spirit she little dreams of.

I know no entertainment that gives such pleasure to any person of sentiment or humour, as the theatre. – But I am sorry to say, there are few English comedies a lady can see, without a shock to delicacy. You will not readily suspect the comments gentlemen make on your behaviour on such occasions. Men are often best acquainted with the most worthless of your sex, and from them too readily form a judgment of the rest. A virtuous girl often hears very indelicate things with a countenance no wise embarrassed, because in truth she does not understand them. Yet this is, most ungenerously, ascribed to that command of features, and that ready presence of mind, which you are thought to possess in a degree far beyond us; or, by still more malignant observers, it is ascribed to hardened effrontery.

Sometimes a girl laughs with all the simplicity of unsuspecting innocence, for no other reason but being infected with other people's laughing: she is then believed to know more than she should do. – If she does happen to understand an improper thing, she suffers a very complicated distress: she feels her modesty hurt in the most sensible manner, and at the same time is ashamed of appearing conscious of the injury. The only way to avoid these inconveniences, is never to go to a play that is particularly offensive to delicacy. – Tragedy subjects you to no such distress. – Its sorrows will soften and ennoble your hearts.

'Friendship, Love, Marriage'

... The temper and dispositions of the heart in your sex make you enter more readily and warmly into friendships than men. Your natural propensity to it is so strong, that you often run into intimacies which you soon have sufficient cause to repent of; and this makes your friendships so very fluctuating.

Another great obstacle to the sincerity as well as steadiness of your friendships is the great clashing of your interests in the pursuits of love, ambition, or vanity. For these reasons, it would appear at first view more eligible for you to contract your friendships with the men. Among other obvious advantages of an easy intercourse between the two sexes, it occasions an emulation and exertion in each to excel and be agreeable: hence their respective excellencies are mutually communicated and blended. As their interests in no degree interfere, there can be no foundation for jealousy or suspicion of rivalship. The friendship of a man for a woman is always blended with a tenderness, which he never feels for one of his own sex, even where love is in no degree concerned. Besides, we are conscious of a natural title you have to our protection and good offices, and therefore we feel an additional obligation of honour to serve you, and to observe an inviolable secrecy, whenever you confide in us.

But apply these observations with great caution. Thousands of women of the best hearts and finest parts have been ruined by men who approach them under the specious name of friendship. . . .

There is a different species of men whom you may like as agreeable companions, men of worth, taste, and genius, whose conversation, in some respects, may be superior to what you generally meet with among your own sex. It will be foolish in you to deprive yourselves of an useful and agreeable acquaintance, merely because idle people say he is your lover. Such a man may like your company, without having any design on your person.

People whose sentiments, and particularly whose tastes, corres-pond, naturally like to associate together, although neither of them have the most distant view of any further connection. But as this similarity of minds often gives rise to a more tender attachment than friendship, it will be prudent to keep a watchful eye over yourselves, lest your hearts become too far engaged before you are aware of it. At the same time, I do not think that your sex, at least in this part of the world, have much of that sensibility which disposes to such attachments. What is commonly called love among you is rather gratitude, and a partiality to the man who prefers you to the rest of your sex; and such a man you often marry, with little of either personal esteem or affection. Indeed, without an unusual share of natural sensibility, and very peculiar good fortune, a woman in this country has very little probability of marrying for love.

It is a maxim laid down among you, and a very prudent one it is, That love is not to begin on your part, but is entirely to be the consequence of our attachment to you. Now, supposing a woman to have sense and taste, she will not find many men to whom she can possibly be supposed to bear any considerable share of esteem. Among these few, it is a very great chance if any of them distinguishes her particularly. Love, at least with us, is exceedingly capricious, and will not always fix where reason says it should. But supposing one of them should become particularly attached to her, it is still extremely improbable that he should be the man in the world her heart most approved of.

As, therefore, Nature has not given you that unlimited range in your choice which we enjoy, she has wisely and benevolently assigned to you a greater flexibility of taste on this subject. Some agreeable qualities recommend a gentleman to your common good liking and friendship. In the course of his acquaintance, he contracts an attachment to you. When you perceive it, it excites your gratitude; this gratitude rises into a preference, and this preference perhaps at last advances to some degree of attachment, especially if it meets with crosses and difficulties; for these, and a state of suspense, are very great incitements to attachment, and are the food of love in both sexes. If attachment was not excited in your sex in this manner, there is not one of a million of you that could ever marry with any degree of love.

A man of taste and delicacy marries a woman because he loves her more than any other. A woman of equal taste and delicacy marries him because she esteems him, and because he gives her that preference. But if a man unfortunately becomes attached to a woman whose heart is secretly pre-engaged, his attachment, instead of obtaining a suitable return, is particularly offensive; and if he persists to teaze her, he makes himself equally the object of her scorn and aversion.

The effects of love among men are diversified by their different tempers. An artful man may counterfeit every one of them so as easily to impose on a young girl of an open, generous, and feeling heart, if she is not extremely on her guard. The finest parts in such a girl may not always prove sufficient for her security. The dark and crooked paths of cunning are unsearchable, and inconceivable to an honourable and elevated mind.

The following, I apprehend, are the most genuine effects of an honourable passion among the men, and the most difficult to counterfeit. A man of delicacy often betrays his passion by his too great anxiety to conceal it, especially if he has little hopes of success. True love, in all its stages, seeks concealment, and never expects success. It renders a man not only respectful, but timid to the highest degree in his behaviour to the woman he loves. To conceal the awe he stands in of her, he may sometimes affect pleasantry, but it sits aukwardly on him, and he quickly relapses into seriousness, if not into dulness. He magnifies all her real perfections in his imagination, and is either blind to her failings, or converts them into beauties. Like a person conscious of guilt, he is jealous that every eye observes him; and to avoid this, he shuns all the little observances of common gallantry.

His heart and his character will be improved in every respect by his attachment. His manners will become more gentle and his conversation more agreeable; but diffidence and embarrassment will always make him appear to disadvantage in the company of his mistress. If the fascination continue long, it will totally depress his spirit, and extinguish every active, vigorous, and manly principle of his mind. You will find this subject beautifully and pathetically painted in Thomson's Spring.

When you observe in a gentleman's behaviour these marks which I have described above, reflect seriously on what you are to do. If his attachment is agreeable to you, I leave you to do as nature, good sense, and delicacy shall direct you. If you love him, let me advise you never to discover to him the full extent of your love, no not although you marry him. That sufficiently shews your preference, which is all he is intitled to know. If he has delicacy, he will ask for no stronger proof of your affection, for your sake; if he has sense, he will not ask it for his own. This is an unpleasant truth, but it is my duty to let you know it. Violent love cannot subsist, at least cannot be expressed, for any time together, on both sides; otherwise the certain consequence, however concealed, is satiety and disgust. Nature in this case has laid the reserve on you.

. . .

In short, I am of opinion, that a married state, if entered into from proper motives of esteem and affection, will be the happiest for yourselves, make you most respectable in the eyes of the world, and the most useful members of society. But I confess I am not enough of a patriot to wish you to marry for the good of the public. I wish you to marry for no other reason but to make yourselves happier. When I am so particular in my advices about your conduct, I own my heart beats with the fond hope of making you worthy the attachment of men who will deserve you, and be sensible of your merits.

. . .

There is one advice I shall leave you, to which I beg your particular attention. Before your affections come to be the least engaged to any man, examine your tempers, your tastes, and your hearts, very severely, and settle in your own minds, what are the requisites to your happiness in a married state; and as it is almost impossible that you should get every thing you wish, come to a steady determination what you are to consider as essential, and what may be sacrificed.

If you have hearts disposed by nature for love and friendship, and possess those feelings which enable you to enter into all the refinements and delicacies of these attachments, consider well, for Heaven's sake, and as you value your future happiness, before you give them any indulgence. If you have the misfortune (for a very great misfortune it commonly is to your sex) to have such a temper and such sentiments deeply rooted in you, if you have spirit and resolution to resist the solicitations of vanity, the persecution of friends (for you will have lost the only friend that would never persecute you), and can support the prospect of the many inconveniences attending the state of an old maid, which I formerly pointed out, then you may indulge in that kind of

sentimental reading and conversation which is most correspondent to your feelings.

But if you find, on a strict self-examination, that marriage is
absolutely essential to your happiness, keep the secret inviolable
in your own bosoms, for the reason I formerly mentioned; but
shun as you would do the most fatal poison, all that species of
reading and conversation which warms the imagination, which
engages and softens the heart, and raises the taste above the level
of common life. If you do otherwise, consider the terrible conflict
of passions this may afterwards raise in your breasts.

If this refinement once takes deep root in your minds, and you
do not obey its dictates, but marry from vulgar or mercenary
views, you may never be able to eradicate it entirely, and then it
will embitter all your married days. Instead of meeting with sense,
delicacy, tenderness, a lover, a friend, an equal companion, in a
husband; you may be tired with insipidity and dulness; shocked
with indelicacy, or mortified by indifference. You will find none
to compassionate, or even understand your sufferings; for your
husbands may not use you cruelly, and may give you as much
money for your clothes, personal expence, and domestic necess-
aries, as is suitable to their fortunes. The world would therefore
look on you as unreasonable women, and that did not deserve to
be happy, if you were not so. – To avoid these complicated evils, if
you are determined at all events to marry, I would advise you to
make all your reading and amusements of such a kind, as do not
affect the heart nor the imagination, except in the way of wit or
humour.

Notes

1 *A Comparative View of the State and Faculties of Man with those of the
   Animal World* (1765). The passage referred to reads: 'If we impress
   their minds with a belief that they were made only to be domestic
   drudges, and the slaves of our pleasures, we debase their minds, and
   destroy all generous emulation to excel; whereas, if we use them in a
   more liberal and generous manner; a decent pride, a conscious
   dignity, and a sense of their own worth, will naturally induce them to
   exert themselves to be what they would wish to be thought, and are
   entitled to be, our companions and friends' (7th edn., 1777, pp. 116–
   17).
2 Misquoted from James Thomson, *The Seasons* (1730), 'Autumn', ll.
   606–8.

1.7   Mary Wollstonecraft, from *Thoughts on the Education of Daughters: with Reflections on Female Conduct, in the more important Duties of Life*, 1788

'Matrimony'

Early marriages are, in my opinion, a stop to improvement. If we were born only 'to draw nutrition, propagate and rot', the sooner the end of creation was answered the better; but as women are here allowed to have souls, the soul ought to be attended to. In youth a woman endeavours to please the other sex, in order, generally speaking, to get married, and this endeavour calls forth all her powers. If she has had a tolerable education, the foundation only is laid, for the mind does not soon arrive at maturity, and should not be engrossed by domestic cares before any habits are fixed. The passions also have too much influence over the judgment to suffer it to direct her in this most important affair; and many women, I am persuaded, marry a man before they are twenty, whom they would have rejected some years after. Very frequently, when the education has been neglected, the mind improves itself, if it has leisure for reflection, and experience to reflect on; but how can this happen when they are forced to act before they have had time to think, or find that they are unhappily married? Nay, should they be so fortunate as to get a good husband, they will not set a proper value on him; he will be found much inferior to the lovers described in novels, and their want of knowledge makes them frequently disgusted with the man, when the fault is human nature.

When a woman's mind has gained some strength, she will in all probability pay more attention to her actions than a girl can be expected to do; and if she thinks seriously, she will chuse for a companion a man of principle; and this perhaps young people do not sufficiently attend to, or see the necessity of doing. A woman of feeling must be very much hurt if she is obliged to keep her children out of their father's company, that their morals may not be injured by his conversation; and besides, the whole arduous task of education devolves on her, and in such a case it is not very practicable. Attention to the education of children must be irksome, when life appears to have so many charms, and its pleasures are not found fallacious. Many are but just returned from a boarding-school, when they are placed at the head of a family, and how fit they are to manage it, I leave the judicious to judge. Can they improve a child's understanding, when they are scarcely out of the state of childhood themselves?

Dignity of manners, too, and proper reserve are often wanting. The constant attendant on too much familiarity is contempt. Women are often before marriage prudish, and afterwards they think they may innocently give way to fondness, and overwhelm the poor man with it. They think they have a legal right to his affections, and grow remiss in their endeavours to please. There are a thousand nameless decencies which good sense gives rise to, and artless proofs of regard which flow from the heart, and will reach it, if it is not depraved. It has ever occurred to me, that it was sufficient for a woman to receive caresses, and not bestow them. She ought to distinguish between fondness and tenderness. The latter is the sweetest cordial of life; but, like all other cordials, should be reserved for particular occasions; to exhilarate the spirits, when depressed by sickness, or lost in sorrow. Sensibility will best instruct. Some delicacies can never be pointed out or described, though they sink deep into the heart, and render the hours of distress supportable . . .

Reason must often be called in to fill up the vacuums of life; but too many of our sex suffer theirs to lie dormant. A little ridicule and smart turn of expression, often confutes without convincing; and tricks are played off to raise tenderness, even while they are forfeiting esteem.

Women are said to be the weaker vessel, and many are the miseries which this weakness brings on them. Men have in some respects very much the advantage. If they have a tolerable understanding, it has a chance to be cultivated. They are forced to see human nature as it is, and are not left to dwell on the pictures of their own imaginations. Nothing, I am sure, calls forth the faculties so much as the being obliged to struggle with the world; and this is not a woman's province in a married state. Her sphere of action is not large, and if she is taught to look into her own heart, how trivial are her occupations and pursuits! What little arts engross and narrow her mind! 'Cunning fills up the mighty void of sense'; and cares, which do not improve the heart of understanding, take up her attention. Of course, she falls a prey to childish anger, and silly capricious humors, which render her rather insignificant than vicious.

In a comfortable situation, a cultivated mind is necessary to render a woman contented; and in a miserable one, it is her only consolation. A sensible, delicate woman, who by some strange accident, or mistake, is joined to a fool or a brute, must be wretched beyond all names of wretchedness, if her views are confined to the present scene. Of what importance, then, is intellectual improvement, when our comfort here, and happiness hereafter, depends upon it.

Principles of religion should be fixed, and the mind not left to fluctuate in the time of distress, when it can receive succour from no other quarter. The conviction that every thing is working for our good will scarcely produce resignation, when we are deprived of our dearest hopes. How they can be satisfied, who have not this conviction, I cannot conceive; I rather think they will turn to some worldly support, and fall into folly, if not vice. For a little refinement only leads a woman into the wilds of romance, if she is not religious; nay, more, there is no true sentiment without it, nor perhaps any other effectual check to the passions.

2

SEXUALITY

Conduct literature equated 'natural' femininity with passive asexual virtue. In contrast, in the texts included here women are defined entirely by their active, and therefore suspect, sexuality. At first glance, then, these first two sections might be taken to illustrate the familiar opposition between women as angels and women as whores, between women as the embodiment of moral value and women as the source of moral disorder. But the binary categories are too simple. As a detailed comparative reading across the two sections makes clear, these contradictory representations are actually ideologically inseparable. In the introduction to Section 1, I suggested that conduct literature should be read in the light of other, more overtly political, discourses, and that its potentially disruptive, and often barely disguised, sub-text is the control of (female) sexuality. Read in juxtaposition with the passages here, those alliances and that sub-text become all the more apparent. The private moral constraints urged by the conduct manual can be read as part of more public discourses of economic utility and social intervention, articulated here through the objectification and limitation of female sexuality.

The passages fall into three main categories – medical litera-ture (2.6, 2.7, 2.8, 2.10), including an early sex manual claiming authorship by 'A Physician'; anti-female satire (2.1, 2.4); and documents dealing with the problem of prostitution (2.2, 2.3, 2.5, 2.9) – but connections and overlaps between these categories are immediately obvious. Implicitly or explicitly, all the passages (with the possible exception of Martha Mears's *Pupil of Nature*, 2.10) take male sexuality as the norm: female sexuality is thus deviant, or at best serves a passively functional role. Not surprisingly, this is most obvious in *The Pleasures of Conjugal Love* (2.6) and (allowing for Mandeville's irony) *A Modest Defence of Public Stews* (2.2), texts which pander to the fantasies and fears of a male audience, and which are more explicitly, negatively and violently echoed in Gould's conventional anti-female satire *Love Given O're* (2.1). But in the medical texts, too, female sexuality is represented as aberrant and mysterious. Thus the 'Inconstancy of [women's] Imagination' in *Conjugal Love* recurs in James's authoritative *Medicinal Dictionary* (2.8) in the 'remarkable . . . variety of forms' assumed by hysteria, the condition to which, apparently, all women except married mothers are liable. And in *The Ladies Dispensatory* (2.7), a text directed specifically at women, menstruation is an '*extraordinary* Discharge' (my emphasis), necessary because the economy of the female body fails to regulate itself in 'due Time and Proportion'. (For interesting overlaps between the terms used here and in texts which discuss the economy of the female mind, see 3.1, 3.7.)

Paradoxically, this physiological inadequacy is ascribed to women's biological function as 'the Vehicle through which the human Species should be propagated'. At the same time, the myth of rampant female sexuality ('Ev'ry woman is at heart a rake' – see 2.1, 2.4, 2.5) is given a scientific explanation as resulting inevitably from the female body's constant readiness to conceive (2.2, 2.5). (It was commonly assumed that ovulation was stimulated by intercourse, and that orgasm facilitated conception.) Female sexuality is simultaneously and inseparably constructed as both natural and unnatural, and its potentially anarchic power contained by reducing it to the socially sanctioned duty of motherhood.

The ideological status of marriage and motherhood is much clearer in these texts than in the conduct manuals, where their economic importance was masked by discourses of natural femininity and romantic affection. Here, discourses of nature, morality and feeling collude more visibly with those of economic self-interest and social stability, and particularly so in the texts on prostitution. Thus Defoe (2.3) defends marriage by defining 'the great Use of Women in a Community' as being to 'supply it with Members that may be serviceable', and makes the startlingly utilitarian suggestion that women over child-bearing age should not be allowed to marry since that 'loses to the World the Produce of one Man'. Appeals to the wealthy middle class for subscriptions to the Magdalen House charity (2.9) are based on the same criteria: in the preface to the first sermon, the reform of prostitutes is offered as a means of bolstering national strength through an efficiently reproductive population, and subscription thus becomes a patriotic duty. In both texts, women are objects of exchange within a mercantilist discourse which conflates economic self-interest and moral rectitude. In terms of sexual as well as economic ideology, there is a clear continuity between their self-righteous defence of the bourgeois marriage, and Mandeville's defiantly libertine argument for nationalized brothels (2.2), in which sexually active women provide a 'legal Evacuative' for the body politic (cf. passage 2.1, ll. 80–4).

In one way, then, the restriction of female sexuality to motherhood is dedicated to the expansionist ideology of an upwardly mobile middle class; at the same time, it is used conservatively to protect that class position against encroachment from above and below. In *The Ladies Dispensatory* (2.7), for example, the 'natural Duty' of breast-feeding (however advisable in purely hygienic terms) is actually presented as a means of social control, protecting the middle class from moral infection by lower-class wet-nurses and by mothers who reject respectable domesticity for the upper-class indulgences of public life. And in several texts, female freedom is associated with social and moral corruption in a slightly different way: educating 'Shopkeepers Daughters' above their station is cited (2.5) as a significant cause of 'Disorders in the married State', generally, and prostitution in particular – given inappropriate social expectations, these young women are left with no other means of supporting themselves. (See 2.3, 2.5, 2.9, and, for other texts dealing with issues of an appropriate education, female employment, and the role of women in maintaining class hierarchies, cf. 3.4, 3.6, 3.8, 3.9.)

In the extract from *The Present State of Matrimony* by 'Philogamus' (2.5), almost all these contradictory discourses are very obviously present. Here, women have both 'stronger Inclinations' and 'a natural Modesty'; too free an education is seen as responsible for present moral degeneration, so women must be restricted to a modern version of the classical 'gynaeceum' to maintain their 'angelical Nature' by protecting them from themselves. This harshly repressive regime, offered in the explicit interests of family and commonwealth, is represented as part of a natural process through metaphors of husbandry (!); and at the end of the extract 'true Love' is promised as the reward for subjection in a romantic idealization of marriage which recalls Wilkes in Section 1 (1.3, and cf. 4.13).

In these contexts, Martha Mears's self-consciously gender-based stress on pregnancy as a natural state (2.10) looks rather less innovative. In midwifery as in other spheres, men were taking over from women (cf. 3.8), and Mears, importantly, opposes these 'interested men' who have defined pregnancy as a disease. She also appeals to anti-slavery rhetoric in advocating female solidarity across class barriers. But these radical alliances (cf. 3.5, 5.3, 5.5, 5.6) are potentially undermined by her privileging of motherhood in what are still, essentially, bourgeois and male-centred terms. (For a rather different view of her post-Rousseauian idealization of the life of country women, see 4.5.) As Mary Wollstonecraft's writings demonstrate (and cf. Section 5), it was not yet possible even for radical women to escape the conduct ideology which made sexual autonomy impossible to reconcile with acceptable femininity.

The question of how dominant constructions of female sexuality affected women's writing and subjectivity is raised again by the two fictionalized accounts of prostitutes' experiences included here. Defoe's utilitarian analysis of prostitution ends with a paradigmatic seduction narrative – the account of a prostitute subsequently hanged for pick-pocketing – and the sympathy evoked by the first-person voice complicates any simple moral conclusion and disrupts his functional objectification of women. (And there is an obvious further generic comparison to be made between this text and Defoe's first-person narratives *Moll Flanders* and *Roxana*.) A similar cautionary tale, though in the third person, is included in the Magdalen House material (2.9). Seduction narratives were very popular throughout the century and, particularly under the influence of sentimentalism, they manifest a characteristic duality in the representation of prostitutes between 'pestilent Whore' and fallen woman, and more generally between women as sexually guilty and women as victims (cf. 1.5, 4.7; for conservative attacks on this kind of writing, see

3.9, 4.18; for debates about attitudes to the 'fallen woman', see 1.6, 3.5, 3.9, 5.5.). The role of sexual victim as used in the Magdalen House sermons, for example, is simply a form of objectification. There, static vignettes of innocent motherhood are evoked to titillate and flatter the self-interested sensibilities of a (male) audience. But, like so many manifestations of the cult of sensibility, the role of victim could also be enabling: when appropriated by women writers it offered a subject-position from which to articulate, in however limited a way, female sexual experience.

2.1   [Robert Gould], from *Love Given O're: or, a Satyr against the Pride, Lust, and Inconstancy, &c. of Woman*, 1682

Woman! by Heav'ns the very Name's a Crime,
Enough to blast, and to debauch my Rhime.
35 Sure Heav'n it self (intranc't) like *Adam* lay,
Or else some banish'd Fiend usurp't the sway
When *Eve* was form'd; and with her, usher'd in
Plagues, Woes, and Death, and a new World of Sin.
The fatal Rib was crooked and unev'n,
40 from whence they have their Crab-like Nature giv'n;
Averse to all the Laws of Man, and Heav'n.
     O *Lucifer*, thy Regions had been thin,
Were't not for Womans propagating Sin:
'Tis they alone that all true Vices know;
And send such Throngs down to thy Courts below:
More Souls they've made obedient to thy Raign,
Than Heav'n, and Earth, and Seas beside, contain.
True, the first Woman gave the first bold Blow,
And bravely sail'd down to th'Abyss below;
50 But had the great Deed still been left undone,
None of the daring Sex, no, hardly one,
But in the very self-same path would go,
Tho' sure 'twou'd lead 'em to eternal woe:
Find me ye pow'rs, find one amongst 'em all,
That does not envy *Eve* the glory of the Fall:
Be cautious then, and guard your Empire well;
For shou'd they once get power to rebel,
They'd surely raise a Civil War in Hell,

Add to the pains you feel; and make you know,
60   W'are here above, as Curst as you below.
     How happy had we been, had heav'n design'd
Some other way to propagate our kind?
For whatsoe'ere those All-discerning Pow'rs
Created sweet, Wife! Nauseous Wife! turn'd sow'r;
Debauch'd th'innocent, Ambrosial meat,
And (like *Eves* Apple) made it Death to eat:
But curst be the vile Name, and curst be they,
Who are so tamely Dull as to obey.
The Slaves they may command; Is there a Dog,
70   Who, when he may have freedom, wears a Clog?
But Man, base Man, the more imprudent Beast,
Drags the dull weight when he may be releas't:
May such ye Gods (too many such we see)
While they live here, just only live, to be
The marks of Scorn, Contempt, and Infamy.
But if the Tyde of Nature boist'rous grow,
And would Rebelliously its Banks o'erflow,
Then chuse a Wench, who (full of lewd desires)
Can meet your flouds of Love with equal fires;
80   And will, when e're you let the Deluge flie,
Through an extended Sluce strait drain it dry;
That Whirl-pool Sluce which never knows a Shore,
Ne're can be fill'd so full as to run ore,
For still it gapes, and still cries – room for more!
Such only damn the Soul; but a damn'd Wife,
Damns that, and with it all the Joys of Life:
And what vain Blockhead is so dull, but knows,
That of two Ills the least is to be chose.
     But now, since Womans boundless Lust I name,
90   Womans unbounded Lust I'le first proclaim:

          . . .

     Who knew not (for to whom was she unknown)
Our late illustrious *Bewley*? (true, she's gone
105   To answer for the num'rous Ills sh'as done;
Who, tho' in Hell (in Hell, if any where)
Hemm'd round with all the flames and tortures there,
Finds 'em not fiercer, tho' she feels the worst,

Then when she liv'd, her own wild flames of Lust.)
110 As *Albions* Isle fast rooted in the Main,
Does the rough Billows raging force disdain,
Which tho' they foam, and with loud terrors rore,
Yet they can never reach beyond their shore.
So she with Lusts Enthusiastick Rage,
Sustain'd all the salt Stallions of the Age.
Whole Legions she encounter'd, Legions tir'd;
Insatiate yet, still fresh Supplies desir'd.
Illustrious Bawd! whose Fame shall be display'd,
When Heroes Glories are in Silence laid,
120 In as profound a Silence, as the Slaves
Their conquering Swords dispatch'd into their Graves.
But Bodies must decay; for 'tis too sure,
There's nothing from the Jaws of Time secure.
Yet, when she found that she could do no more,
When all her Body was one putrid Sore,
Studded with Pox, and Ulcers quite all o're;
Ev'n then, by her delusive treach'rous Wiles,
(Which show'd most specious when they most beguil'd)
Sh'enrolled more Females in the List of Whore,
130 Than all the Arts of Man e're did before.
Prest with the pond'rous guilt, at length she fell;
And through the solid Centre sunk to Hell:
The murm'ring Fiends all hover'd round about,
And in hoarse howls did the great Bawd salute;
Amaz'd to see a sordid lump of Clay,
Stain'd with more various bolder Crimes than they:
Nor were her torments less; for the dire Train,
Soon sent her howling through the rowling flames,
To the sad Seat of everlasting pain.

. . .

And now, if so much to the World's reveal'd,
Reflect on the vast Stores that lie conceal'd:
How, when into their Closets they retire,
Where flaming Dil—s does inflame desire,
150 And gentle Lap-d—s feed the am'rous fire:
Lap-d—s! to whom they are most kind and free,
Than they themselves to their own Husbands be.

How curst is Man! when Bruits his Rivals prove,
Ev'n in the sacred bus'ness of his Love.
Great was the wise Man's saying, great, as true;
And we well know, than he none better knew;
Ev'n he himself acknowledges the Womb
To be as greedy as the gaping Tomb:
Take Men, Dogs, Lions, Bears, all sorts of Stuff,
160   Yet will it never cry – there is enough.
Nor are their Consciences (which can betray
Where e're they're sworn to love) less large than they;
Consciences, so lewdly unconfin'd!
That ev'ry one wou'd, cou'd they act their mind,
To their own single share engross ev'n all Mankind.
And when the Mind's corrupt, we all well know,
The actions that proceed from't must be so.
Their guilt's as great who any ills wou'd do,
As their's who freely do those ills pursue:
170   That they would have it so their Crime assures;
Thus if they durst, all Women wou'd be Whores.

2.2 'Colonel Harry Mordaunt' [Bernard Mandeville], from *A Modest Defence of Public Stews: or, an Essay upon Whoring,* 1724; 1740 edn

We come now to the last great Point propos'd, *viz.* that this Project of the *Publick Stews* will prevent, as much as possible, the Debauching of modest Women, and thereby reduce Whoring to the narrowest Bounds in which it can possibly be contain'd.

To illustrate this Matter, we must slip a little back to consider the Constitution of Females, while they are in a State of Innocence; and when we have taken a View of the Fortifications, which Nature has made to preserve their Chastity, we shall find out the Reason why it is so often surrender'd, and be the better able to provide for its Defence.

Every Woman who is capable of Conception, must have those Parts which officiate, so fram'd, that they may be able to perform whatever is necessary at that Juncture. Now, to have those Parts so rightly adapted for the Use which Nature design'd them, it is requisite that they should have a very quick Sensation, and, upon the Application of the *Male Organ*, afford the Woman an exquisite Pleasure; for, without this extravagant Pleasure in Fruition, the recipient Organs could never exert themselves to promote Conception as they now do, in such an extraordinary Manner . . . .

To counterballance this violent natural Desire, all young Women have strong Notions of Honour carefully inculcated into them from their Infancy. Young Girls are taught to hate a *Whore*, before they know what the Word means; and when they grow up, they find their worldly Interest entirely depending upon the Reputation of their Chastity. This sense of Honour and Interest, is what we may call artificial Chastity; and it is upon this Compound of natural and artificial Chastity, that every Woman's real actual Chastity depends.

. . . Most Women, indeed, let them be ever so fully resolv'd to comply, make as great a Shew of Resistance as they can conveniently counterfeit; and this the Sex would pass upon the World for a Kind of innate Modesty; but it is very easily accounted for.

As soon as Women have entertain'd any Degree of Love, they make it their whole Study to raise and maintain an equal Degree of Passion in the Men; and they are very sensible how far the bare Appearance of Modesty will prevail to render them amiable. The Pain they suffer in smothering their Desires, is fully recompenc'd by that secret Pleasure which a Lover's Eagerness gives them, because they esteem it a Proof both of the Sincerity and Violence of his Passion. A Woman is, not without some Reason, afraid, lest a Man's Love should diminish after Enjoyment, and would gladly bribe his After-Love, by the great Value she seems to put upon her Chastity before she makes him a Present of it.

Besides, not to mention the actual Pleasure a Woman receives in Struggling, it is a Justification of her in the Eye of the Man, and a Kind of *Salvo* to her Honour and Conscience, that she never did fully comply, but was in a Manner forc'd into it. This is the plain natural Reason why most Women refuse, to *surrender* upon Treaty, and why they delight so much in being *storm'd*.

Having thus taken a cursory View of the Sex, in their several Classes, and according to their several Circumstances, we may conclude, preferring Truth to Complaisance, that by far the greater Part of Womenkind hold their Virtue very precariously; and that Female Chastity is, in its own Nature, built upon a very *Ticklish* Foundation.

... The only Way to preserve Female Chastity, is to prevent the Men from laying Siege to it: But this Project of the *Publick Stews* is the only Way to prevent Men's laying Siege to it: Therefore, this Project is the only Way to preserve Female Chastity. . . .

Since the Torrent of Lewdness, then, is too strong to be oppos'd by open Force, let us see if we can find out an Expedient to divert it by Policy, and prevent the Mischief, tho' we can't prevent the Crime.

Most *Authors*, who have writ of Government, have chose to express their Sentiments by comparing the Publick Body with the Body Natural; and Mr. *Hobbs*, in his *Leviathan*, has carry'd the *Allegory* as far as it will go. To make Use of it in the present Instance, we may look upon *Whoring* as a Kind of Peccant Humour in the Body-Politick, which, in order to its Discharge, naturally seizes upon such external Members as are most liable to Infection, and at the same Time most proper to carry off the Malignity. If this Discharge is promoted by a License for *Publick Stews*, which is a Kind of legal Evacuative, the Constitution will certainly be preserved: Whereas, if we apply Penal Laws, like violent Astringents, they will only drive the Disease back into the Blood; where, gathering Strength, and at last assimilating the whole Mass, it will break out with the utmost Virulence, to the apparent Hazard of those sound Members, which otherwise might have escaped the Contagion. As we may observe in a *Clap*, where Nature of her own Accord expels the noxious Humour thro' the same Passages by which it was at first received; but if we resist Nature in this Discharge, and repel the Venom by too hasty an Application of *Stypticks*, the Disease, then, turns to a *Pox*, seizes the Vitals, and (to use *Solomon's* Words) *like a Dart, strikes thro' the Liver*. But, leaving *Allegory* as more proper for *Rhetorick* or *Poetry*, than such serious Debates, since this Project of the *Publick Stews* is the only Expedient now left for the Preservation of Female Chastity, the Question is, Whether or no this Expedient will really answer the End propos'd.

To prove the Affirmative, requires no more but that we look into ourselves, and examine our own Passions; for Love ever was and will be the same in all Men, and in all Ages. The first amorous Emotions that young Men feel are violent; they are plagued with a Stimulation which raises a vehement Desire: The Passion is strong, but then it is general: It is Lust, not Love: And, therefore, the natural Impatience of *Lust* will prompt them to take the speediest way for present Gratification, and make them prefer the ready and willing Embraces of a Courtezan, before the doubtful and distant Prospect of enjoying a modest Damsel, whose Coyness will cost so much Pains, as well as Time, to overcome; and, when overcome, may probably occasion a future Uneasiness, and give them more Trouble after Enjoyment than they had before.

Besides this, if their first Affections should happen to be engaged to a particular Object, which is very rare; and that this particular Object was in their Power to compass, which is still rarer; yet there is naturally in young Men a certain secret Shame, which attends their first Sallies, and prevents their declaring a private Passion, 'till it grows so violent, that they are forced to give it vent upon the Publick; and by that Means get into a regular Method of making themselves easy, without doing their Modesty any Violence.

But tho' the natural Bent of Men's Minds inclines them to an easy Purchase of Pleasure in their first Amours; yet publick Whoring lies at present under so many Disadvantages, the publick Women, for want of good Regulation, are so infamous in the Principles and Practice, the Places of Resort so vile, and so scandalously imposing in the common Expence, and, lying under the Lash of the *Civil* Power, so pester'd with the mercenary Officiousness of *Reforming Constables* and, which is worst of all, the Plague of *Claps* and *Poxes* is so inevitable, that Men, contrary to their Inclinations, are often forced to enter upon private Intrigues; either without trying the Publick, or after meeting with some Misfortunes in the Tryal.

Now if we see daily so many Young Men who prefer the publick Commerce under all these Disadvantages, what Success may we not expect from this happy Establishment of the *Stews*, when the Young Women's Behaviour will be regulated after a civil decent Manner; when the Houses of Entertainment will be so Commodious, and the Expence of Accommodation so reasonable; when the horrid Dread of *Claps* is entirely remov'd; and when the Laws, instead of disturbing such Assemblies, will be employ'd in their Protection, to give them the greater Countenance and Encouragement? Surely we may hope for a thorough Reformation.

. . .

When this Project is first set on Foot, the vast Choice and Variety there is at present of these Women, will give us an Opportunity of making a very beautiful Collection; and will, doubtless, for some Time, occasion a considerable run upon the Publick; so that *Private Whoring*, the only Nursery of our Courtezans, may probably remain too long neglected: For the whole Body of our incontinent Youth, like a standing Army, being employ'd in constant Action, there cannot well be spar'd a sufficient Detachment to raise the necessary Recruits.

But however true this may be, we shall thereby suffer no Inconvenience; for if the Supplies of young Women, which we may reasonable expect from the Northern and Western parts of these Kingdoms, or from such Places as are remote and out of the Influence of this *Scheme:* I say, if these Supplies should not prove sufficient to answer the greatness of the Demand, and that the Reputation of the *Stews*, upon this Account, should begin to flag, why then the worst Accident that can befal, is a gradual Relapse into our former State of *Private Whoring;* and this no farther than is just necessary to recruit the *Stews*, and thereby make them retrieve their former Character; For every Woman that is debauch'd more than is barely necessary, only brings so much additional Credit and Reputation to the *Stews*, and in some Measure atones for the Loss of her own Chastity, by being a Means to preserve that of others; so that whenever the Tide of private Lewdness runs too high, and exceeds the just and ordinary Bounds, it must of Course, by encouraging the *Publick Stews*, immediately suffer a proportionable Ebb: That is to say, it must be reduc'd again so low, that there will remain but just sufficient Quantity to supply the *Stews;* which is as low as in the Nature of the Thing, is possible.

I might here lavish out Encomiums, and take Occasion to dwell upon those many Advantages that will accrue to the *Nation* by this admirable Scheme, but shall only take Notice of this peculiar Excellence, which it has above all other Schemes, that it necessarily executes itself.

But since the Necessity of debauching a certain Number of young Women, is entirely owing to the Necessity of supplying the *Publick Stews;* a Question may very reasonably arise, whether this

Project might not be vastly improv'd, even to the total Extirpation of *Private Whoring*, by an Act *for encouraging the Importation of Foreign Women.*

2.3 [Daniel Defoe], from *Some Considerations upon Street-Walkers with A Proposal for lessening the present Number of them,* [1726]

. . . in charitable Compassion to so great a Part of the most beautiful of our Species, as may find themselves reduc'd to this Condition, which they must know and feel to be the Extremity of Unhappiness; I would lay out a Word or two in proposing something which might serve at least to lessen the Number of such as are to be miserable hereafter, since the living Set are past Redemption.

The great Use of Women in a Community, is to supply it with Members that may be serviceable, and keep up a Succession. They are also useful in another Degree, to wit, in the Labour they may take for themselves, or the Assistance which they may afford their Husbands or Parents. It will readily be allowed, that a Street-walking Whore can never answer either of these Ends; Riot and Diseases prevent one, and the Idleness which directs her to this Course of Life incapacitates her for the other. How very useless then is such a Subject? Sure no body will urge, that the Consumption of Commodities and Manufactures which she helps towards, is a sufficient Atonement for the Mischief she does, and the want of that Good she is incapable of doing: And yet how many of this Kind are there, whose Lives and Services are irrecoverably lost to their Country, and yet continue a pernicious Charge upon it? Sure if there be any way of reforming this, both a religious and a political Consideration should set all good Men upon seeking it, and when found, upon pursuing it. The Discovery of the Cause of a Mischief must always precede the Cure of it; and to inquire into this, I don't find that upon strict Calculation the Number of the Female Sex so far exceeds ours, as to set the Surplus a wandring in this manner, as has been suggested. I believe the Numbers of both Sexes are very well equalled by the Hand of Providence, considering the Accidents common to both; and that the main Cause is, that Neglect of Matrimony which the Morals of the present Age inspire Men with. Multitudes of Men overlooking all Considerations but Fortune, decline Marriage, or at least defer it till that Article is easy; while the Proportion of Women, who arrive at Puberty in this Time, and are not provided for by their Kindred, prompted by Nature, and urged by Wants, are forced to become the Instruments of satisfying those Desires in Men which were given for a better Use, and which are the greatest Temptations to Matrimony.

Some Remedy might be apply'd to this by our Laws giving more Encouragement to Matrimony. What if some Immunities attended that State, some Exemptions from Taxes, or the like? or what if the old *Roman* Law, entitling the Parents of three or more Children to certain Privileges, were put in force among us, or something grounded upon that Hint? I am perswaded, such Encouragements to Virtue would have a better Effect than all the Whippings, *Bridewels* and *Work-Houses*, which are invented as Discouragements to Vice.

Next to no Marriage, Inequality in Marriage is the greatest Mischief; I mean such Inequality as concerns Age and Constitution. Rationally speaking, no Woman ought to be allowed to marry after her Capacity of Child-bearing has left her. Such a Conjunction, supposing every one virtuous, loses to the World the Produce of one Man; but supposing Things as they may be, corrupts the Virtue of several Women, whom Dislike to old Wives put young Fellows upon seducing. These are the Causes of the shocking Rabble of Harlots, which infest our Publick Ways; Man's Solicitation tempts them to Lewdness, Necessity succeeds Sin, and Want puts an End to Shame. If some Care were taken to encourage Virtue in the manner I have hinted above, we might live to see less of these Abominations; if not, we may yet find them increase upon us. Meanwhile, let us provide for such Amendment; and by cutting off the rotten Branches in this Season, prevent the Corruption of more in the next. If we grow more virtuous, it must be by degrees; but we may grow less vicious at once. Let the Whipping-Post, Work-House, and Transportation, be employ'd to dissipate the present Set of Street-Walking Strumpets; and let us by gentler Allurements to Virtue, destroy the Hopes of any Succession of such miserable Sinners.

. . .

P.S. I cannot but on this Occasion give you, *Sir*, a genuine Letter from One of the unhappy Persons I have troubled you about, and who was afterwards executed for picking a Gentleman's Pocket, to Mrs. –, who kept a noted Bawdy-House in *Great P–ney-street;* by which the miserable Condition of these Creatures will more fully appear, and consequently, the great Necessity there is to suppress them.

MADAM,

'The forlorn Condition I am in, the many unmerited Injuries I have suffer'd from you, and the great Use I have formerly been of to you, I thought might be sufficient to incite you to afford me a little charitable Assistance; but in vain: so that you reduce me to the unhappy Necessity of reminding you of the Miseries of my past Life, not a few of which were owing to you, and which, if you have not joined a sear'd Conscience to a hardened Heart, must extort from you that Compassion I call for.

'You know, Madam, my Father, who was by his Rank a Gentleman, was by his Fortune unable to make any other Provision for me, than by giving me an Education suitable to that Rank; which Education has been my greatest Curse, as it has enabled me to feel more bitterly the Ills which I have undergone. The want of Means to support my Character, soon after his Death laid me open to the Sollicitations of Sir *James* –, whose great Fortune made it proper for me to bear with the first Insolence of his Proposals, rather than by shocking him, destroy the Hopes I had form'd of making him like me in an honourable Way. But why do I say this to you? Alas, Madam, I am distracted! I write like what I was, tho' I feel with Bitterness what I am.

'The History of his Triumph, his forsaking and deceiving me concerning the Maintenance which he promis'd and pretended to secure for me, are but too well known to you; they were the Means of my Acquaintance with you. I know not how you and he had concerted Matters before-hand; but when he brought me to your House, he represented it to me as a new Lodging which he had taken for me; after having gutted and sent away all the Goods and Furniture I had in the former, which I thought to find with you, but never heard of since. The necessitous Condition which I found my self reduc'd to by this new Villany of his, soon made me compliant with your Requests. What and how much Shame I have suffered for your Benefit, I can't bear to think of: I say, for your Benefit; for so you manag'd it, that almost all my Wages of Sin were Diseases. Oh, would to God that, according to the Scripture, they had been instant Death.

'Those Maladies, which Intemperance as well as Incontinence contributed to, soon render'd me unfit for your Purpose; the little Beauty which recommended me to you was fled, and I was no longer a Temptation to Sin. You therefore, cruel Woman, turn'd me out of Doors, poorer than you receiv'd me. I had Cloaths when I came to you splendid enough to adorn Beauty; when I left you, scarce Rags to cover it. In this sad Condition, I fell into more and new Vices, which I think of with Horror; I grew harden'd to Shame, and therefore forgot all Thoughts of Sin. Drunkenness, which was at first a Relief, now became an incurable Disease; and all the little Gains that my shameful Occupation brought me in, were laid out upon intoxicating vulgar Drams. Work-Houses and Whippings have been employ'd in vain upon me; still as I was released, my Wants threw me into my old Ways; till at last, oh Shame to think of! by frequent Converse with Thieves and Pickpockets, I learn'd their Arts; and, intic'd by their Gains, practised them. I stand at present committed to this Place for picking a Gentleman's Pocket. I am now awaken'd from my Sins, and wish for that Death which I am told attends me: but such is my miserable Condition, that I can't prepare properly for it without your Assistance. I have no Friends to apply to; they all forsook me before I came to you; you are the only Person I deserve any thing from upon Earth; what I deserve from Heaven, distracting Thought! – But I may repent, and assuredly shall, if the want of due Relief drives me not to Despair. Farewel, Madam; I am the same that you knew me in nothing but the Name . . . .'

Newgate

2.4 [Joseph Dorman], from *The Female Rake: or, Modern Fine Lady. An Epistle from Libertina to Sylvia,* [1736]

While you, my Dear, with Philosophic Eyes,
Look with Contempt, on all beneath the Skies,
Of Wisdom fond, the diff'rent Orbs Survey,
And count the Stars which form the milky Way;

Who like a Solomon, by Age grown Wise,
Can Pleasures past most prudently despise;
Gravely pronounce all Vanity, which you
By Years deny'd, no longer can pursue:
Who with much reading can, at length, discover

10   That Fifty is no charm t'engage a Lover, –
Say; did you quit this odious vicious Town
While you'd a Charm which you cou'd name your own?
Nay, while with Art, you could your Face repair,
Or black-lead Combs disguise the whit'ning Hair?
If this is, *Sylvia*, as you know it, true,
You fled no Pleasure; Pleasure, fled from you.

. . .

'Till Time had stol'n the Light'ning from her Eyes,
Sylvia, was never known to Moralize;
She gave a Loose to ev'ry gay Desire,

50   And own'd the tender Flame she cou'd Inspire;
No priestly Doubts, cou'd on her Joys break in,
Imprudence only was a mortal Sin:
Conscience undisturb'd, she calmly slept,
And Virtue suffer'd nought – the Secret kept.
    Think not that I from Virtue e'er will stray,
By chusing Fops, whose Vanities betray.
Virtue, we know, subsists in other's Thought,
And she is virtuous, who was never caught:
Our Virtue then, is Prudence in our Choice,

60   On that alone depends the publick Voice:
You, ever chaste, a Groupe of Youths enjoy'd,
But one Intrigue, *Mirtilla's* Fame destroy'd.
The World by Outside judges, and we see
Fame takes its Rise, from what we seem to be:
A Vestal thus, Imprudence shall undo,
While Caution makes a Vestal – ev'n of you.

. . .

    Life is, you say, no more than transient Breath,

120   And ev'ry gasp we fetch, we draw in Death;
Wherefore, we shou'd this trifling World despise,
And think of nothing, but eternal Joys;
Life yields but few, and those not free from Pain,

Therefore from those it yields, we shou'd refrain.
Does not this say, your Patrimony's small,
'Twere better, therefore, you had none at all:
More prudent, sure, wou'd be th'Advice to save,
And make the most of ev'ry Doit we have.
    Does Reason teach us, that th'Almighty can
130   Conceive Delight in Miseries of Man;
That he has made our State of Life much worse
Than that of Beasts; with Appetites to curse?
Reason, you say, shou'd stubborn Passions break;
And yet you'll own, that Reason, is too weak:
Thus, the most boasted Gift of bounteous Heav'n,
Is vainly, by your own Confession, giv'n.

     . . .

    I dare not think thus wickedly, I own,
Of the All-merciful, Tremendous *One*.
Eternal Goodness, Reason says, can ne'er
Give me my Passions, but to prove a Snare.
Life is replete with Ills; by gracious Heav'n
To mitigate those Ills, were Passions giv'n;
These we may gratify, and treat as Jests,
The idle Menaces of greedy Priests,
Who for their Lucre feign'd a Heav'n and Hell,
170   T'enhance our Fears, and idle Pardons sell.

     . . .

    I know no Fear but one; and Love of Fame
Keeps me still anxious to preserve my Name:
'Tis for this Reason I observe your Rule,
Close with the Man of Sense, and shun the Fool:
This gives some Pain, and oft a well-made Fop
Has tempted me, to let your Maxim drop,
Follow *Paulina*, who no Pleasure flies,
220   Laughs at all Censure; stedfastly denies
Well witness'd Facts, and swears them monstrous Lies:
You may believe, or not, – just as you please,
For either Way, *Paulina* is at ease;
Enjoys her Fortune, finds the same Respect,
Or where she's shunn'd, repays it with Neglect.
    Martia, more anxious, like a Bully swaggers,

Threatens with pois'nous Draughts, or Mid-night
    Daggers;
Talks of some daring Friend, whose ready Sword
Will take Revenge for a reflecting Word.
230   *Herculean* labour! Loss to *Britain's* Crown,
What Numbers must he, ev'ry day, mow down!
What Numbers, *Martia*, has thy cruel Breath
Doom'd, by this Hero's Sword, to unripe Death!
For *Martia*, fond of Youth, her Arts employs,
And throws out ev'ry Bait to take in Boys:
Elated, these to the first Friend declare
How much they are indebted to the Fair;
The Favours they've receiv'd, in Publick Boast
Describe, and make her hidden Charms their Toast.
240   *Ametra* judges right, that Joy's no Sin,
At Scandal laughs, and publickly lies-in:
The poor and strong from her receive their Pay,
Grown weak or pert, for others they make Way.
Why shou'd the World *Ametra's* Actions scan,
Is then Variety reserv'd for Man ?
They, without Scandal, quit the Wife's Embrace,
And oft the Chambermaid supplies her Place:
A Countess weeps, a Peasant is caress'd,
And this, with Men, is treated as a Jest.
250   May not *Ametra*, then, without Reproach,
Enjoy the Lacky who's behind her Coach:
Love while she likes, and when she's cloy'd forsake,
Turn off one Lover, and another take?
Thus does she argue, and 'tis thus she does,
Treating her Fav'rites, as she uses Cloaths;
Wears them while fresh, and while they please the Eye,
Then for her Woman's use, she throws them by.
      From these, Example I shall never take,
I'll be the Prudent, tho' a Female Rake;
260   For Prudence is not to the Male confin'd,
Our Sex can boast as great a Strength of Mind.
I ev'ry Taste enjoy; yet, with some Pain,
I, hitherto have liv'd without a Stain;
But then this Pain, does ampler Pleasure give,
T'observe how artfully I can deceive.

Now learn how prudently I play my Game,
Nor fear, hereafter, I shall blot my Fame.

. . .

The Man, who on his Impudence relies,
And boasts a gen'rous Scorn of all Disguise,
Who boards the Fair, as Soldiers storm a Town,
And with G-d D-ye's thinks to bear her down;
Whose Rhet'rick is, Nay – Z-ds, I know you well,
You are afraid – by God I scorn to tell,
B-d, I am sound – D-n it, nay – why so coy;
Are not you Women, form'd, like us, for Joy?
290   Such Men, I say, whate'er their Rank may be,
A second Time, find no Access to me.
In ev'ry publick Place these Men I fly,
A bow from them's sufficient to destroy.
As noisy Bullies boast their great Exploits,
And talk of Conquests in imagin'd Fights;
So, these vain Bablers, with audacious Mein,
Will Favours boast, from those they ne'er have seen.
    The feather'd Fop, who makes his Dress his Care,
Shou'd not be trusted by the prudent Fair;
300   Fond of himself, and of his Conquest proud,
He will proclaim her Infamy aloud.
From others Follies, I have learn'd the Wit,
T'avoid those Shelves, on which I've seen them split.
    There is a set of Men, from which I chuse,
Who will no Favours of the Fair abuse;
Who live luxurious, on the publick Sweat,
Drink richest Wines, provoking Viands eat:
For whom, *Burgundia* does her Vine produce,
For whom, *Tokay* sends forth its flagrant Juice;
310   Whom neither Care nor Study does exhaust,
Who for their Appetites will spare no Cost;
Who are as anxious to preserve their Fame,
(By which they live,) as the most prudent Dame.
These are the Men with whom no Risque we run,
To ease that Burthen, Custom has laid on.
Be satisfied, and banish ev'ry Fear,
(Pleasure's my Chace, yet Reputation's Dear,)

Nor tremble while I rake, with so much Care.

LIBERTINA

2.5 'Philogamus', from *The Present State of Matrimony: or, the Real Causes of Conjugal Infidelity and Unhappy Marriages*[1], 1739

I shall not enter into the Question, which are most inclined to Wickedness, the Men, or the Women: But it is out of all Question, that both are come to a most enormous Pass. Men are undoubtedly more wicked in other Respects; and commit greater Numbers of different Crimes than Women. There are ten Thousand other Crimes, that Women are entirely ignorant of. But whether we are partial to our selves, or not, I will not define; nevertheless, as to Lubricity, it is generally supposed by us, that Women are more inclined than Men. Their Souls seem to be of a more amorous Temper: Their Constitutions are more turned to supply that Passion: Love, and the Effects of it, is the darling and predominant Passion of the Sex. Whether some great Men wrong them, when they say, that

Every Woman is at Heart a Rake:[2]

Or, that the greatest Hero in other Respects; the greatest Conqueror, the best and wisest Man in the World, would be despised by every Woman in her Heart, if he was not qualified for her Ends, I will not pretend to say; but charitably believe it is more a poetical or rhetorical Exaggeration, than a real Truth. But it is beyond all Dispute, that they are not guilty, nor even inclined to any proportionable Number of other enormous Crimes.

As Women were principally designed for producing the Species, and Men for other greater Ends: we cannot wonder, if their Inclinations and Desires tend chiefly that Way. The great Concern of every Commonwealth, is to keep them within due Bounds; which this present Generation exceeds, to a most flagrant and exorbitant Degree: Not to be railing and exclaiming against them, if, being deprived of the main End of their Creation, as to this Life, they fall into very great Disorders.

Neither is it necessary to determine, whether Conjugal Infidelity be a greater Crime in the Woman, than the Man. It is undeniably a very great one in both. If both the Criminals are married Persons, still greater: I say *Criminals;* since it is a Crime by all Laws, Divine and Human. Every Kingdom, Nation, and

People, a Degree above Savages, universally esteemed it as such. That it is deemed a Crime, by the universal Voice of Nature. However, it is generally supposed a greater Crime in the Woman than the Man. Because she not only imposes a spurious Breed on her Husband's Family; makes a Foreigner Heir to his Estate; depriving sometimes his own real Children begotten afterwards, of their just Inheritance; or, at least, his right Heirs and next Relations; but makes the Son of a Man his Heir, who has done him the greatest Injury. But suppose so: Does not the Adulterer concur in all these Injuries? Is he not then equally guilty, at least as to that Part? The greatest Crime on the Woman's Side, is the breach of the high Trust her Husband reposes in her for his Offspring; which he cannot impose upon her, nor make her believe the Child is her own, when it is not, as she can him: Since she ought to be subject to her Husband, as her Head and Lord, on whom he reposes the greatest Trust in Nature, it is the highest Infidelity to betray this sacred Trust; and even a greater, than it would be in him to have Children by another single Woman. The Adultress breaks through all those Ties; but the Man, in that Case, breaks but one Part of them: Which nevertheless is a grievous Crime. But if he is criminal with another married Woman, he is equally guilty; and frequently is the Occasion of the weaker Vessel's paying him in his own Coin.

. . .

Another Cause of Conjugal Infidelity, and Disorders in the married State, is the wrong, I may say, the wretched Way of educating our Youth: Particularly our young Ladies. When all the Care in the World should be applied, to lay a Foundation of that Virtue, which is to be the Guard and Fence, against the almost only Passion, their angelical Nature brings into the World along with them. And this before their latent Materials are set afloat: Which might be kept dormant: Or, at least, not nigh so apt to Break out into Torrents, when they come to Maturity. I beg you, Sir, to reflect a little, how our young Misses of Rank and Quality, and even some Shopkeepers Daughters are educated. How different from the Ways of old! In Days of Yore, the Daughters of Kings and Princes, were educated in the inward Recesses of their Palaces: Which had a peculiar Name appropriated to it. I think the *Greeks* called it *Gynacaeum:* Or the Womens

Apartment. More sacred from the Access of Men, than Monasteries are abroad. Where they were kept, till given in Marriage, much more retired, than Nurseries ought to be for little Children with us. There they were employed under the Mother's Eye; or under the Care of such chast and prudent Matrons to teach and instruct them, as they had been educated themselves. No Men were permitted to come nigh them; scarce the Father, with Relations now and then, just to have a Sight of their blooming Innocence: Proper Arts and Employments adapted to their State, took up their leisure Hours: The Needle, or the Loom, the Pencil, or the Lute, according to the more delicate Taste of the Sex, employed their Time, almost as much as dressing, visiting, and conquering Hearts do now. . . . Where they were formed from their Youth, to believe, that the Life of Ladies of the most eminent Quality, was not to be a Life of revelling, visiting, and gadding about; but to be employed in educating their beauteous Offspring, in the Ways of Virtue and Modesty: And to make the Husband's Home, the chief Comfort and Enjoyment of his Life: When tired with publick Employments, he found his well managed Family all in Joy to receive him. This is a short and imperfect Sketch of the Education of our female Youth in Days of old; delivered down to us in the grave Histories of the Antients. We even see something of it in the very Romances of old Times. Which, though they inspired too much of an amorous Softness, in a Sex, whose Nature is more bent that Way: And for that Reason decried by the more rigid and severe: Yet they generally give an Idea of the antient Way of educating young Ladies, infinitely beyond our modern Ways. They display Virginal and Conjugal Chastity in the brightest Colours; with as great Examples of the Deformity of Coquetry and Infidelity. Our wise Forefathers very justly thought the Care and Education of Women to be no indifferent Thing, with respect to the Commonwealth. As the Depravation of our Male Youth is one of the greatest Detriments to a State; that of the Women must have the next Place to it. It has a very great Share in the most flagrant and destructive Disorders. If, with all the Care we can take, great Disorders will happen, what must be the Consequences of our modern Education? So diametrically opposite to that of our wise Ancestors. Let us compare them together, and see, if great Part of the reigning Exorbitances are not to be imputed to it. I do not contradict myself, if I allow, that Women are more inclined to criminal Excesses of that kind, than Men, when they are left without Restraint: And when I say, that they are infinitely more chast than Men, if they are educated with proper Care. But then, as their tender and delicate Complexion is infinitely more susceptible of Passion in that Respect; and more formed by Nature for it; they must be more nicely guarded from all Objects, too apt to excite that Flame. Yet we may say; if they are more easily corrupted, they are more easily preserved; if taken in Time, and cultivated to Virtue from their tender Infancy. The more tender a Plant is, the more capable of being formed to any Shape; though perhaps not so capable of retaining it, as a more stubborn one, without proper Ways and Means to keep it in it's primary Bent. We have some Examples, modern as well as antient, of more heroick Virtue of that Kind than in our Sex, under the greatest Temptations, and severest Trials. I am sorry, they are not so frequent as in past Ages. However, if Nature for just Reasons, has given the Fair-Sex stronger Inclinations; it has also given them a natural Modesty and Check upon them, which we have not. That this Modesty is from their Nature, if not perverted, is evident from all Accounts of the antient Heathens, and the most barbarous Nations, where a virginal Modesty still appears in them, abstracting from Religion, and external Education; though these may be vast Helps, but then, as Tinder, and light combustible Matter must be kept at a greater Distance from the Fire, than more solid Materials, so they must be kept at a greater Distance from inflaming Objects. But do we do so, with respect to our young Women? Are not our young Misses bred up among Men, almost as soon as severed from their Nurses? Are they not admitted into promiscuous Company, as soon as they are able to go abroad, for fear they should not learn the Art of Love and Gallantry time enough.

. . .

Since therefore we consider, under this Article, the Disorders of Marriage proceeding from the two foregoing Causes, *viz.* The too great Liberty allowed our Women, and the want of true Love in the young Couple, before the indissolvable Knot is tied; our Business is to prevent these great Inconveniences; and since the antient heroick Way of making Love is not to be expected, nor the *Italian* Locks and Bolts to be allowed in a free Nation, as ours is, the great Difficulty is, to contrive proper Ways and Means to keep them in due Restraint; by which I do not mean a corporal Restraint, but a just Decorum, suitable to the virginal, or matrimonial State. The first may be more strict, and even involuntary sometimes, because young Virgins are neither capable, nor ought to be entire Mistresses of themselves: The latter is to be voluntary, and only bounded by the Rules of Duty and Decency. The best way to procure this voluntary Restraint in married Women, is to endeavour to create an inviolable Love in the young Couple before Marriage, that when they come to be joined in those strict Bonds, they may be persuaded, that they have obtained what they sought with so much Anxiety, and would preserve with the Loss of all that was dear to them.

Notes

1 Marriages were not regularized until 1753 when Hardwicke's Marriage Act made the publishing of banns and a properly conducted church wedding legally necessary. The effect was to stop both the increasingly common instant weddings, often performed for unscrupulous reasons, and the custom of accepting betrothal as binding and therefore as sanctioning pre-marital sexual relations. Texts like this one contributed to the climate in which the Marriage Act was passed, seeing rising numbers of irregular marriages and illegitimate births as evidence of a decline in public morality.
2 Alexander Pope, 'Epistle to a Lady' (1735), l. 216. Pope's formulation of what was already a satiric commonplace reverberates throughout the eighteenth century (cf. 2.1, 2.4, 3.5).

2.6 'A Physician', from *The Pleasures of Conjugal Love Explained. In an Essay Concerning Human Generation*, [1740]

'At What Age a Young Man and a Young Woman Ought to Marry'

. . . some Physicians have maintained, that Women were hotter than Men, because they are sooner ripe for Business, for if generally speaking, say they, they have more Blood, they have also more Heat, because the natural Heat resides after a more eminent manner, where there is most of that Humour.

They add, that we observe Women to be more ingenious and active than Men, because having more Blood they have also more Spirits, which are the Cause of their Activity, they have also sooner Hair on their Privities, and some have been seen to have their Privities veiled before they have enter'd the Age of Discretion. . . .

Besides, they are much more amorous than Men, and, as Sparrows, do not live long, because they are too hot and too susceptible of Love, so Women last less Time, because they have a devouring Heat that consumes them by Degrees.

There are *Messalina's*[1] found to this very day, who, by Reason of their excessive Heat, would be in a condition to dispute with several Men in effect, they suffer Cold with more Constancy, and if their natural Heat, of which they have a large store, did not resist the Coldness of Winter, we should hear more Women than Men complain of the Rigour of the Season.

If I might be allow'd some Digression from the subject I treat of, I think, I might without any manner of difficulty prove the contrary of what is said of the Constitutions of Women. I could show, that the great quantity of Blood proceeds rather from the Mediocrity than any Excess of Heat; that Women are rather fickle and light than ingenious; that if they Engender and grow old sooner, it shows the weakness of that Heat: That Excess of Love cannot be particularly ascribed to the force of this same Heat, but to the Inconstancy of their Imagination, or rather to the Providence of Nature, that has made them to serve us for Play-toys after our more serious Occupations. After all, if they are not susceptible of Cold, we must not look for the Cause thereof, but in the ordinary plight of Body, which is always opposite to the Generation of the most active Qualities.

Man, to the contrary, acts with more firmness, feeds more happily, defends himself with more Courage and Presence of Mind, reasons with more Strength, and contributes towards the getting of Children with more Alacrity. He acts particularly in Generation, where he communicates himself, and by other Actions of the Body and Mind gives proofs of his Strength and Heat; whereas the Woman only suffers the Impressions a Man makes upon her, and often is not ready so soon as he to furnish wherewithal to form a Man. In short, she is only to Conceive, to give Suck, and to breed up Children.

Note

1 The wife of the Roman Emperor Claudius, she became identified
with sexual misconduct, on the probably unjust evidence of contemporary scandal (cf. 5.6).

2.7   from *The Ladies Dispensatory: or, Every Woman her own Physician*, 1740

'The Preface'

The delicate Texture of a Woman's Constitution, as on the one
Hand it renders her the most amiable Object in the Universe, so
on the other it subjects her to an infinite Number of Maladies, to
which Man is an utter Stranger, or which he is acquainted with
only from Report and Observation. Being designed by the great
Author of Nature for the Vehicle thro' which the human Species
should be propagated, and the Repository where every original
vital Particle should be kept and nourished for a certain Time,
while it encreases from infinitely small to a very considerable
Magnitude, it was proper that her Parts should be suited to these
Ends; which they could not be, according to Reason, without
subjecting the whole Machine to its present Inconveniences. That
lax and pliant Habit, capable of being dilated and contracted on
every Occasion, must necessarily want that Degree of Heat and
Firmness which is the Characteristick of Man, and which enables
him to digest and evacuate his Nutriment in due Time and
Proportion. Hence arises that monthly Plenitude which calls for
an extraordinary Discharge, and for which Nature has provided
in the Situation and Form of certain Vessels. Now this periodical
Secretion, as it is unlike any Thing known in other Animals; so it
occasions various Symptoms and Cases that deserve the utmost
and nicest Regard of Physicians, as they resemble no other
Diseases that fall under their Inspection. And if we add to this, the
Dangers, Difficulties, and various Symptoms attendant on Child-
bearing, all which, as well as the former, are treated of at large in
the following Sheets, I make no question but the Necessity and
Usefulness of Books in general on the Diseases of Women, will be
acknowledged not only by ev'ry one of that Sex, but also by every
one of ours who considers the Matter, and is endued with
Sentiments truly generous and humane.

. . .

. . . there is one Particular, of the highest Regard to all Mothers of Children, which I must beg Leave a little to insist on in this Preface: I mean, the advising them to nurse their own Offspring, where it is not utterly inconsistent with some present Disorder. This is not only a Duty incumbent on them, but the most likely Means to preserve their own Health, and prevent many of the Diseases to which they are too often subject. . . .

But, say some, if the Child lives and thrives, what Matter is it whose Milk he sucks? Why do they not say, what Matter of whose Body he is born, or of whose Blood and Spirits he consists? Is not the Blood in the Breasts, tho' altered by Heat in Colour, the same it was in the Womb? And is not the Provision of Nature herein wonderful, that when the Blood has done its Part in forming and finishing the Child in the Womb, it then ascends up higher, ready to issue forth in salutary Streams, for the Support and Establishment of the first Principles of Life, and to recruit the new-born Babe with its proper and natural Sustenance?

It is not without Reason thought, that the good or ill Qualities of the Milk have a considerable Influence on the Mind and Body, and contribute, as much as any Thing, towards the forming a Similitude of Disposition and Temper in the one, as well as of Strength and Beauty in the other. . . .

What Madness is it then to leave a Body and a Mind, formed upon noble and generous Principles, to be corrupted by the base Mixture and Allay of a Stranger's Milk, especially if your Nurse (which too frequently happens) should prove dishonest, intemperate, or lewd? And there is not always that Care which ought to be, even in the Choice of them. Is it fit we should suffer the Infant to be thus perniciously infected, and to draw his Life out of a mean ignoble Body? . . .

But besides all this, there is another Consideration, not to be overlooked or unregarded: That those Mothers who do, as it were, discharge their Children from them, and thus dispose of them, do at least weaken, if not dissolve that Bond of Love and Tenderness which Nature ties between them. For as soon as the Child is out of Sight, that Ardency of natural Affection insensibly decays, and we hear no more of that Impatience and Solicitude, which would otherwise discover itself, than if the Object of it were laid in the Grave. I might add, that the Thoughts and Inclinations also of the Infant, are apt to fix and center in the Person from whom it has derived its Nourishment, and with whom it has been most conversant, without any apparent Want or Desire of its Mother. When therefore the first Tenderness and Affection are thus biass'd and perverted, whatever After-love Children thus educated may shew their Parents, it seems, in a great Measure, owing to opinion and Custom, rather than to a true Principle of Nature. . . .

And no less vehement, on the Head, is a celebrated Divine of our national Church, with a few of whose Thoughts I shall conclude. We must be so faithful, says he, as to tell nice and delicate Mothers, that nursing of their Children is a natural Duty; and because it is so, of a more necessary and indispensable Obligation, than any positive Precept of Revealed Religion; and that the general Neglect of it is one of the great and crying Sins of this Age and Nation. – It is a sort of exposing Children, which frequently, in the Consequence of it, is little better than laying them in the Streets. – The Objections of *Trouble* and *Restraint* which it lays on Women of high Rank, are altogether insufficient. As to the Trouble, no Person can be discharg'd from any Duty on that Account, since God, who made it a Duty, foresaw the Trouble of it when he made it so. And as to the Restraint, it can only restrain from spending the Morning in superfluous Dressing, the Day in formal and impertinent Visits, the Evening at lascivious Plays, and much of the Night in Gaming and Revelling. Nor can State and Dignity excuse them; because whatever Rank the Mother is of, the Child bears a Proportion to it, and there is the same Equality between the greatest Lady and her own Child, as between the meanest Beggar and hers. The Generation of the Infant is the Effect of Desire; but the Care of it argues Virtue and Choice.

2.8   R. James M.D., from *A Medicinal Dictionary*, 1743

HYSTERICA: . . . the frequency of this Disease is not more remarkable than the Variety of Forms, by which it discovers itself, as it assumes the Appearance of almost every Distemper with which miserable Mortals are afflicted. For it always produces

Symptoms peculiar to whatever Part of the Body it seizes; and, unless the Physician be a Person of Judgment and Penetration, he will be deceived, and imagine such Symptoms to belong to some Disease essential to the Part affected, and not to the Hysteric Passion. . . .

It is to be observed, that all Women are not equally subject to this Disorder, but that it more particularly seizes Virgins, before their first menstrual Discharge, such as are marriageable, young Widows, and Wives; especially if they are full of Blood and Moisture, and have not borne Children: As, also, such as are brought up in Idleness, or are of a soft Texture, and delicate Constitution. . . .*Forestus* . . . says, that robust, masculine Women, if they are corpulent, full of Blood, and continent, tho' inclined to Venereal Enjoyments, and live at Ease, feeding upon hot, moist, and flatulent Diet, and indulging themselves in generous Wines, and Delicacies, which prove a Stimulus to Venery, are frequently seized with this Disorder, without a suppression of the Menses. . . . Besides, we have, among others, the Testimony of *Aretaeus*, that young Women, whose nervous Systems are delicate and weak, who are of a tender Habit, and subject to exorbitant Sallies of lawless Passion, are in greater Danger of this spasmodic Disease, than those who are robust, hardy, laborious, and of a more steady Mind. 'Tis also observable, that Women of sanguine, choleric Constitutions, and prone to impetuous Commotions of Mind, are subject to severe Convulsions of the nervous Parts. . . .

There still remains another highly natural, and efficacious Method of Cure, which is, that to be expected from Marriage. Reason, Experience, and the Authorities of the greatest Physicians, concur in pronouncing Matrimony highly beneficial in removing hysteric Disorders.

2.9   from *An Account of the Rise, Progress, and Present State of the Magdalen Hospital, for the reception of Penitent Prostitutes. Together with Dr. Dodd's Sermons . . .*, 1770[1]

from *The First Sermon, preached before the President, vice-Presidents, Treasurer and Governors, April 28 1759.*

Preface

The great decrease of our people is a subject of common observation, and doubtless one source of it is that abominable lust, and prevalent promiscuous commerce of the sexes, which, to the prejudice of honourable matrimony, so notoriously abounds. As very many of the objects in the *Magdalen-House* are extremely young, the preserving them from that immediate destruction into which they must otherwise have fallen, it is hoped, is an object not unworthy men who love their country, and wish to promote its happiness. And as many of them have been deluded, in the most *scandalous* manner, some, I may say, without a figure, almost in their *hanging sleeves,* and have been kept purposely in black and total ignorance of their crime, to which they were unwittingly introduced; surely, it is but a debt we owe to such, to give them the means of instruction, and *one* chance at least for eternal life, which they could otherwise never have found.

Sermon

'Tis true, that to common and superficial observers of things, nothing seems a more detestable object, more worthy our hatred and scorn, than a common and pestilent Prostitute. And indeed were those in that miserable condition, either placed in it by their own choice, or detained in it by their own free-will: had a vicious inclination at first introduced, or did the same vicious inclination continue them in it, amidst repeated opportunities to retrieve and return; we would then grant they were wholly unworthy the least compassion, and more beneath humanity than the beast that perisheth. But when we are fully convinced, that different, far different is the truth of the case; then compassion pleads their cause, and humanity urgeth us to their succour and redress.

For, though the great author of our being hath, for wise and good ends, implanted the same passions in either sex, and therefore transgression is as possible, and of consequence as excusable on the weaker side, as it is on the stronger; yet fact abundantly demonstrates to us, that men, for the most part, are the seducers; and the generality of those, who now claim our aid, have been introduced to their misery by the complicated arts of seduction, and by every unjustifiable method, which cruel and brutish lust suggests to the crafty seducer.

And it is well known how much harder that case, in this particular, is with the female sex, than with our own. – One false step for ever ruins their fair fame; blasts the fragrance of virgin innocence, and consigns them to contempt and disgrace! While the author of their distress may triumph in his villainy! and – shame to human nature – not be branded with one mark of reproach for the ruin of a fellow-creature!

from *The Third Sermon, preached at the anniversary meeting of the Governors, March 18 1762*

. . . Nor can it be an unpleasing reflection, that amidst the prevalence of selfishness, of dissipation, and of disregard to serious religion, (too justly complained of, I fear, in the present day) yet a general philanthropy happily abounds through the nation. . . . And public charity rears up her lovely head, and triumphs! *There*, she shews you Christian knowledge widely spread throughout the earth; and thousands of children instructed in the principles of evangelical truth.[a] *There* she shews you the desolate and afflicted widow, with her orphans around her, forgetting awhile the deprivation of former comforts, and their sad downfall from a state of plenty and of peace; while the generous hand of pity, by administering to their support, is supplying the loss of the affectionate husband, and indulgent father. *There* she shews you the sick, the wounded, and the lame, smiling amidst their anguish, and blessing the benevolence which affords them such seasonable relief. . . . *There* she points to the refuge of indigent pregnant women, awhile unmindful of their pangs, and gratefully acknowledging that goodness, which hath consulted their security and comfort, at the hour of sorrow and extremity. *There* she presents to your sight the retreats, of phrensy, at lucid intervals thankful in her cells, for those kind edifices, which screen from public view the most formidable disguises, and mortifying abasements of human nature. *There* she shews you the chambers of deserted infants, of little out-casts, and unfriended orphans, kindly sheltered from the rude blasts of infamy, of ignorance, of ruin; and made instrumental to the commerce, the defence, and the domestic necessities of the nation.[b] And *there* she shews you happy PENITENTS exulting in the goodness of their God; and pouring out their tears and thanks to heaven and their benefactors, for restoring them to all things dear and valuable to human creatures upon earth.

. . .

Indeed, I cannot but observe here, that so scanty are the means of subsistence allowed the female sex; so few the occupations which they can pursue, and those so much engrossed by our sex: so small are the profits arising from their labours, and so difficult often the power of obtaining employment, especially for those of doubtful character; and frequently, so utter their unskilfulness in any branches of their common industry, from a mistaken neglect of their parents in their education; – and several of whom, while they absurdly expend much on boarding-schools, think it beneath them to have their daughters taught a trade. – So scanty are the means of subsistence, arising from these and the like causes, that, it is but too well known, many virtuous and decent young women, left desolate with poor unfriended children, have been compelled to the horrid necessity (and we want not to be told, what numbers in this great city lie in wait to improve, and turn to their own advantage that necessity) of procuring bread by prostitution!

from *The Fourth Sermon, n.d.*

But alas! wretched and ruined, introduced to shame and sorrow, reputation and virtue lost, cast off and abandoned by all – whither could they fly, or where obtain relief? They cannot, must not utterly perish in want and nakedness: – perhaps too, the anguish and misfortunes of some of them have been aggravated, by the necessity of supporting a little hapless infant, heir of its mother's infamy and suffering! Oh dreadful alternative to the mother, either to see her child, her much loved, tho' unfortunate child, perish with hunger and with thirst, – or to obtain its support by the horror of prostitution! yet to this dire necessity many broken-hearted mothers have been reduced! and thus the best and most tender parental affection has reigned in the woman's breast, while the poor afflicted wretch has been compelled to a way of life most detestable and shocking to her!

You would not doubt the reformation of such a one, if an opportunity to reform and to regain her credit in the world could be given her. But *here*, and *here only*, such an opportunity is given; an opportunity, already embraced by many, and by many, we have the utmost reason to believe, truly improved.

'An Authentic Narrative of a Magdalen'

Of this number was *A.F.* an hapless young woman, of about
sixteen years of age, admitted into the MAGDALEN HOUSE
under a load of infamy and horror, in *December* 1761. She was the
favourite daughter of her father, a person of a decent and
respectable character in life, who, though he had several children, regarded this with eyes of peculiar tenderness and affection. Pleasing and delicate in her person, she had always hitherto
shewn an equally amiable mind, and returned her father's regard
with becoming attention. But alas! an insidious seducer soon
found the way to her heart; and under the delusive pretensions of
courtship and marriage, in an unguarded hour, ruined and
withdrew her from her father's house. He, in all the frantic rage
of distress, sought the child of his tenderest affection. He found,
forgave, and brought her home. But, whether through an
infatuation for her seducer, (which, however strange, is found
but too often the case) whether through the admonitions of her
afflicted parents too repeatedly urged, or through restraint, not
known before; once more, in an evil hour, she left her father's
house, and soon, abandoned by her seducer, plunged into total
licentiousness and debauchery.

Her father, who felt such anguish as none but the parental
heart can in any degree conceive, now gave up his child as
irretrievably lost. Happening, however, some time after, to pass
along the street, he saw a young creature, highly dressed, throw
herself into a chair, which waited at the door of one of those many
infamous houses in this city, to convey her to her lodgings, after
the debaucheries of the place. Let the parent guess what He must
have felt, when he perceived this gay victim of licentiousness to be
– his child, his favourite child – his daughter! He stood struck
with horror and amazement, whilst she – pierced no doubt to the
heart, yet unwilling to humble herself, and confess her guilt,
turned from him, and by her immediate order, was carried off,
leaving the parent who had passed so many sollicitous hours for
her, almost petrified with grief, and unable to move!

There is great reason to believe that this occasional but
affecting interview touched her to the quick, and was the
foundation of that resolve which she soon after put into practice.
For, the fury of unbridled passion beginning to abate, and the

distresses of her detested course of life daily increasing; the early impressions of parental tenderness naturally coincided with these to awaken reflection, and to shew her herself.

Alarmed at the view, she wished, she determined to return, and try what repentance could do. For which purpose she applied to the MAGDALEN HOUSE, and found a ready admission. For how could admission be refused to one so young, labouring under such a burden of misery, and with such probable expectations of sincere amendment?

Those expectations were not disappointed: she continued three years in the House; during the whole of which her behaviour was decent, consistent, and commendable. But, though reconciled to God, though conscious of the sincerity of her heart, she could find no solid satisfaction, till reconciled to the father whom she had so much injured, and to whose soul she had given such unspeakable anguish. The father, however, was now deaf to all her solicitations. In vain she wrote, in vain she pleaded: every effort proved ineffectual to procure that pardon, without which her heart can never know peace.

A person who deeply interests himself in favour of the Objects of the Charity, wrote to her father. The following was the answer he received.

'*SIR*,
'I had the honour of yours, and with it a renewal of my sorrow of heart; which proceeded, not from your relation of an amendment of life in a long lost and abandoned child, but from the remembrance of her unhappy fall. Did you but know, Sir, with what care and industry an affectionate father and mother (possessed of but little, perhaps worthy of more,) have discharged their duty, there is nothing but your great goodness of heart could induce you to be so generous an advocate of one, that has forfeited so much. But what can I say on this afflicting subject, with any degree of propriety, to keep clear of offending the fathers of an unhappy many; whilst my indignation for the conduct of one, causes such perturbation of body and mind, as renders me defenceless both in words and actions.

'Un-neglected by precept and example, unprovoked by want or ill usage, she sacrificed all that was binding, to a lawless unruly passion, and plunged herself into that long scene of misery, which

91

must have been longer still, were she not rescued by the humane hands of this noble Charity. Happy is it for her, that you, Sir, have condescended to say, she has approved herself worthy of it; and happier still will she be, if she continues to deserve, from those bountiful hands which protect, and have led her back to those paths of virtue from whence she strayed.

'Pardon me, Sir, that I detain you so long on a melancholy subject, persuaded as I am, that your tenderness of heart has suffered by many such doleful tales; and I hope you will forgive me when I say, that I am not sufficiently prepared for the sorrowful interview you desire, with my once most tenderly beloved daughter. But, as your kind and fatherly letter has conveyed some consolation to a long disturbed and afflicted heart, by telling me that her repentance has begot compassion in you, and the rest of the worthy Governors of that blessed Charity; I will not appear so obdurate and unrelenting to say, that I will never see her; but, in time, on her persevering in good works, and finishing her reformation, agreeable to the time instituted by that excellent Charity; I may not only see her, but also have pity, and restore her to that care and protection, which never departed from me, until she departed from them. . . .'

. . . Her heart was sincere, and her reformation real. Received home with joy, she proved by her whole behaviour the truth of her repentance, and conducted herself in every manner suitable to her circumstances, and agreeable to her parent.

Sollicitous for her welfare, he soon after gained her an establishment in a family of worth and distinction, where getting an unfortunate scratch upon the leg, and through attention to her duty neglecting it, bad consequences ensued; a mortification speedily came on, and an amputation of her leg was found unavoidable.

She bore the dreadful tidings with great composure and resignation; sent to the Chapel of the *Magdalen Hospital*, earnestly requesting the prayers of all her sister penitents for her, and underwent the cruel operation with a patience and resolution which surprized those who performed it.

It is easy to conceive, from a habit of body so wretched as that which rendered the amputation necessary, what must have been the consequences of such an expedient: a total mortification came on; and in a few days after she expired; expired with blessings on the Charity, as the great means of her salvation; expired with all that serenity of soul, with all that humility, yet confidence of hope, which nothing but true christian principles can inspire; but which those principles will always inspire into the breast of the real Penitent.

Notes

(a) The Societies for propagating and promoting Christian Knowledge, [established 1699] with which the Charity Schools are connected.

(b) The Foundling Hospital [opened 1741], the Marine Society [for Educating Poor Destitute Boys to the Sea], the Asylum, etc. etc.

1 The Magdalen House Charity for penitent prostitutes was established by private subscription in 1758, a practical application of the concerns about the 'torrent of lewdness' and the falling population which lie behind passage 2.5. It offered shelter and an ascetic regime of work and worship for prostitutes who petitioned for entry, were judged genuinely penitent and who were not 'infected with the foul disease'. Of the 1,036 prostitutes who passed through the Hospital in the first ten years, 509 were 'reconciled to, & received by their Friends or placed in Services in reputable Families, and to Trades'.

2.10 Martha Mears 'Practitioner in Midwifery', from *The Pupil of Nature; or Candid Advice to the Fair Sex*, 1797

'Essay I'

'Follow Nature' is the great lesson which the wisest and best of men have never been tired of repeating.[1] That simple yet important piece of advice includes, in two words, an admirable summary of human prudence. FOLLOW NATURE – trace her footsteps – listen to her voice – mark well her conduct in all her works. She will teach you to do what is right and to avoid what is dangerous or improper: she will hold out the fairest models of excellence for your imitation: she will bring you back from your wanderings, and lead you securely along the delightful paths of truth and happiness. Resign yourself then with confidence to this unerring guide; and if at any time you should be tempted to forsake her, check the fatal impulse by instantly recollecting, that you are not more liable to lose your way even in the darkness of ignorance, than in the twilight of superficial knowledge – in pursuing meteors of fancy, or the false glare of imposture and pretended science.

But general precepts are of very little use, unless they are unfolded and applied to particular cases. It is my intention therefore to shew that the study of nature alone will direct us to the proper treatment of women after conception, – to the surest means of preserving the health, and of promoting the vigour, growth, and beauty of their offspring. The idea is rather new in appearance than reality. It has not, indeed, been laid down as a principle, or made the foundation of any system of midwifery; but its truth has been admitted by physicians of the greatest eminence in every age and every country. I claim no other merit but that of a well-meant endeavour to present it in a clear and interesting light. I have little more to do than to copy some pages from the volume of nature: – happy, if I could preserve the beautiful simplicity of the original! – happier still, if I could impress upon the minds of my fair countrywomen a few of its salutary maxims! I do not mean to amuse them with an idle parade of learning: I do not come dressed out in a rich wardrobe of words, to dazzle their attention: such pomp, such ornaments would ill become the humble handmaid of nature. Yet, in spite of prejudice, I hope my own sex will grant a candid hearing to one who is herself a mother; – who has united the advantages of experience with those of a regular education and a moderate share of practice; – who knows no language but that of the heart; – and whose fondest wish, in the present attempt, is to allay the fears of pregnant women, to inspire them with a just reliance on the powers of nature, and, above all, to guard them and their lovely children against the dangers of mismanagement, of rashness, of unfeeling and audacious quackery. . . .

A state of pregnancy has too generally been considered as a state of indisposition or disease: this is a fatal error and the source of almost all the evils to which women in childbearing are liable. The joy of becoming a mother, the anticipated pleasure of presenting a fond husband with the dearest pledge of mutual love is chilled by imaginary terrors. A certain change at first is felt: some emotions of fear are then excited: these are increased by the fairy tales of old nurses, – by the rules without number, and the medicines without necessity which interested men so often prescribe. Even where advice may seem proper, we should always be sparing of our cautions. The very means of safety awaken an idea of danger; and that idea is more to be dreaded, because harder to be removed than the worst of maladies.

We must begin, then, by banishing the false alarms which so absurd a mistake may give rise to. We must hasten to convince the timid female, that the very state, at which she has been taught to tremble, brings her nearer to the perfection of her being; and, instead of disease, affords a much stronger presumption of health and security. See the benignity of nature in all her other works! – Cast your eyes abroad in the season of love, when each plant tends to re-produce itself by its flowers and its fruit, – when the birds of song redouble their melody, and those that excel in the beauty of their colouring array themselves in their finest plumage! – Then tell me if you can suppose that nature is less attentive to her darling object, woman, when preparing her for the great purpose of perpetuating the human species.

'Essay VI'

Women who follow very hardy occupations in the country, and to whom what fortune has denied in point of affluence, is abundantly compensated by a large stock of health, feel no inconvenience from their usual employments in the early months of pregnancy: they seldom or never miscarry: they have few complaints: they require no indulgence, but a little abatement of their toil, when they become unwieldy; and as the womb partakes of the general vigour and activity of the whole frame, it expels its burthen in due time with much ease; and the recovery from childbed is so rapid as scarcely to leave any remembrance of its having been a state of pain or labour. Such persons want no instructions concerning exercise. They have nothing to fear but extraordinary shocks either of body or mind, – the tempest of the passions, or external violence. They know very well, and therefore need not be cautioned against the bad consequences of any straining efforts, – any over-exertion in lifting or carrying heavy weights, – in a word, any painful and exhausting task. They follow simple nature in every thing, even in regulating the proper periods of labour and rest. They go to bed with the lamb, and they rise with the lark: their slumbers are sound, and their wakings chearful.

It is not so with poor married women in great cities. The impure, confined air they breathe relaxes the frame and destroys its activity. What they eat, what they drink, is often improper, sometimes pernicious. Their meals and their hours of rest are equally irregular. Night is too often changed, as it were, in to day; and the victim of poverty is forced from her bed at one, two, three, or four o'clock in the morning, according to the caprice, or the sordid views of some selfish, unfeeling, marble-hearted employer to labour for sixteen or eighteen hours at the washing-tub, – to waste all the necessary supplies of strength and of life in unseasonable, unhealthy, and long continued toil! Is it possible that one woman can treat another with such cruelty, and yet lay claim to the title of a good housewife! Is it possible that you can sleep while you are robbing a fellow creature of needful repose? Can you view with pleasure the work done, when you consider that a miscarriage may be the consequence, or that you may be in reality the murderer both of a parent and a child? Perhaps your unfortunate hireling is obliged to conceal her condition, in order to get employment: – but, how wretched is the excuse, that you did not know her to be pregnant? Let her condition be what it may, surely the day is long enough for the toils of cheerless poverty, without adding thereto the night also. Do not prescribe such hard terms to those whom hunger and distress leave at your mercy. Your tasks should be moderate, and your pay liberal. The example of others is no reason for your continuing a practice inconsistent with humanity. It is a sort of domestic slave-trade, the abolition of which will do equal honour to your heart and your understanding.

From what has been said on the subject of exercise, ladies of fortune will easily perceive, that luxury is not a more fatal enemy than indolence. They both produce nearly the same effects: they tend to increase, in a state of pregnancy, the natural disposition to fulness: the system is loaded: the blood loiters in its course: the juices, retarded in their circulation, stagnate and grow foul: the whole body becomes languid and inactive: the powers of the womb in particular are enfeebled or perverted; and various disorders, abortion, or long, severe, and dangerous labours are the usual consequences. To prevent these, pregnant ladies must not only avoid all excesses of the table, they must also resist the soft allurements of lazy unnerving indulgence.

Note

1 The advice to 'follow nature' is a moral commonplace throughout the eighteenth century, but in a text of this type and date, a likely specific source would be Rousseau's *Émile* (1762).

3

EDUCATION

Women's education was fiercely debated in the eighteenth century and the importance of education as an ideological apparatus is evident throughout the texts included here. Arguments about whether, and how, women should be educated are always part of wider political debates, and in terms of sexual politics they raise the fundamental question of difference itself. Education was the issue on which feminists began to challenge assumptions about women's natural inferiority, offering telling critiques of the conduct-book construction of femininity. The obvious inadequacies of women's education were for them a means of proving the circularity of the conservative view. According to that view, a limited curriculum was justified by a female 'nature' which, the feminists pointed out, the curriculum had itself created. As Mary Astell put it in 1696, 'the Incapacity, if there be any, is acquired not natural' (see 5.1). But the differences between 'radical' and 'conservative' educational theories are far from clear-cut, as the passages here and in Section 5 demonstrate. (For a full sense of the debate, the two sections should be read together.) The conservative texts all stress the need to give women a serious, if limited, education in keeping with their providential role as rulers of the domestic economy. The radical potential in this image of female power is developed by advocates of more innovative models of female education, but even in the most progressive texts, such models are in constant negotiation with the dominant ideology of feminine propriety and with other, in some cases contradictory, political allegiances.

Throughout the century, theorists disagreed on how to define
the qualities and potential of the female mind, on how girls'
education should differ from that of boys, and on the social roles
and intellectual rewards available to the educated woman. At the
beginning of the period, very few girls received much of a formal
education (see 3.1, 5.1, 5.2). By the mid-century, the pressures of
an expanding bourgeoisie and competitive marriage market had
established some degree of education as the norm for daughters
of the middle class, but the issue remained contentious. The
rising numbers of educated women were cited as proof of
England's cultural superiority (3.7), but the girls' boarding-
schools which proliferated during the century became syn-
onymous with low moral standards and national decline (3.6),
and the satiric stereotype of the sexually unattractive learned
woman remained powerfully influential (3.3, 3.9; and cf. 2.5, 4.9,
4.10, 4.11, 4.17).

The dominant view informing these contradictory popular
images, and which changed little during the century, is represented by the first two passages included here. The extract from
Fénélon's influential *Treatise on the Education of Daughters* (3.1) is
from the 1805 translation, a measure of the continuing importance (or renewed need) at the end of the century of a text first
translated into English in 1707. His terms are familiar: women
are 'by nature weaker than men' and the 'irregularities' of
uneducated women are blamed for revolutions of all kinds (cf.
2.1); education is the means by which that disruptive energy
('curiosity' or 'a roving imagination') can be safely contained. The
discourse of complementarity is used to promote a strictly
hierarchical system based on separate spheres – women have the
power to 'civilize and govern' the family in support of men's
authority in 'public affairs' (cf. 3.7, 3.8, 3.9, and 1.1, 2.5).

The extract from Hester Chapone's *Letters on the Improvement of
the Mind* (3.2) concentrates more specifically on the curriculum
suitable for a girl in training for her civilizing role. The detailed
curriculum described in Chapone's manual had an extensive
influence, not least because, in a typical slippage between text and
female author, Chapone herself was taken to personify her own
educated ideal of virtuous self-effacement (see 4.19; for other
examples of this identification of text with author, see 4.10, 4.11,
4.17, 4.18). Again the stress is on moderation, on decorative

accomplishments ('the graces of imagination'), on the fear of overloading the delicate mind or transgressing an allotted role, so that the 'male' subjects – the classics, science, religious controversy – are to be avoided (for a female claim to science, see 4.17; for a feminist defence of a different curriculum, see 5.2). According to Fénélon, education teaches 'the value of silence' (cf. 3.7, 1.6), and in both these texts women with too much and too little education are equally open to 'vanity and luxury', the temptations of the public world. The discourse of containment, familiar from the texts on female sexuality, is rewritten in terms of the female mind.

The ideological effects of this essentially contradictory consensus position were less easily contained. Its concern to perpetuate traditional gender roles through a defence of female seriousness actually opened up possibilities of other kinds of fulfilment for women, and put the conduct-book construction of femininity under pressure to accommodate, or refute, those possibilities. That process can be traced in several of the texts included here, and is conducted largely through debates about what women are being educated for. Thus Vicesimus Knox's fictional correspondent (3.3) articulates the social displacement experienced by the educated woman, but ends by asserting her commitment to intellectual 'satisfaction' for its own sake, in spite of its 'disagreeable consequences'. Mary Wollstonecraft (3.4) is similarly concerned with social displacement, but in more starkly economic terms. Her text is an interesting reworking of the frequent conservative fear of education as a means to disruptive social mobility (cf. 2.5, 2.9). In a painful account of the limited employment opportunities available to the woman with an education and no fortune, she exposes the financial motivation frequently responsible for educating daughters and explores the peculiarly liminal class position of the governess or female companion (cf. 3.8). As so often in Wollstonecraft, sensibility is offered as compensation for material suffering: in another striking parallel with more conservative texts, she offers women consolation through religious sublimation (cf. 3.9, and 1.2, 1.7, 4.2, 5.1).

The wider political contexts of these issues are seen most clearly in the three final texts. Here, the need to adjust and reassert

traditional gender roles is explicitly part of anti-Jacobin discourses following the French Revolution (cf. 4.19). Thus the
passage from Hawkins's *Letters on the Female Mind* (3.7) deflects
Helen Maria Williams's radical questions, '*A King or no King? A
Nobility or no Nobility*', on to definitions of the female mind as
apolitical, implicitly accusing Williams of unnaturally transgressing her gender role. Hawkins's text is the most unproblematically
traditional of the three. In Wakefield and More, the conservative
position is visibly influenced by Enlightenment views of women's
capacities. In a potentially radical gesture, Wakefield (3.8)
appropriates the new utilitarianism of Adam Smith to claim wider
employment for women, but uses that claim defensively to
enforce a rigid class hierarchy. More, too, appeals to gender
solidarity (3.9) in a very clever reworking of feminist rhetoric for
rather different ends: she urges patriotic women to reject the
temptations of knowledge offered by 'the new German
enlighteners' whose dangerous ideas can lead only to 'those
gratifications which custom, not religion, has tolerated in the
male sex'.

Catherine Macaulay (3.5), like Wollstonecraft, was one of the
radical theorists More identifies as having succumbed to 'the
writings of the French infidels' (see also 5.5, 5.6). *Letters on
Education* is strongly influenced by Rousseau's *Émile* (cf. 2.10), but
it rewrites Rousseau in maintaining that girls should be educated
alongside boys. The inevitable result, Macaulay argues, will be a
revolutionary change in sexual power relations, the tyranny of
'passion' overthrown by rational friendship (cf. 5.1). Macaulay's
celebration of chastity cannot escape the terms of conduct-book
propriety, but its implications are actually to destroy the basis of
that system of difference. Her ideal of womanhood is
androgynous rather than feminine: '*manly*, noble, full of strength
and majesty' (my emphasis). For Hawkins, Wakefield, and More,
sexual difference is fixed, part of the Providential order; for
Macaulay, it is culturally determined, open to redefinition under
the scrutiny of Enlightenment rationalism. But Macaulay's is an
isolated voice: though education for (middle-class) women was
established at least in principle during the eighteenth century, its
overwhelming effect was to reinforce rather than undermine
obtaining gender definitions.

3.1 François de Salignac de la Mothe-Fénélon, trans. Rev. T. F. Dibdin, from *Treatise on the Education of Daughters*, 1687; first English translation 1707; this translation 1805

'On the Importance of the Education of Daughters'

The Education of Girls is, in general, exceedingly neglected: custom, and maternal caprice, often appear to have the entire regulation of it. It absolutely seems as if we supposed the sex to be in need of little or no instruction. On the other hand, the Education of *Boys* is considered as a very important concern, affecting the welfare of the public; and although it be frequently attended with errors and mistakes, great abilities are nevertheless thought necessary for the accomplishment of it. . . . In regard to Girls, some exclaim, 'why make them learned? curiosity renders them vain and conceited: it is sufficient if they be one day able to govern their families, and implicitly obey their husbands!' Examples are then adduced of many women whom science has rendered ridiculous; and on such contemptible authority we think ourselves justified in blindly abandoning our daughters to the conduct of ignorant and indiscreet mothers.

It is true, that we should be on our guard not to make them ridiculously learned. Women, in general, possess a weaker but more inquisitive mind than men; hence it follows that their pursuits should be of a quiet and sober turn. They are not formed to govern the state, to make war, or to enter into the church; so that they may well dispense with any profound knowledge relating to politics, military tactics, philosophy, and theology. The greater part of the mechanical arts are also improper for them: they are made for moderate exercise; their bodies as well as minds are less strong and energetic than those of men; but to compensate for their defects, nature has bestowed on them a spirit of industry, united with propriety of behaviour, and an economy which renders them at once the ornament and comfort of home.

But admitting that women are by nature weaker than men, what is the consequence? What, but that the weaker they are, the more they stand in need of support. Have they not duties to perform, which are the very foundation of human existence? Consider, it is women who ruin or uphold families; who regulate the *minutiae* of domestic affairs; and who consequently decide upon some of the dearest and tenderest points which affect the happiness of Man. They have undoubtedly the strongest influence on the manners, good or bad, of society. A sensible woman, who is industrious and religious, is the very soul of a large establishment, and provides both for its temporal and eternal welfare. Notwithstanding the authority of men in public affairs, it is evident, that they cannot effect any lasting good, without the intervention and support of women.

The *world* is not a phantom, it is the *aggregate of all its families;* and who can civilize and govern these with a nicer discrimination than women? besides their natural assiduity and authority at home, they are peculiarly calculated for it, by a carefulness, attention to particulars, industry, and a soft and persuasive manner. . . .

Such then, are the occupations of the female sex, which cannot be deemed of less importance to society than those of the male. It appears that they have a house and establishment to regulate, a husband to make happy, and children to rear. Virtue is as necessary for men as for women; and without entering upon the comparative good or ill which society experiences from the latter sex, it must be remembered that they are *one half of the human race*, REDEEMED BY THE BLOOD OF JESUS CHRIST, AND DESTINED TO LIFE ETERNAL.

Lastly, do not forget that if women do great good to the community when well educated, they are capable of infinite mischief when viciously instructed. It is certain that a bad education works less ill in a male, than in a female breast; for the vices of men often proceed from the bad education which their mothers have given them, and from passions which have been instilled into them at a riper age, from casual intercourse with women.

What intrigues does history present to us – what subversion of laws and manners – what bloody wars – what innovations in religion – what revolutions of states – all arising from the irregularities of women? Ought not these considerations to impress us with the importance of female education?

'Errors in the Ordinary Mode of Education'

. . . weariness and idleness, united with ignorance, beget a pernicious eagerness for public diversions; hence arises a spirit of curiosity, as indiscreet as it is insatiable.

Those who are instructed and busied in serious employments, have, in general, but a moderate curiosity. What they know gives them an indifference for many things of which they are ignorant; and convinces them of the inutility and absurdity of those things, with which narrow minds, that know nothing, and have nothing to exercise themselves upon, are extremely desirous of becoming acquainted.

On the contrary, young women, without instruction or application, have always a roving imagination. In want of substantial employment, their curiosity hurries them on to vain and dangerous pursuits. Those who have somewhat more vivacity, pique themselves on a superior knowledge, and read, with avidity, every book which flatters their vanity: they become enamoured of novels, plays, and 'Tales of Wonder', in which love and licentiousness predominate: they fill their minds with visionary notions, by accustoming themselves to the splendid sentiments of heroes of romance, and hence are rendered unfit for the common intercourse of society. . . .

Some there are who push their curiosity still further, and without the least qualifications, presume to decide upon theological points. – But those who have not sufficient grasp of intellect for these curiosities, have other pursuits, better proportioned to their talents: they are extremely desirous of knowing what is said, and going on in the world – a song – news – an intrigue – to receive letters, and to read those that other people receive; these things delight prodigiously; they wish every thing to be told them, and to tell every thing in turn: they are vain, and vanity is a sure incentive to talk. They become giddy, and volatility prevents those reflections from rising which would show them the value of silence.

3.2 Hester Chapone, from *Letters on the Improvement of the Mind, addressed to a Young Lady*, 1773

'On Politeness and Accomplishments'

With regard to accomplishments, the chief of these is a competent share of reading, well chosen and properly regulated; and of this I shall speak more largely hereafter. Dancing and the knowledge of the French tongue are now so universal that they cannot be dispensed with in the education of a gentlewoman; and indeed they both are useful as well as ornamental; the first, by forming and strengthening the body, and improving the carriage; the second, by opening a large field of entertainment and improvement for the mind. I believe there are more agreeable books of female literature in French than in any other language; and, as they are not less commonly talked of than English books, you must often feel mortified in company, if you are too ignorant to read them. Italian would be easily learnt after French, and, if you have leisure and opportunity, may be worth your gaining, though in your station in life it is by no means necessary.

To write a free and legible hand, and to understand common arithmetic, are indispensable requisites.

As to music and drawing I would only wish you to follow as Genius leads: . . . it is of great consequence to have the power of filling up agreeably those intervals of time, which too often hang heavily on the hands of a woman, if her lot be cast in a retired situation. Besides this, it is certain that even a small share of knowledge in these arts will heighten your pleasure in the performances of others: the taste must be improved before it can be susceptible of an exquisite relish for any of the imitative arts. . . . As I look upon taste to be an inestimable fund of innocent delight, I wish you to lose no opportunity of improving it, and of cultivating in yourself the relish of such pleasures as will not interfere with a rational scheme of life, nor lead you into dissipation, with all its attendant evils of vanity and luxury.

As to the learned languages, though I respect the abilities and application of those ladies, who have attained them, and who make a modest and proper use of them, yet I would by no means advise you – or any woman who is not strongly impelled by a particular genius – to engage in such studies. The labour and time which they require are generally incompatible with our natures and proper employments: the real knowledge which they supply is not essential, since the English, French, or Italian tongues afford tolerable translations of all the most valuable productions of antiquity, besides the multitude of original authors which they furnish; and these are much more than sufficient to store your mind with as many ideas as you will know how to manage. The danger of pedantry and presumption in a woman – of her exciting envy in one sex and jealousy in the other – of her exchanging the graces of imagination for the severity and preciseness of a scholar, would be, I own, sufficient to frighten me from the ambition of seeing my girl remarkable for learning. Such objections are perhaps still stronger with regard to the abstruse sciences. . . .

Though *religion* is the most important of all your pursuits, there are not many *books* on that subject, which I should recommend to you at present. Controversy is wholly improper at your age, and it is also too soon for you to enquire into the evidence of the truth of revelation, or to study the difficult parts of scripture . . ..

The principal study I would recommend, is *history*. I know of nothing equally proper to entertain and improve at the same time, or that is so likely to form and strengthen your judgment, and, by giving you a liberal and comprehensive view of human nature, in some measure to supply the defect of that experience, which is usually attained too late to be of much service to us. . . .

The faculty, in which women usually most excel, is that of imagination; and, when properly cultivated, it becomes the source of all that is most charming in society. Nothing you can read will so much contribute to the improvement of this faculty as *poetry;* which, if applied to its true ends, adds a thousand charms to those sentiments of religion, virtue, generosity, and delicate tenderness, by which the human soul is exalted and refined.

3.3   Vicesimus Knox, from *Essays Moral and Literary*, 1779

'On the Insensibility of the Men to the Charms of a Female Mind Cultivated with Polite and Solid Literature. In a Letter.'

SIR,

I am the only daughter of a clergyman, who, on the death of my mother, which happened when I was about three years old, concentrated his affections in me, and thought he could not display his love more effectually than in giving me a good education. His house was situated in a solitary village, and he had but little parochial duty, so that there was scarcely any thing to divert his attention from this object. He had ever been devoted to letters, and considered learning, next to virtue, as the noblest distinction of human nature.

As soon as I could read, I was initiated in Lilly's Grammar, and, before I was eight years old, could repeat every rule in it with the greatest accuracy. I was taught indeed all kinds of needle-work; but two hours every day were invariably set apart for my improvement in Latin. . . .

My father was so well pleased with my proficiency, and with the task of instructing the object of his dearest love, that he resolved to carry my improvements higher, and to open to my view the spacious fields of Grecian literature. The Greek Grammar I mastered with great ease, and I found a sweetness in the language which amply repaid me for the little difficulties I sometimes encountered. . . . I was enabled to drink at the fountain-head, while others were obliged to content themselves with the distant and polluted stream. I found that no translations whatever, however accurately they might exhibit the sense of originals, could express the beauties of the language, I was possessed of a power of inspecting those volumes, in admiration of which the world has long agreed, but from which my sex has been for the most part unreasonably excluded. It was a noble privilege, and I value myself upon it; but I hope and believe I did not despise those who had not partaken of it solely for want of opportunities.

The French and Italian languages became easy after my acquaintance with the Latin, and my father was of opinion that they are indispensably necessary to the modern scholar. . . .

After having laid a foundation in the languages, which I believe is seldom done with success but at an early age, my father allowed me to feast without controul on the productions of my own country. The learning I had acquired enabled me to read them critically, and to understand all their allusions. The best writers abound so much in quotations, that I cannot help thinking that they who are unacquainted with the ancient languages, must often be mortified at their inability to unlock the concealed treasure.

All the classical poets, from Shakespeare to Pope, were my study and delight. History, which my father always recommended as peculiarly suited to adorn the female mind, was a favourite pursuit. . . . After reading a life, or the history of any particular event, I was always desired by my father to give my sentiments upon it in writing; an exercise which I found to be attended with great advantage.

I never penetrated deeply into the sciences, yet I could not rest satisfied without a superficial knowledge of astronomy, of the solar system, of experimental philosophy, and of geography, mathematical, physical, and political. This little was necessary for rational conversation, and I had neither time nor taste for scientific refinements. Poetry was my delight, and I sometimes wrote it, as the partiality of my poor father led him to assert, in a pleasing manner.

I do not make it a merit of my own, because it was entirely owing to my father's direction, that with all my attention to books I did not neglect the ornamental accomplishments. My father excelled in music, and he taught me to play on the harpsichord. He engaged a good master to instruct me in dancing, and he always cautioned me against that neglect of dress and of accurate cleanliness, which, he said, had sometimes involved literary ladies in deserved disgrace. He likewise inculcated the necessity of avoiding a pedantic manner of conversation, and strictly charged me never to be overbearing, or to shew in the company of others the least appearance of conscious superiority. I believe I may venture to say, that I complied with his directions, and that I talked with perfect ease among the superficial, and neither expressed nor felt contempt, except where vanity and affectation were combined with ignorance.

Yet, notwithstanding my improvements, and my earnest endeavours to prevent them from becoming invidious, I find myself received in the world with less cordiality than I had reason to expect. My own sex stand too much in awe of me to bear me any affection. When I come into their company, an universal silence would prevail, if it were not interrupted by myself. Though I cannot say that I am treated rudely, yet I can easily perceive that the civilities I receive are constrained; and I have every reason to believe, that no small pains are taken to traduce my character, and to ridicule my taste in dress, and all the circumstances of external behaviour. It is kindly hinted, that a little awkwardness and impropriety may be excused in a learned lady, and that dress and decorum are beneath the notice of a poetess.

I have no reason to think that my person is particularly disagreeable; yet I know not how it is, I am avoided by gentlemen who are ambitious of the company of other ladies. They have dropt, in the hearing of some of my friends, that though they think me extremely clever, yet they cannot reconcile the ideas of female attractions and the knowledge of the Greek. They do not mean to detract from my praise; but they must own, that I am not the woman after their hearts. They entertain a notion, that a lady of improved understanding will not submit to the less dignified cares of managing a household. She knows how to make verses, says the witling, but give me the woman who can make a pudding.

I must confess, I ever thought it the most valuable recommendation of a wife to be capable of becoming a conversable companion to her husband; nor did I ever conceive that the qualifications of a cook-maid, a laundress, or a house-keeper were the most desirable accomplishments in a partner for life. A woman of improved understanding and real sense is more likely to submit to her condition, whatever it may be, than the uneducated or the half-learned; and such an one will always be willing to superintend oeconomy when it becomes her duty; and to take an active part in household management, when the happiness of him she loves, and of herself, depends upon her personal interference.

The education of children in the earlier periods, particularly of daughters, naturally belongs to the mother. Her inclination to improve them, seconded by her ability to take the proper methods, must be attended with the most valuable effects. The world is acquainted with the happy consequences of a Cornelia's parental care. But it seems probable, that little nourishment of mind can be imbibed from a mother, whose ideas hardly ever wandered beyond the limits either of a kitchen or a dressing-room. Neither is there sufficient reason to conclude, that she whose intellectual acquisitions enable her to entertain her husband, and to form the minds of her children, must be incapable or unwilling to superintend the table, and give a personal attention to domestic oeconomy.

That learning belongs not to the female character, and that the female mind is not capable of a degree of improvement equal to that of the other sex, are narrow and unphilosophical prejudices. The present times exhibit most honourable instances of female learning and genius. The superior advantages of boys education are, perhaps, the sole reason of their subsequent superiority. Learning is equally attainable, and, I think, equally valuable, for the satisfaction arising from it, to a woman as a man. For my own part, I would not lose the little I possess, to avoid all those disagreeable consequences of which I have just now complained.

3.4 Mary Wollstonecraft, from *Thoughts on the Education of Daughters: with Reflections on Female Conduct, in the more Important Duties of Life*, 1788

'Unfortunate Situation of Females, Fashionably Educated, and Left without a Fortune'

I have hitherto only spoken of those females, who will have a provision made for them by their parents. But many who have been well, or at least fashionably educated, are left without a fortune, and if they are not entirely devoid of delicacy, they must frequently remain single.

Few are the modes of earning a subsistence, and those very humiliating. Perhaps to be an humble companion to some rich old cousin, or what is still worse, to live with strangers, who are so intolerably tyrannical, that none of their own relations can bear to live with them, though they should even expect a fortune in reversion. It is impossible to enumerate the many hours of anguish such a person must spend. Above the servants, yet considered by them as a spy, and ever reminded of their inferiority when in conversation with the superiors. If she cannot condescend to mean flattery, she has not a chance of being a favorite; and should any of the visitors take notice of her, and she for a moment forget her subordinate state, she is sure to be reminded of it.

Painfully sensible of unkindness, she is alive to every thing, and many sarcasms reach her, which were perhaps directed another way. She is alone, shut out from equality and confidence, and the concealed anxiety impairs her constitution; for she must wear a cheerful face, or be dismissed. The being dependant on the caprice of a fellow-creature, though certainly very necessary in this state of discipline, is yet a very bitter corrective, which we would fain shrink from.

A teacher at a school is only a kind of upper servant, who has more work than the menial ones.

A governess to young ladies is equally disagreeable. It is ten to one if they meet with a reasonable mother; and if she is not so, she will be continually finding fault to prove she is not ignorant, and be displeased if her pupils do not improve, but angry if the proper methods are taken to make them do so. The children treat them with disrespect, and often with insolence. In the mean time life glides away, and the spirits with it; 'and when youth and genial years are flown', they have nothing to subsist on; or, perhaps, on some extraordinary occasion, some small allowance may be made for them, which is thought a great charity.

The few trades which are left, are now gradually falling into the hands of the men, and certainly they are not very respectable.

It is hard for a person who has a relish for polished society, to herd with the vulgar, or to condescend to mix with her former equals when she is considered in a different light. What unwelcome heart-breaking knowledge is then poured in on her! I mean a view of the selfishness and depravity of the world; for every other acquirement is a source of pleasure, though they may occasion temporary inconveniences. How cutting is the contempt she meets with! – A young mind looks round for love and friendship; but love and friendship fly from poverty: expect them not if you are poor! The mind must then sink into meanness, and accommodate itself to its new state, or dare to be unhappy. Yet I think no reflecting person would give up the experience and improvement they have gained, to have avoided the misfortunes; on the contrary, they are thankfully ranked amongst the choicest blessings of life, when we are not under their immediate pressure.

How earnestly does a mind full of sensibility look for disinterested friendship, and long to meet with good unalloyed. When fortune smiles they hug the dear delusion; but dream not that it is one. The painted cloud disappears suddenly, the scene is changed, and what an aching void is left in the heart! a void which only religion can fill up – and how few seek this internal comfort!

A woman, who has beauty without sentiment, is in great danger of being seduced; and if she has any, cannot guard herself from painful mortifications. It is very disagreeable to keep up a continual reserve with men she has been formerly familiar with; yet if she places confidence, it is ten to one but she is deceived. Few men seriously think of marrying an inferior; and if they have honor enough not to take advantage of a woman who loves, and thinks not of the difference of rank, they do not undeceive her until she has anticipated happiness, which, contrasted with her dependant situation, appears delightful. The disappointment is severe; and the heart receives a wound which does not easily admit of a compleat cure, as the good that is missed is not valued according to its real worth: for fancy drew the picture, and grief delights to create food to feed on.

If what I have written should be read by parents, who are now going on in thoughtless extravagance, and anxious only that their daughters may be *genteelly educated*, let them consider to what sorrows they expose them; for I have not over-coloured the picture.

Though I warn parents to guard against leaving their daughters to encounter such misery; yet if a young woman falls into it, she ought not to be discontented. Good must ultimately arise from every thing, to those who look beyond this infancy of their being; and here the comfort of a good conscience is our only stable support. The main business of living of our lives is to learn to be virtuous; and He who is training us up for immortal bliss, knows best what trials will contribute to make us so; and our resignation and improvement will render us respectable to our selves, and to that Being, whose approbation is of more value than life itself.

3.5   Catherine Macaulay Graham, from *Letters on Education*, 1790

Part One, Letter IV

The moderns, in the education of their children, have too much followed the stiff and prudish manners of ancient days, in the separating the male and female children of a family. This is well adapted to the absurd unsocial rigour of Grecian manners; but as it is not so agreeable to that mixture of the sexes in a more advanced age, which prevails in all European societies, it is not easy to be accounted for, but from the absurd notion, that the education of females should be of an opposite kind to that of males. How much feebleness of constitution has been acquired, by forming a false idea of female excellence, and endeavouring, by our art, to bring Nature to the ply of our imagination. Our sons are suffered to enjoy with freedom that time which is not devoted to study, and may follow, unmolested, those strong impulses which Nature has wisely given for the furtherance of her benevolent purposes; but if, before her natural vivacity is entirely subdued by habit, little Miss is inclined to show her locomotive tricks in a manner not entirely agreeable to the trammels of custom, she is reproved with a sharpness which gives her a consciousness of having highly transgressed the laws of decorum; and what with the vigilance of those who are appointed to superintend her conduct, and the false biass they have imposed on her mind, every vigorous exertion is suppressed, the mind and body yield to the tyranny of error, and Nature is charged with all those imperfections which we alone owe to the blunders of art. . . .

There is another prejudice, Hortensia, which affects yet more deeply female happiness, and female importance; a prejudice, which ought ever to have been confined to the regions of the east, because [it is more suitable to that] state of slavery to which female nature in that part of the world has ever been subjected, and can only suit with the notion of a positive inferiority in the intellectual powers of the female mind. You will soon perceive, that the prejudice which I mean, is that degrading difference in the culture of the understanding, which has prevailed for several centuries in all European societies. Our ancestors, on the first revival of letters, dispensed with an equal hand the advantages of a classical education to all their offspring; but as pedantry was the fault of that age, a female student might not at that time be a very agreeable character. True philosophy in those ages was rarely an attendant on learning, even in the male sex; but it must be obvious to all those who are not blinded by the mist of prejudice, that there is no cultivation which yields so promising a harvest as the cultivation of the understanding; and that a mind, irradiated by the clear light of wisdom, must be equal to every task which reason imposes on it. The social duties in the interesting characters of daughter, wife, and mother, will be but ill performed by ignorance and levity; and in the domestic converse of husband and wife, the alternative of an enlightened, or an unenlightened companion, cannot be indifferent to any man of taste and true knowledge. Be no longer niggards, then, O ye parents, in bestowing on your offspring, every blessing which nature and fortune renders them capable of enjoying! Confine not the education of your daughters to what is regarded as the ornamental parts of it, nor deny the graces to your sons. Suffer no prejudices to prevail on you to weaken Nature, in order to render her more beautiful; take measures for the virtue and harmony of your family, by uniting their young minds early in the soft bonds of friendship. Let your children be brought up together; let their sports and studies be the same; let them enjoy, in the constant presence of those who are set over them, all that freedom which innocence renders harmless, and in which Nature rejoices. By the uninterrupted intercourse which you will thus establish, both sexes will find, that friendship may be enjoyed between them without passion. The wisdom of your daughters will preserve them from the bane of coquetry, and even at the age of desire, objects of temptation will lose somewhat of their stimuli, by losing their novelty. Your sons will look for something more solid in women, than a mere outside; and be no longer the dupes to the meanest, the weakest, and the most profligate of the sex. They will become the constant benefactors of that part of their family who stand in need of their assistance; and in regard to all matters of domestic concern, the unjust distinction of primogeniture will be deprived of its sting.

Part One, Letter XXIV, *'Chastity'*

But the most difficult part of female education, is to give girls such an idea of chastity, as shall arm their reason and their sentiments on the side of useful virtue. For I believe there are more women of understanding led into acts of imprudence by the ignorance, the prejudices, and the false craft of those by whom they are educated, than from any other cause founded either in nature or in chance. You may train up a docile idiot to any mode of thinking or acting, as may best suit the intended purpose; but a reasoning being will scan over your propositions, and if they find them grounded in falsehood, they will reject them with disdain. When you tell a girl of spirit and reflection that chastity is a sexual virtue, and the want of it a sexual vice, she will be apt to examine into the principles of religion, morals, and the reason of things, in order to satisfy herself on the truth of your proposition. And when, after the strictest enquiries, she finds nothing that will warrant the confining the proposition to a particular sense, she will entertain doubts either of your wisdom or your sincerity; and regarding you either as a deceiver or a fool, she will transfer her confidence to the companion of the easy vacant hour, whose compliance with her opinions can flatter her vanity. Thus left to Nature, with an unfortunate biass on her mind, she will fall a victim to the first plausible being who has formed a design on her person. Rousseau is so sensible of this, that he quarrels with human reason, and would put her out of the question in all considerations of duty. But this is being as great a fanatic in morals, as some are in religion; and I should much doubt the reality of that duty which would not stand the test of a fair enquiry; beside, as I intend to breed my pupils up to act a rational part in the world, and not to fill up a niche in the seraglio of a sultan, I shall certainly give them leave to use their reason in all matters which concern their duty and happiness, and shall spare no pains in the cultivation of this only sure guide to virtue. I shall inform them of the great utility of chastity and continence; that the one preserves the body in health and vigor, and the other, the purity and independence of the mind, without which it is impossible to possess virtue or happiness. I shall intimate, that the great difference now beheld in the external consequences which follow the deviations from chastity in the two sexes, did in all probability arise from women having been considered as the mere property of the men; and, on this account had no right to dispose of their own persons: that policy adopted this difference, when the plea of property had been given up; and it was still preserved in society from the unruly licentiousness of the men, who, finding no obstacles in the delicacy of the other sex, continue to set at defiance both divine and moral law, and by mutual support and general opinion to use their natural freedom with impunity. I shall observe, that this state of things renders the situation of females, in their individual capacity very precarious; for the strength which Nature has given to the passion of love, in order to serve her purposes, has made it the most ungovernable propensity of any which attends us. The snares, therefore, that are continually laid for women, by persons who run no risk in compassing their seduction, exposes them to continual danger; whilst the implacability of their own sex, who fear to give up any advantages which a superior prudence, or even its appearances, give them, renders one false step an irretrievable misfortune. That, for these reasons, coquettry in women is as dangerous as it is dishonorable. That a coquet commonly finds her own perdition, in the very flames which she raises to consume others; and that if any thing can excuse the baseness of female seduction, it is the baits which are flung out by women to entangle the affections, and excite the passions of men.

I know not what you may think of my method, Hortensia, which I must acknowledge to carry the stamp of singularity; but for my part, I am sanguine enough to expect to turn out of my hands a careless, modest beauty, grave, manly, noble, full of strength and majesty; and carrying about her an aegis sufficiently powerful to defend her against the sharpest arrow that ever was shot from Cupid's bow. A woman, whose virtue will not be of the kind to wrankle into an inveterate malignity against her own sex for faults which she even encourages in the men, but who, understanding the principles of true religion and morality, will regard chastity and truth as indispensible qualities in virtuous characters of either sex; whose justice will incline her to extend her benevolence to the frailties of the fair as circumstances invite, and to manifest her resentment against the underminers of female happiness; in short, a woman who will not take a male rake either for a husband or a friend. And let me tell you, Hortensia, if women had as much regard for the virtue of chastity as in some cases they pretend to have, a reformation would long since have taken place in the world; but whilst they continue to cherish immodesty in the men, their bitter persecution of their own sex will not save them from the imputation of those concealed propensities with which they are accused by Pope[1], and other severe satirists on the sex.

Note

1 In his 'Epistle to a Lady' (see 2.5, note 2).

3.6 Clara Reeve, from *Plans of Education; with Remarks on the Systems of other Writers*, 1792

When we consider the great increase of boarding schools, we ought not to be surprised at the increase of evils arising from them. In every town, village, and even hamlet, there are persons found who take upon them the great and important charge of female education: and over their doors are seen in letters of gold,
    'A Boarding School for Young Ladies'
Adventurers of all kinds have found resources in this profession: needy foreigners, without friends or characters; broken traders;

ladies of doubtful virtue; ladies' waiting-maids; nay, even low and menial servants, have succeeded in raising a boarding school. What must we think of the negligence and credulity of such parents as intrust their most precious treasures, their children, the sacred deposits of heaven and their country, to the care of the unknown – perhaps, ignorant, – perhaps, unprincipled people?

We do not mean to include all boarding schools under this description; we know that there are some, which answer every purpose of virtuous and ingenuous education, such as we encourage and recommend; but we insist, that far the greater number are either useless, or pernicious, especially to the lower classes of people: and even among those of the better kinds, the attention is chiefly paid to external accomplishments, while the moral duties, and the social virtues are neglected, or slightly attended to.

How often do we see the young girls come from those schools, full of pride, vanity, and self-consequence! – ignorant of the duties and virtues of a domestic life, insolent to their inferiors, proud and saucy to their equals, impertinent to their parents; without that sweet modesty and delicacy of mind and manners, which are the surest guards of female virtue, and the best omens of their future characters as wives, mothers, and mistresses of families; and which nothing can compensate for the want of.

3.7   Laetitia Matilda Hawkins, from *Letters on the Female Mind, Its Powers and Pursuits. Addressed to Miss H. M. Williams, with particular reference to Her Letters from France*,[1] 1793

Letter I

But the points of, *A King or no King? A Nobility or no Nobility?* are not those, my dear madam, which I mean to discuss with you, I would rather convince you that they are points neither you nor I can discuss with propriety or success; that there is but one side a female can take in politics, without injuring the feminine character, and that till we either are fitted by education to investigate all the abstract science of jurisprudence, or till intuition shall be judged the only requisite for deciding the most important questions, we must be content with a minor species of fame.

In this first address to you, I would confine myself to the consideration of this simple proposition – *What are the objects on which the female genius may be most properly exercised?* But this question involves in it one previous to it, and that is, *What are the peculiar properties of the female mind?* which, with your leave, we will first regard.

It cannot, I think, be truly asserted, that the intellectual powers know no difference of sex. Nature certainly intended a distinction; but it is a distinction that is far from degrading us. Instances, without doubt, may be adduced, where talents truly masculine, and of superior masculine excellence, have been bestowed on the softer sex; but they are so rare, that the union is not to be looked for. In general, and almost universally, the feminine intellect has less strength but more acuteness; consequently, in our exercise of it, we shew less perseverance and more vivacity. We are not formed for those deep investigations that tend to the bringing into light reluctant truth; but when once she has appeared, when *vera incessu patuit Dea*,[2] then it is within the female province to give her spirit and decoration, which the less flexible and less volatile male mind would fail in attempting.

That we were not designed for the exertion of intense thought, may be fairly inferred from the effect it produces on the countenance and features. The contracted brow, the prolated visage, the motionless eye-ball, and the fixed attitude, though they may give force and dignity to the strong lines of the male countenance, can give nothing to soft features that is not unpleasant: no other idea can be conveyed but that of Armida accoutred in Clarinda's armour:[3] the new character is unsuitable and unmanageable, not only useless but oppressive.

In contemplating this subject, I have always imagined this difference to subsist between the minds of the different sexes. Male genius fetches its treasures from the depths of science, and the accumulated wisdom of ages: the female finds her's in the lighter regions of fancy and the passing knowledge of the day. There are, unquestionably, approximations between them that render it sometimes difficult to ascertain the precise point at which they diverge, as in all other works of the creation links are found which form, by regular gradations, the various dissimilarities of being into one regular progression; but still the generic and specific distinction exists, though to our obtuse faculties scarcely perceptible but when magnified by some degrees of distance.

In this age of liberality and refinement in female education, (for which no one is more thankful than myself) whatever is ingenious, shrewd, elegant, and sportive; whatever requires pathos and the energy of plaintive eloquence, may be looked for from our young women; and their invention renders the field assigned them a source of inexhaustible production, in which, while by confining their attention, they do not weaken their powers, they need fear no rival; but if they prefer the mine to the flowery face of nature, if they will dig for casual diamonds instead of weaving fragrant garlands, let them not be disappointed if they fail, or angry if the trespass is retorted more to their harm.

When I confine the powers of women to lighter subjects of exertion, I would not be understood as insinuating, that they are incapable of any thing *serious:* I mean only that they misapply them, when, descending below the level of necessity, they fancy they find pleasure in what they are not fitted to comprehend. Dividing subjects of thought into *abstruse, serious,* and *light,* I consider only the former and the latter as peculiarly appropriated by either sex; the center is common to both: it is the key-note uniting two chords, equally useful and necessary to both.

The peculiar properties of the female mind I should therefore reckon acuteness of perception, vivacity of imagination, and a concatenation of invention that disdains all limit. The corporeal part of our composition here lends its aid, and while it produces, perhaps, only pains to the body, adds every possible intellectual charm to the mind: our irritable nerves are our torments and our grace; what we conceive quickly and clearly, we feel exquisitely. . . .

If this desultory sketch is believed to comprehend nearly the whole brief catalogue of female powers, where shall we look for subjects fitted to their exertions? Let not the advocate for female excellence be alarmed; the field is ample, and little is excluded from its boundary; every shrub, every flower of literature is contained within it; forest trees only are excluded: and surely no woman, who has ever contemplated the oak, will complain that she is not permitted to bear it away from its native soil. . . .

Arithmetic, geography, natural philosophy, natural history, civil history, biography may be added, with undoubted propriety, to the attainment of all the languages a female inclination *points* to; and when relieved by a taste for and a perfection in music, an adroitness and delicacy in the exercise of the imitative arts, we pronounce the mind, where they have fixed their abode, an accomplished one; and if they meet a bodily form, on which the less important but more shewy cares of the dancing-master have been happily bestowed, the world pronounces, and pronounces truly, that this is an accomplished woman. – Whoever thou art that claimest this character, let me, as a sister and a friend, conjure thee to give to it its last polish, that of moral virtue, in all its beautiful variety of modulation, and I will say – Thou art a gem.

from *Letter II*

The study, my dear madam, which I place in the climax of unfitness, is that of *politics;* and so strongly does it appear to me barred against the admission of females, that I am astonished that they ever ventured to approach it. . . .

I am well aware, that the influence of those, to whose care we are consigned in the early part of education, is too strong to be easily kept dormant or annihilated. We are in religion and politics, in general, what our parents are; and if we err, we find in their example a satisfactory excuse. I do not ask women to have no opinion on the subject; but, for decorum's sake, do not encourage them to a tilting match with their acquaintance, on a point to them incomprehensible: let them enjoy in peace the traditionary creed of their forefathers; let them change it for any that they think carries more authority with it; but let it be in silence.

Notes

1 Helen Maria Williams, poet and novelist, published her first collection of *Letters from France* in 1790, followed by further volumes throughout the 1790s. A first-hand account of the events of the French Revolution from a sympathetic point of view, they were extremely popular but also widely criticized (cf. 4.19).
2 Virgil, *Aeneid*, I.405, in Dryden's translation: 'And by her graceful walk the Queen of Love is known'.
3 Characters in Tasso's epic poem *Gerusalemme Liberata* (1581): Armida, niece of a magician, lures Christian knights into her enchanted garden; Clarinda is an Amazon.

3.8   Priscilla Wakefield, from *Reflections on the Present Condition of the Female Sex; with Suggestions for its Improvement*, 1798

Chapter I

It is asserted by Doctor Adam Smith,[1] that every individual is a burthen upon the society to which he belongs, who does not contribute his share of productive labour for the good of the whole. The doctor, when he lays down this principle, speaks in general terms of man, as a being capable of forming a social compact for mutual defence, and the advantage of the community at large. He does not absolutely specify, that both sexes, in order to render themselves beneficial members of society, are equally required to comply with these terms; but since the female sex is included in the idea of the species, and as women possess the same qualities as men, though perhaps in a different degree, their sex cannot free them from the claim of the public for their proportion of usefulness. That the major part of the sex, especially of those among the higher orders, neglect to fulfil this important obligation, is a fact that must be admitted, and points out the propriety of an enquiry into the causes of their deficiency.

The indolent indulgence and trifling pursuits in which those who are distinguished by the appellation of gentlewomen, often pass their lives, may be attributed, with greater probability, to a contracted education, custom, false pride, and idolizing adulation, than to any defect in their intellectual capacities. The contest for equality in the mental capacity of the sexes has been maintained, on each side of the question, with ingenuity; but as judgment only can be formed from facts, as they arise in the present state of things, if the experiments have been fairly tried, the rare instances of extraordinary talents, which have been brought forward to support the system of equality, must yield to the irresistible influence of corporeal powers. Which leads to a conclusion, that the intellectual faculties of each sex are wisely adapted to their appropriate purposes, and that, laying aside the invidious terms of superiority and inferiority, the perfection of mind in man and in woman, consists in a power to maintain the distinguishing characteristics of excellence in each. But this concession by no means proves, that, even in this enlightened age and country, the talents of women have ever been generally exerted to the utmost extent of their capacity, or that they have been turned towards the most useful objects; neither does it imply that the cultivation they receive is adequate to bring into action the full strength of those powers which have been bestowed on them by nature. The intellectual faculties of the female mind have been too long confined by narrow and ill-directed modes of education, and thus have been concealed, not only from others, but from themselves, the energies of which they are capable.

Chapter V

Society may be resolved into four classes or degrees: the first comprehends the nobility, and all those who, either by the influence of high offices or extensive hereditary possessions, rival them in power: the second contains those, who by the application of their talents to learning, commerce, manufactures, or agriculture, procure a respectable subsistence approaching to opulence: to the third may be referred those, whose honest and useful industry raises them above want, without procuring for them the means of splendid or luxurious gratification: the fourth is composed of the labouring poor. The rank of women being determined by the accident of their birth, or their connexions in marriage, a correspondent arrangement is, with equal propriety, applicable to them, as to the other sex.

An enquiry into the objects of attainment, employments, and pursuits of the different classes of the one sex, will throw light upon those that ought to occupy the corresponding ranks of the other.

Noblemen, and gentlemen of independent property, receive a course of instruction adapted to prepare them for filling up the highest offices in the different departments of the state, consistently with their own dignity and the service of their country; or to maintain the inviolability of our valuable constitution, as distinguished ornaments in the senate, or at the bar.– The learned professions, or the lucrative and respectable avocations of commercial life, are sources of honour and wealth to the inferior gentry and merchants. Farmers, tradesmen, and artificers, besides the general acquisition of the simpler branches of learning, attain the knowledge of some peculiar art, or branch of commerce, by which they are enabled to gain a competent support.

The necessity of directing the attention of females to some certain occupation is not so apparent, because custom has rendered them dependant upon their fathers and husbands for support; but as some of every class experience the loss of those relations, without inheriting an adequate resource, there would be great propriety in preparing each of them, by an education of energy and useful attainments, to meet such disasters, and to be able, under such circumstances, to procure an independence for herself. There is scarcely a more helpless object, in the wide circle of misery which the vicissitudes of civilized society display, than a woman genteelly educated, whether single or married, who is deprived, by any unfortunate accident, of the protection and support of male relations: unaccustomed to struggle with difficulty, unacquainted with any resource to supply an independent maintenance, she is reduced to the depths of wretchedness, and not unfrequently, if she be young and handsome, is driven by despair to those paths which lead to infamy. Is it not time to find a remedy for such evils, when the contentions of nations has produced the most affecting transitions in private life, and transferred the affluent and the noble to the humiliating extremes of want and obscurity? When our streets teem with multitudes of unhappy women, many of whom might have been rescued from their present degradation, or who would perhaps never have fallen into it, had they been instructed in the exercise of some art or profession, which would have enabled them to procure for themselves a respectable support by their own industry.

This reasonable precaution against the accidents of life is resisted by prejudice, which rises, like an insurmountable barrier, against a woman, of any degree above the vulgar, employing her time and her abilities towards the maintenance of herself and her family: degradation of rank immediately follows the virtuous attempt, as it did formerly among the younger branches of the noble families in France. But the nature of truth is immutable, however it may be obscured by error: that which is a moral excellence in one rationable being, deserves the same estimation in another; therefore, if it be really honourable in a man to exert the utmost of his abilities, whether mental or corporal, in the acquisition of a competent support for himself and for those who have a natural claim upon his protection, it must be equally so in a woman; nay, perhaps still more incumbent, as in many cases there is nothing so inimical to the preservation of her virtue as a state of poverty, which leaves her dependant upon the generosity of others, to supply those accommodations which use has rendered necessary to her comfort.

There appears then no moral impediment to prevent women from the application of their talents to purposes of utility; on the contrary, an improvement in public manners must infallibly result from it. As their influence over the other sex is universally acknowledged, it may be boldly asserted, that a conversion of their time from trifling and unproductive employments, to those that are both useful and profitable, would operate as a check upon luxury, dissipation, and prodigality, and retard the progress of that general dissoluteness, the offspring of idleness, which is deprecated by all political writers, as the sure forerunner of national decay.

Chapter VIII

Transitions in private life from affluence to poverty, like the sable pageantry of death, from their frequency, produce no lasting impressions upon the beholders. Unexpected misfortunes befal an acquaintance, who has been caressed in the days of prosperity. The change is lamented, and she is consoled by the visits of her friends in the first moments of affliction. She sinks gradually into wretchedness: she becomes obscure, and is forgotten. The case would be different could avocations be suggested, which would enable those, who suffer such a reverse of fortune, to maintain a decent appearance, and procure them a degree of respect. It is far from my present design to point out all the various pursuits which may consistently engage the talents, or employ the industry, of women whose refinement of manners unfit them for any occupation of a sordid, menial kind: such an undertaking would require an extensive acquaintance with the distinct branches of the fine arts, which adorn, and of the numerous manufactures which enrich, this country. But a few remarks, upon the nature of those employments which are best adapted to the higher classes of the sex, when reduced to necessitous circumstances, may, perhaps, afford useful hints to those who are languishing under the pressure of misfortune, and induce abler pens to treat a subject hitherto greatly neglected.

Numerous difficulties arise in the choice of occupations for the purpose. They must be such as are neither laborious nor servile; and they must, of course, be productive, without requiring a capital.

For these reasons, pursuits which require the exercise of intellectual, rather than bodily powers, are generally the most eligible.

Literature affords a respectable and pleasing employment, for those who possess talents and an adequate degree of mental cultivation. For although the emolument is precarious, and seldom equal to a maintenance, yet, if the attempt be tolerably successful, it may yield a comfortable assistance in narrow circumstances, and beguile many hours, which might otherwise be passed in solitude or unavailing regret. The fine arts offer a mode of subsistence, congenial to the delicacy of the most refined minds; and they are peculiarly adapted, by their elegance, to the gratification of taste. The perfection of every species of painting is attainable by women, from the representation of historic facts, to the minute execution of the miniature portrait, if they will bestow sufficient time and application for the acquisition of the principles of the art, in the study of those models, which have been the means of transmitting the names and character of so many men, to the admiration of posterity. The successful exercise of this imitative art requires invention, taste, and judgment: in the two first, the sex are allowed to excel; and the last may be obtained by a perseverance in examining, comparing, and reflecting upon the works of those masters who have copied nature in her most graceful forms. . . .

But as neither exalted genius, nor the means of cultivating that portion of it which nature has bestowed, to the utmost extent, are likely to be very generally possessed; it is fortunate for those who are less liberally endowed, that there are many profitable, though inferior branches of design, or of arts connected with it. The drapery and landscape, both of portraits and historical pieces, are often entrusted the pupils of the master, and constitute a branch of the art, for which women might be allowed to be candidates. The elegant as well as the humourous designs which embellish the windows of print-sellers, &c. also sketches for the frontis-pieces of books, and other ornaments of the same kind, must employ many artists; nor does it appear that any good reason for confining them to one sex has been assigned.

Colouring of prints is a lucrative employment. There was, a few years ago, in London, a French woman, who had a peculiar method of applying water-colours to prints, by which she might have gained a very liberal income, had her industry and morals been equal to her ingenuity. Designs for needle-work, and ornamental works of all kinds, are now mostly performed by men, and those who have a good taste obtain a great deal of money by them; but surely this employment is one, among many, which has been improperly assumed by the other sex, and should be appropriated to women. The delicate touches of miniature painting, and painting in enamel, with devices for rings and lockets in hair-work, are more characteristic of female talents than of masculine powers. The delineation of animals or plants for books of natural history, and colouring of maps or globes, may be followed with some advantage. Patterns for calico-printers and paper-stainers are lower departments of the same art, which might surely be allowed as sources of subsistence to one sex, with equal propriety, as to the other

. . . . The profession of an actress is indeed most unsuitable to the sex, in every point of view; whether it be considered with respect to the courage requisite to face an audience, or the variety of situations incident to it, which expose moral virtue to the most severe trials. Let the daughters of a happier destiny, whilst they lament the evils to which some of their sex are exposed, remember those unpropitious circumstances, that have cast them into a line of life, in which it is scarcely possible to preserve that purity of sentiment and conduct, which characterizes female excellence. When their errors are discussed, let the harsh voice of censure be restrained, by the reflection, that she who has made the greatest advances towards perfection, might have fallen, had she been surrounded by the same influences.

The species of agriculture which depends upon skill in the management of the nursery ground, in rearing the various kinds of shrubs and flowers, for the supply of gentlemen's gardens and pleasure-grounds, would supply an elegant means of support to those women who are able to raise a capital for carrying on a work of that magnitude. Ornamental gardening, and the laying out of pleasure-grounds and parks, with the improvement of natural landscape, one of the refinements of modern times, may likewise afford an eligible maintenance to some of those females, who, in the days of their prosperity, displayed their taste in the embellishment of their own domains.

Chapter IX

The next class of women which comes under animadversion, includes several gradations, involving the daughters of every species of tradesmen below the merchant, and above the meaner mechanic; consequently, very different degrees of refinement befit the individuals who form the extreme links, which are separated, insensibly as it were, from the other divisions towards which they approximate. The peculiar duties of each, will vary according to her respective situation; but humility, sobriety, modesty of deportment, an industrious disposition, and an adjustment of their manners to their circumstances, are the characteristic ornaments of their general condition.

. . .

The knowledge of a trade is a probable means, which ought not to be neglected, of enabling them to give their assistance towards the support of their family; but should it be more eligible for the husband and wife to unite in the prosecution of the same design, her former subjection to regular application, would render her more apt in accommodating herself to her husband's business. Thus the benefit of apprenticing girls of this rank to some trade is equally apparent, whether they marry or live single.

Men monopolize not only the most advantageous employments, and such as exclude women from the exercise of them, by the publicity of their nature, or the extensive knowledge they require, but even many of those which are consistent with the female character. Another heavy discouragement to the industry of women, is the inequality of the reward of their labour, compared with that of men; an injustice which pervades every species of employment performed by both sexes[a].

In employments which depend upon bodily strength, the distinction is just; for it cannot be pretended that the generality of women can earn as much as men, where the produce of their labour is the result of corporeal exertion; but it is a subject of great regret, that this inequality should prevail, even where an equal share of skill and application is exerted. Male stay-makers, mantua-makers, and hair-dressers, are better paid than female artists of the same professions; but surely it will never be urged as an apology for this disproportion, that women are not as capable of making stays, gowns, dressing hair, and similar arts, as men: if they are not superior to them, it can only be accounted for upon this principle, that the prices they receive for their labour are not sufficient to pay them for the expence of qualifying themselves for their business; and that they sink under the mortification of being regarded as artizans of inferior estimation, whilst the men, who supplant them, receive all the encouragement of large profits and full employment, which is ensured to them by the folly of fashion. The occasion for this remark is a disgrace upon those who patronize such a brood of effeminate beings in the garb of men, when sympathy with their humbler sisters should direct them to act in a manner exactly opposite, by holding out every incitement to the industry of their own sex. This evil, indeed, calls loudly upon women of rank and fortune for redress: they should determine to employ women only, wherever they can be employed: they should procure female instructors for their children: they should frequent no shops that are not served by women: they should wear no clothes that are not made by them: they should reward them as liberally as they do the men who have hitherto supplanted them. Let it be considered a common cause, to give them every possible advantage. For once, let fashion be guided by reason; and let the mode sanction a preference to women in every profession, to which their pretensions are equal with those of the other sex. This is a patronage which the necessitous have a right to expect from the rich and powerful, whether they are poor by birth, or are unfortunately become so, by that mutability of fortune, to which every rank is liable.

The instruction of youth in all its various departments, offers an eligible means of support for those women, who have been qualified for the office by suitable acquirements. A person who undertakes to superintend the whole of a child or children's education, whether in a private family as governess, or as the manager of a public seminary, ought to possess many rare endowments, and such a turn of thinking, and style of behaviour, as are to be gained only by association with the best company. Those, therefore, who have been placed in the midst of such society, by their early prospects, are the only proper candidates for these offices. The entire exclusion of men from the teaching of girls, would provide a new species of employment for the daughters of tradesmen, were they to have them completely instructed in any one distinct branch of knowledge which masters teach, with a view to supplying their places. This would ensure them a respectable opportunity of maintaining themselves, should occasion require it, at any period of life, and would be a far more valuable gift than a moderate dowry, which, when once consumed, is irrecoverable; whilst a talent, that can be resumed at discretion, is like a bank, to which application may always be made.

Chapter X

The manner in which the labouring poor should pass their time, requires but few observations; for their lot dooms them, even in those countries where their situation is most favourable, to incessant toil, as a necessary means of subsistence: but the rigour of the labour of the female poor should be moderated by the consideration of their inferiority of strength; and if their condition will admit of improvement, an enquiry into the means most likely to effect it properly, belongs to the subject of these reflections.

The internal comfort of a cottage, and the virtues of its inhabitants, depend greatly, if not principally, upon the mother of the family. Oeconomy, cleanliness, industry, and above all these, good temper, are the attractions which draw the husband to his own fire-side, after the labour of the day is over; but when the wife is slatternly, idle, negligent in providing those small accommodations that are the effects of good management, it discourages him from entrusting her with the disposal of the wages which he has laboriously earned: especially if to these defects be added the intolerable evil of a scolding tongue, he is driven from home to seek recreation in company, and is too frequently tempted to expend that pittance in excess, which should be appropriated to the support of the family.

Very different are the appearances of comfort in the houses of the poor, according to the management of the wife, even where the earnings are equal. In some, the children are covered with rags, and brought up in the streets to profligacy and ruin: in others, all who are capable of being employed, are busied in something useful, proportioned to their age, and their clothes creditably mended to the utmost. There is a pretty great certainty, that in those families where neatness and industry reign, there is no dram-drinking, nor any score run up at the chandler's shop; for the true oeconomist will always be in the habit of paying as she goes on, well knowing that if she be incapable of discharging her debts every week, at least, it will be impossible to release herself from the accumulation of months. If her husband brings home his money regularly, she contrives to amass such sums as shall enable her to buy the articles of consumption in tolerable quantities, not by ounces and penny-worths; a system to which the wasteful prodigal is reduced, by squandering that substance in excess, or superfluity, which should be reserved for the necessities of the household.

A discrimination in charitable donations, according to the visible effects of good conduct, if generally adopted by the wealthy, would operate as a stimulus upon the negligent to amend, and be a means of augmenting the number of comfortable cottages. But whilst the bounty of the rich continues to be bestowed upon those whose appearance is the most wretched, without allowing time to enquire whether the cause of that excessive misery consists in misconduct or unavoidable misfortune, the importunate, the dissolute, the idle, and the improvident, will gain an advantage over the modest, industrious, frugal sufferer, who disdains to solicit compassion by the artificial distress of dirt and rags. The misery of the poor, like that of other ranks, chiefly originates in their vices: whatever, therefore, conduces to reform their morals, will increase their comforts and improve their condition.

Notes

(a) This abuse is in no instance more conspicuous than in the wages of domestic servants. A footman, especially of the higher kind, whose most laborious task is to wait at table, gains, including clothes, vails, and other perquisites, at least £50 per annum; whilst a cook-maid, who is mistress of her profession, does not obtain £20, though her office is laborious, unwholesome, and requires a much greater degree of skill than that of a valet. A similar disproportion is observable among the inferior servants of the establishment.

1 In *An Enquiry into the Nature and Causes of the Wealth of Nations* (1776).

3.9 Hannah More, from *Strictures on the Modern System of Female Education*, 1799

'Introduction'

It is a singular injustice which is often exercised towards women, first to give them a very defective Education, and then to expect from them the most undeviating purity of conduct; – to train them in such a manner as shall lay them open to the most dangerous faults, and then to censure them for not proving faultless. Is it not unreasonable and unjust, to express disappointment if our daughters should, in their subsequent lives, turn out precisely that very kind of character for which it would be evident to an unprejudiced by-stander that the whole scope and tenor of their instruction had been systematically preparing them?

Some reflections on the present erroneous system are here with great deference submitted to public consideration. The Author is apprehensive that she shall be accused of betraying the interests of her sex by laying open their defects: but surely, an earnest wish to turn their attention to objects calculated to promote their true dignity, is not the office of an enemy. So to expose the weakness of the land as to suggest the necessity of internal improvement, and to point out the means of effectual defence, is not treachery, but patriotism.

Chapter I:*'Address to women of rank and fortune, on the effects of their influence on society. – Suggestions for the exertion of it in various instances.'*

At this period, when our country can only hope to stand by opposing a bold and noble *unanimity* to the most tremendous confederacies, against religion, and order, and governments, which the world ever saw; what an accession would it bring to the public strength, could we prevail on beauty, and rank, and talents, and virtue, confederating their several powers, to come forward with a patriotism at once firm and feminine for the general good! I am not sounding an alarm to female warriors, or exciting female politicians: I hardly know which of the two is the most disgusting and unnatural character. Propriety is to a woman what the great Roman critic says action is to an orator; it is the first, the second, the third, requisite. A woman may be knowing, active, witty, and amusing; but without propriety she cannot be amiable. Propriety is the centre in which all the lines of duty and of agreeableness meet. It is to character what proportion is to figure, and grace to attitude. It does not depend on any one perfection; but it is the result of general excellence. It shews itself by a regular, orderly, undeviating course; and never starts from its sober orbit into any splendid eccentricities; for it would be ashamed of such praise as it might extort by any aberrations from its proper path. It renounces all recommendation but what is characteristic; and I would make it the criterion of true taste, right principle, and genuine feeling, in a woman, whether she would be less touched with all the flattery of romantic and exaggerated panegyric than with that beautiful picture of correct and elegant propriety, which Milton draws of our first mother, when he delineates

'Those thousand *decencies* which daily flow
From all her words and actions'.[1]

. . .

But there is another object to which I would direct the exertion of that power of female influence of which I am speaking. Those ladies who take the lead in society are loudly called upon to act as the guardians of the public taste as well as of the public virtue. They are called upon therefore, to oppose with the whole weight of their influence, the irruption of those swarms of publications now daily issuing from the banks of the Danube, which, like their ravaging predecessors of the darker ages, though with far other arms, are overrunning civilized society. Those readers, whose purer taste has been formed on the correct models of the old classic school, see with indignation and astonishment the Huns and Vandals once more overpowering the Greeks and Romans. They behold our minds, with a retrograde but rapid motion, hurried back to the reign of 'chaos and old night', by distorted and unprincipled compositions, which unite the taste of the Goths with the morals of Bagshot[(a)],

Gorgons, and Hydras, and Chimeras dire![2]
They terrify the weak, and disgust the discerning, by wild and

mis-shapen superstitions, in which, with that *consistency* which forms so striking a feature of the new philosophy, those who most earnestly deny the immortality of the soul are most eager to introduce the machinery of ghosts.

The writings of the French infidels were some years ago circulated in England with uncommon industry and with some effect: but the plain sense and good principles of the far greater part of our countrymen resisted the attack, and rose superior to the trial. Of the doctrines and principles here alluded to, the dreadful consequences, not only in the unhappy country where they originated and were almost universally adopted, but in every part of Europe where they have been received, have been such as to serve as a beacon to surrounding nations, if any warning can preserve them from destruction. In this country the subject is now so well understood, that every thing that issues from the *French* press is received with jealousy; and a work, on the first appearance of its exhibiting the doctrines of Voltaire and his associates, is rejected with indignation. . . .

Let not those to whom these pages are addressed deceive themselves by supposing this to be a fable; and let them inquire most seriously whether I speak truth, in asserting that the attacks on infidelity in Great Britain are at this moment principally directed against the female breast. Conscious of the influence of women in civil society, conscious of the effect which female infidelity produced in France, they attribute the ill success of their attempts in this country, to their having been hitherto addressed to the male sex. They are now sedulously labouring to destroy the religious principles of women, and in too many instances have fatally succeeded. For this purpose, not only novels and romances have been made the vehicles of vice and infidelity, but the same allurement has been held out to the women of our country, which was employed by the first philosophist to the first sinner – Knowledge. Listen to the precepts of the new German enlighteners, and you need no longer remain in that situation in which Providence has placed you! Follow their examples, and you shall be permitted to indulge in all those gratifications which custom, not religion, has tolerated in the male sex!

Let us jealously watch every deepening shade in the change of manners; let us mark every step, however inconsiderable, whose tendency is downwards. Corruption is neither stationary nor retrograde; and to have departed from modesty, is already to have made a progress. It is not only awfully true, that since the new principles have been afloat, *women* have been too eagerly inquisitive after these monstrous compositions; but it is also true that, with a new and offensive renunciation of their native delicacy, *many women of character* make little hesitation in avowing their familiarity with works abounding with principles, sentiments, and descriptions, 'which should not be so much as named among them'. By allowing their minds to come in contact with such contagious matter, they are irrecoverably tainting them; and by acknowledging that they are actually conversant with such corruptions, (with whatever reprobation of the author they may qualify their perusal of the book,) they are exciting in others a most mischievous curiosity for the same unhallowed gratification. Thus they are daily diminishing in the young and the timid those wholesome scruples, by which, when a tender conscience ceases to be intrenched, all the subsequent stages of ruin are gradually facilitated.

We have hitherto spoken only of German *writings;* but because there are multitudes who seldom read, equal pains have been taken to promote the same object through the medium of the stage: and this weapon is, of all others, that against which it is, at the present moment, the most important to warn the more inconsiderate of my countrywomen.

As a specimen of the German drama, it may not be unseasonable to offer a few remarks on the admired play of the *Stranger*.[3] In this piece the character of an *adulteress*, which, in all periods of the world, ancient as well as modern, in all countries, heathen as well as christian, has hitherto been held in detestation, and has never been introduced but to be reprobated, is for the first time presented to our view in the most pleasing and fascinating colours. . . .

About the same time that this first attempt at representing an adultress in an exemplary light was made by a German dramatist, which forms an aera in manners; a direct vindication of adultery was for the first time attempted by a *woman*, a professed admirer and imitator of the German suicide Werter. *The Female Werter*, as she is styled by her biographer, asserts, in a work intitled 'The Wrongs of Women',[4] that adultery is justifiable, and that the restrictions placed on it by the laws of England constitute one of the *Wrongs of Women*.

And this leads me to dwell a little longer on this most destructive class in the whole wide range of modern corruptors, who effect the most desperate work of the passions, without so much as pretending to urge their violence in extenuation of the guilt of indulging them. They solicit this very indulgence with a sort of cold-blooded speculation, and invite the reader to the most unbounded gratifications, with all the saturnine coolness of a geometrical calculation. Theirs is an iniquity rather of phlegm than of spirit: and in the pestilent atmosphere they raise about them, as in the infernal climate described by Milton,

> The parching air
> Burns frore, and frost performs th'effect of fire.[5]

This cool, calculating, intellectual wickedness eats out the very heart and core of virtue, and like a deadly mildew blights and shrivels the blooming promise of the human spring. Its benumbing touch communicates a torpid sluggishness, which paralyzes the soul. . . .

But let us take comfort. These projects are not yet generally realised. These atrocious principles are not yet adopted into common practice. Though corruptions seem with a confluent tide to be pouring in upon us from every quarter, yet there is still left among us a discriminating judgment. Clear and strongly marked distinctions between right and wrong still subsist. While we continue to cherish this sanity of mind, the case is not desperate. Though that crime, the growth of which always exhibits the most irrefragable proof of the dissoluteness of public manners; though that crime, which cuts up order and virtue by the roots, and violates the sanctity of vows, is awfully increasing,

> 'Till senates seem,
> For purposes of empire less conven'd
> Than to release the adult'ress from her bonds;[6]

yet, thanks to the surviving efficacy of a holy religion, to the operation of virtuous laws, and to the energy and unshaken integrity with which these laws are *now* administered; and most of all perhaps to a standard of morals which continues in force, when the principles which sanctioned it are no more; this crime, in the female sex at least, is still held in just abhorrence; if it be practised, it is not honourable; if it be committed, it is not justified; we do not yet affect to palliate its turpitude; as yet it hides its abhorred head in lurking privacy; and reprobation *hitherto* follows its publicity.

But on YOUR exerting your influence, with just application and increasing energy, may in no small degree depend whether this corruption shall still continue to be resisted. For, from admiring to adopting, the step is short, and the progress rapid; and it is in the moral as in the natural world; the motion, in the case of minds as well as of bodies, is accelerated as they approach the centre to which they are tending.

O ye to whom this address is particularly directed! an awful charge is, in this instance, committed to your hands; as you discharge it or shrink from it, you promote or injure the honour of your daughters and the happiness of your sons, of both which you are depositaries. And, while you resolutely persevere in making a stand against the encroachments of this crime, suffer not your firmness to be shaken by that affectation of charity, which is growing into a general substitute for principle. Abuse not so noble a quality as Christian candour, by misemploying it in instances to which it does not apply. Pity the wretched woman you dare not countenance; and bless HIM who has 'made you to differ'. If unhappily she be your relation or friend, anxiously watch for the period when she shall be deserted by her betrayer; and see if, by your Christian offices, she can be snatched from a perpetuity of vice. But if, through the Divine blessing on your patient endeavours, she should ever be awakened to remorse, be not anxious to restore the forlorn penitent to that society against whose laws she has so grievously offended; and remember, that her soliciting such a restoration, furnishes but too plain a proof that she is not the penitent your partiality would believe; since penitence is more anxious to make its peace with Heaven than with the world. Joyfully would a truly contrite spirit commute an earthly for an everlasting reprobation! To restore a criminal to public society, is perhaps to tempt her to repeat her crime, or to deaden her repentance for having committed it, as well as to injure that society; while to restore a strayed soul to God will add lustre to your Christian character, and brighten your eternal crown.

Chapter XIII: *'The practical use of female knowledge, with a sketch of the female character, and a comparative view of the sexes.'*

The chief end to be proposed in cultivating the understandings of women, is to qualify them for the practical purposes of life. Their knowledge is not often like the learning of men, to be reproduced in some literary composition, nor ever in any learned profession; but it is to come out in conduct. A lady studies, not that she may qualify herself to become an orator or a pleader; nor that she may learn to debate, but to act. She is to read the best books, not so much to enable her to talk of them, as to bring the improvement which they furnish, to the rectification of her principles, and the formation of her habits. The great uses of study are to enable her to regulate her own mind, and to be useful to others.

To woman therefore, whatever be her rank, I would recommend a predominance of those more sober studies, which, not having display for their object, may make her wise without vanity, happy without witnesses, and content without panegyrists; the exercise of which will not bring celebrity, but improve usefulness. She should pursue every kind of study which will teach her to elicit truth; which will lead her to be intent upon realities; will give precision to her ideas; will make an exact mind; every study which, instead of stimulating her sensibility, will chastise it; which will give her definite notions; will bring the imagination under dominion; will lead her to think, to compare, to combine, to methodise; which will confer such a power of discrimination that her judgment shall learn to reject what is dazzling if it be not solid; and to prefer, not what is striking, or bright, or new, but what is just. That kind of knowledge which is rather fitted for home consumption than foreign exportation, is peculiarly adapted to women.

It is because the superficial nature of their education furnishes them with a false and low standard of intellectual excellence, that women have sometimes become ridiculous by the unfounded pretensions of literary vanity: for it is not the really learned but the smatterers, who have generally brought their sex into discredit, by an absurd affectation, which has set them on despising the duties of ordinary life. There have not indeed been wanting (but the character is not now common) *précieuses ridicules*,[7] who, assuming a superiority to the sober cares which ought to occupy their sex, have claimed a lofty and supercilious exemption from the dull and plodding drudgeries

> Of this dim speck called earth![8]

who have affected to establish an unnatural separation between talents and usefulness, instead of bearing in mind that talents are the great appointed instruments of usefulness; who have acted as if knowledge were to confer on woman a kind of fantastic sovereignty, which should exonerate her from female duties; whereas it is only meant the more eminently to qualify her for the performance of them. For a woman of real sense will never forget, that while the greater part of her proper duties are such as the most moderately gifted may fulfil with credit, (since Providence never makes that to be very difficult, which is generally necessary,) yet the most highly endowed are equally bound to fulfil them; and the humblest of these offices, performed on Christian principles, are wholesome for the minds even of the most enlightened, and tend to the casting down of those high imaginations which women of genius are too much tempted to indulge.

Notes

(a) The newspapers announce that Schiller's Tragedy of the Robbers, which inflamed the young nobility of Germany to inlist themselves into a band of highwaymen to rob in the forests of Bohemia, is *now acting in England by persons of quality!*[Schiller's play deals with a noble outlaw and was highly influential. 'Bagshot': a reference to Bagshot Heath in Surrey, notorious as a haunt of highwaymen and robbers.]

1 *Paradise Lost*, VIII, ll. 601–2
2 *Paradise Lost*, II, l. 628.
3 By Kotzebue, author of *Lovers' Vows*, the performance of which causes Fanny such moral problems in Jane Austen's *Mansfield Park*.
4 The 'woman' is of course Mary Wollstonecraft, whose husband, William Godwin, in 1798 published *Memoirs of the author of a Vindication of the Rights of Woman* and her *Posthumous Works* which include her novel *Maria, or the Wrongs of Woman*. The *Memoirs* gained great notoriety since, among other things, they openly justified Wollstonecraft and Godwin's initial decision not to marry.
5 *Paradise Lost*, II, ll. 594–5 (slightly misquoted).
6 William Cowper, *The Task* (1784), III, 'The Garden', ll. 61–3 (slightly misquoted).

7 *Les Précieuses Ridicules* (1659): a comedy by Molière in which two young provincial women refuse any suitor who does not behave like the hero of a romantic novel.
8 Milton, *Comus*, ll. 5–6 (slightly misquoted).

4

WRITING

Writing was one career which even a fairly conventional education opened up for women. But to write, or at least to publish, was for the eighteenth-century woman a transgressive act. Though the gendering of mental qualities associated femininity with imagination and creativity (see, for example, 3.2, 3.3, 3.7), publishing exposed an essentially private activity to the public gaze, blurring the conduct-book delineation of separate spheres. The effect, even according to sympathetic contemporary commentators, was a troubling confusion of gender roles: a favourable reviewer sees Elizabeth Carter's poems, for example, as yet further evidence that 'the men prate and dress; the women read and write' (see 4.11); and for Samuel Johnson, in a famous formulation, the increasing numbers of women writers were 'Amazons of the pen'.[1] Women's writing is thus defined as a threat to the existing social order, figured at its most extreme as a loss of chastity, a transgression of the very basis of acceptable femininity (see 4.19, and cf. 3.9). Given this identification of writing with sexual decorum, women's texts were judged according to strict moral criteria, criteria which were always liable to slip from text to author, and which became more rather than less rigid as the number of women writers increased.

The texts in this section highlight the representation of women's writing, its discursive identities, and the ways in which, like definitions of women's education, these derived from, modified, and reinforced ideologies of femininity. The passages in the second half, 'Public images', are from critical works, often by men, which describe (and prescribe for) women's writing as a discrete cultural phenomenon; those in the first half, 'Self-images', are from prefaces and autobiographical pieces by women, raising the question of how women writers constructed themselves for public consumption, how they negotiated the restricted parameters laid down both in criticism and in conduct literature generally. At the same time, the extracts offer some sense of the variety of eighteenth-century women's writing, from Teresia Constantia Phillips's autobiography (4.7) to Clara Reeve's decorous definitions of acceptable fiction (4.18), and from the working-class poet Mary Collier's mock-heroic verse (4.5) to Elizabeth Carter's translation of Epictetus (4.11).

One of the immediately striking features of the critical texts is their creation of a tradition of women's writing – or rather of two traditions. Names familiar both from this section and from elsewhere in the anthology – Rowe (1.2, 4.1), Haywood (1.5, 4.7), Wollstonecraft (1.7, 3.4), Chapone (3.2), More (3.9), Manley (4.3), Phillips (4.7), Centlivre (4.9), Hays (5.5), Robinson (5.6) – are categorized, according to a simple, not to say crude, moral differentiation, as inspired by either 'the modest' or 'a wanton Muse' (4.10). Adapting the formalized roll-calls of pro and anti-female satire (cf. 2.1, 2.4) to the subject of literary women, a text like Duncombe's *Feminiad* (4.10), though celebratory, contributes to an aesthetic orthodoxy which privileges domestic and moral virtues over any other criteria. This orthodoxy clearly affects the terms of Scott's praise for Montagu and Talbot in her feminist response to Duncombe, *The Female Advocate* (4.17), and Reeve's guarded acknowledgment of Eliza Haywood (4.18). Polwhele's virulent anti-Jacobin fantasy *The Unsex'd Females* (4.19), in which radical women, and Wollstonecraft in particular, are attacked through their sexuality, is only the most extreme version of a critical tradition based on the reciprocal identification of writer and text. Even in the sympathetic critical texts, women and their writing are described in gendered, and often sexually charged, terms ('a blooming, studious band', (4.10); 'the prettiest poems that have been published for a long time', (4.11), etc.), the effect of which is to deny them any serious status.

The crippling moralism of these two traditions is potentially present at the beginning of the eighteenth century – in the preface to Rowe's poems, for example (4.1) – but it becomes more inflexible during the second half of the period. In a parallel process, visible here in the reviews of novels (4.12, 4.14, 4.15, 4.16), women become identified primarily with fiction, reinforcing both a hierarchy of genres ruled by the 'male' forms of tragedy and epic and the identification of women's writing with immorality. In the extract from Fordyce's *Sermons to Young Women* (4.13), simply reading novels is taken as proof of Pope's influential dictum 'Ev'ry woman is at heart a rake': 'she who can bear to peruse them must in her soul be a prostitute'. As so often, a fear of female autonomy is expressed in sexual terms. Fordyce's preference for the female passivity of 'the Old Romance' (cf. 2.5) is a measure of the disruptive potential of popular fiction for women: novels of sensibility gave women access to an enabling vocabulary of feeling from which obtaining sexual power relations might be challenged.

The passages in the first part of the section offer various responses to these prescriptive caricatures. In almost every case, women writers start from a defensive position: writing is conceived of as an unnatural activity requiring special justification. Thus Mary Chudleigh offers a deferential apology for the 'plain Dress' of her style (cf. 2.10) and claims (disingenuously?) to appeal only to 'the Ladies' (4.2); more aggressively Susannah Centlivre's anonymous defender (4.9) and the writer of the preface to Rowe's *Poems* (4.1) use their introductions to make powerful points about the inadequacies of women's education; and the religious nonconformist Anne Dutton skilfully negotiates biblical authority for the public/private divide by claiming women's right to 'private Converse' with other individuals through the printed word (4.6).

A recurrent motif is the suggestion that for women writing can only ever be a part-time activity. Duncombe's moralistic view that learning might fill those hours 'Which others waste in visits, cards and noise' (4.10; and cf. 3.9) is endorsed by Chudleigh's again self-deprecatory description of her work as the improving product of 'my leisure Hours, my lonely Moments'. Rather differently for Collier the double 'Drudgery' imposed by gender and class makes learning almost impossible (4.5), and Delarivière Manley's fictional self, Rivella, 'rarely speaks of her own Writings', maintaining a tantalizing public distance between woman and author (4.3). But this kind of playing down of intellectual achievement often works to disrupt the official image of the conventionally modest woman. Many women's texts are at one level self-conscious displays of learning, achieved in spite of educational disadvantages and thus offering irrefutable evidence of female abilities. Their authorial personae inevitably offer role-models to their female readers, role-models which might extend or even contradict the work's overt argument. (For a conservative work in which the authoritative persona contradicts the official message about submissive womanhood, see 3.9.)

In three of the texts in the first half the difficulties of a public image and its possible appropriations are particularly acute. The extract from the introductory chapter to Delarivière Manley's barely disguised autobiography *The History of Rivella* (4.3), the fascinating schizophrenic dedicatory epistle to the *Narrative of the Life of Mrs. Charlotte Charke* (4.8), and the passages from the *Apology for the Conduct of Mrs. Teresia Constantia Phillips* (4.7) are representative of a significant sub-genre of women's writing, that of the scandalous autobiography. These texts were usually written for money by women left destitute by unscrupulous men. Thus they solicit the social as well as financial survival of their authors through a narrative mode in which confession necessitates recounting titillating sexual detail and the role of penitent victim involves a devastating critique of the sexual double standard. Their use of fictional techniques (the third-person narrator or the 'quotations' from the seducer's letters in Phillips, for example, a text exactly contemporary with Richardson's *Clarissa*) is a reminder of the blurred distinctions between the emergent novel and other forms of popular narrative. It also makes visible the relationship between written constructions of the self and available cultural paradigms. By making a display of, albeit 'innocent', sexuality their very condition of writing, these texts violently transgress all norms of acceptable femininity. (For a typical reaction to these autobiographies, see 4.10.) The standard seduction narrative on which they are all based, that of the prodigal daughter seeking reconciliation with a father figure (cf. 1.5, 2.3, 2.9), can thus be read as a bid for moral recuperation. Manley's sophisticated projection of self in *Rivella* is more daring. Playing with the reader's suspicion that this is autobiography, Manley describes Rivella's physical charms through the voice of a male admirer, defending herself against public accusations that 'few . . . could be brought to like her' by tantalizing suggestions that on more intimate knowledge 'none . . . could refrain from loving her'. Both strategies inevitably reproduce already available images of women – as passive penitent, or as sexual mystery – but the tension between them, and the foregrounding of sexual inequality in their basic narratives, make the scandalous autobiography a form of women's writing which persistently escapes prescriptive categories.

Note

1 Samuel Johnson, *The Adventurer*, 115 (11 December 1753).

I. Self-images

4.1 [Elizabeth Singer Rowe], from *Poems on Several Occasions. Written by Philomela*, 1696

'Preface to the Reader'

The *occasion* of this *Preface* is, to give the World some account of the *Author* of these *Poems*, as far as I'm permitted to do it: An Employment I the more willingly chuse, because *our Sex* has some Excuse for a little *Vanity*, when they have so good *Reason* for't, and such a *Champion* among themselves, as not many of the *other* can boast of. We are not unwilling to allow Mankind the *Brutal Advantages* of *Strength*, they are Superior to ours in *Force*, they have *Custom* of their side, and *have Ruled*, and are like to do so, and may freely do it without *Disturbance* or *Envy;* at least they should have none from us, if they cou'd but keep *quiet* among *themselves*. But when they wou'd Monopolize *Sence* too, when neither that, nor Learning, nor so much as *Wit* must be allow'd us, but all *over-rul'd* by the *Tyranny* of the *Prouder Sex;* nay, when some of 'em won't let us say our *Souls* are our *own*, but wou'd perswade us we are no more *Reasonable Creatures* then themselves, or their *Fellow-Animals;* we then must ask their Pardons if we are not yet so COMPLEATLY PASSIVE as to bear all without so much as a *murmur:* We complain, and we think with reason, that our *Fundamental Constitutions* are destroyed; that here's a plain and an open design to render us meer *Slaves*, perfect TURKISH WIVES, without *Properties*, or *Sense*, or *Souls;* and are forc'd to Protest against it, and appeal to all the World, whether these are not *notorious* Violations on the *Liberties of Free-born English Women?* This makes the *Meekest Worm* amongst us all, ready to turn agen when we are thus *trampled* on; But alas! What can we do to *Right* our selves? *stingless* and *harmless* as we are, we can only *Kiss* the *Foot* that *hurts* us. However, sometimes it pleases Heaven to raise up some *Brighter Genius* then ordinary to Succour a Distressed People – ; an *Epaminondas* in *Thebes;* a *Timoleon* for *Corinth;* (for you must know we Read *Plutarch* now 'tis Translated) and a *Nassawps* for *all the World:*[1] Nor is our *Defenceless Sex* forgotten – we have not only *Bunduca's* and *Zenobia's,*[2] but *Sappho's,* and *Behn's,* and *Schurman's,* and *Orinda's,*[3] who have *humbled* the most haughty of our Antagonists, and made 'em do Homage to our *Wit,* as well as our *Beauty.* 'Tis true, their Mischievous and Envious *sex* have made it their utmost endeavours to deal with us, as *Hannibal* was serv'd at *Capua,* and to *Corrupt* that *Virtue* which they can no otherwise *overcome:* and sometimes they prevail'd: But, if some *Angels* fell, others remained in their *Innocence* and *Perfection,* if there were not also some *addition* made to their *Happiness* and *Glory,* by their continuing stedfast. *Angels Love,* but they love *Virtuously* and *Reasonably,* and neither err in the *Object,* nor the *Manner:* And if all our *Poetesses* had done the same, I wonder what our *Enemies* cou'd have found out to have objected against us: However, here they are *silenc'd;* and I dare be bold to say, that whoever does not come extreamly prejudic'd to these *Poems,* will find in 'em that *vivacity* of Thought, that *purity* of Language, that *softness* and *delicacy* in the *Love-part,* that *strength* and *Majesty* of Numbers almost every where, especially on *Heroical* Subjects, and that clear and unaffected *Love* to *Virtue;* that heighth of *Piety* and warmth of *Devotion* in the *Canticles,* and other Religious Pieces; which they will hardly find exceeded in the best *Authors* on those Different Kinds of Writing, much less equall'd by any single Writer.

And now I have nothing more, I think, lies upon my Hands, but to assure the *Reader,* that they were actually Writ by A YOUNG LADY, (... as is well-known to some Persons of Quality and Worth) whose NAME had been prefix'd, had not her own *Modesty* absolutely forbidden it. . . .

Notes

1 Epaminondas: Theban commander under whom Thebes became the most powerful state in Greece. Timoleon: Corinthian who killed his brother when he became tyrannical. Plutarch: Greek biographer, translated into English by Sir Thomas North (1579). Nassawps: unidentified, possibly a reference to William III, prince of Orange-Nassau.
2 Types of the military woman. Bunduca [Bonduca]: version of Boudicca or Boadicea. Zenobia: Syrian ruler who also fought against Rome.
3 Sappho: ancient Greek poet, but probably here refers to French romance writer Madeleine de Scudéry, who called herself 'Sapho' (see 5.1, note 4). Aphra Behn (1640–89): playwright, novelist, poet, translator and the first Englishwoman to make a living from writing (cf. 4.10, 4.18); Anna Maria Van Schurman (1607–78): German poet and scholar, author of a feminist work translated into English as *The Learned Maid* (1659) (cf. 5.4). Orinda: the pen-name of Katherine Philips (1631–64), often favourably compared with Aphra Behn because of her modesty (cf. 4.10, 5.1).

4.2 Mary Chudleigh, from *Essays upon Several Subjects in Prose and Verse*, 1710

'To the Reader'

That the Pleasures of the Mind are infinitely preferable to those of Sense, intellectual Delights, the Joys of Thought, and the Complacencies arising from a bright and inlarg'd Understanding, transcendently greater and more satisfactory than those of the Body, than those that owe their Original to the Animal Life, has, through all Ages, been an acknowledg'd Truth, a Truth that comes attended with all the convincing Evidences that can be desired, and will soon be found to be undeniably so by all such as will be at the Pains of making the Experiment.

Such as have been so happy as to have had a Taste of these Delights, a pleasing Relish of these internal Joys, have always been blest with an inward Satisfaction, an unexpressible Felicity; their Minds have been calm, easy, and intrepid, amidst the greatest Storms, the most deafning Hurricanes of Life, never ruffled by Passions, nor disturbed by the most threatning, the melancholiest Circumstances of Fortune. They have long been the dear, the favourite Companions of my solitary Hours, and while they are mine, I cannot only be contentedly, but even chearfully alone; they fill up all the Spaces, all the Intervals of Time, and make my Days slide joyfully along.

O what Pleasures, what transporting Joys do rational instructive Thoughts afford! What rich Treasures do they yield to the Mind! What unexhausted Stores of Knowledge may be drawn from them! They leave no Vacancies, no room for dull insipid Trifles, debasing Impertinencies, nor any of those troublesome Reflexions which generally proceed from narrow groveling Souls, from Souls that have not learn'd to use their Faculties aright. Though I cannot boast of having mine improv'd, and must with Blushes own my Thoughts are infinitely inferior to multitudes of others; yet, mean as they are, to Me they prove delightful, are always welcome, they present me with new and useful Hints, with something that agreeably, as well as advantageously, entertains my Mind; the Notices they give me, I strive to improve by Writing; that firmly fixes what I know, deeply imprints the Truths I've learned.

The following *Essays* were the Products of my Retirement, some of the pleasing Opiates I made use of to lull my Mind to a delightful Rest, the ravishing Amusements of my leisure Hours, of my lonely Moments.

'Tis only to the *Ladies* I presume to present them; I am not so vain as to believe any thing of mine deserves the Notice of the *Men;* but perhaps some of my own Sex may have occasion for such Considerations as these; to them they may prove beneficial; they'll in 'em be perswaded to cultivate their Minds, to brighten and refine their Reason, and to render all their Passions subservient to its Dictates; they'll there be instructed by great Examples, read of several Men, and some Ladies, that have struggled with Pain, Poverty, Infamy, Death, and whatsoever else has been accounted dreadful among the Suffering incident to Humanity, without being overcome, without losing their Resolution, or lessening their Patience; . . . .

I hope they will pardon the Incorrectness of my Stile: The Subjects of which I write are worthy of their Attention; 'tis those I recommend to them: Truth is valuable though she appears in a plain Dress; and I hope they will not slight her because she wants the Ornaments of Language: Politeness is not my Talent; it ought not to be expected from a Person who has liv'd almost wholly to her self, who has but seldom had the Opportunity of conversing with ingenious Company, which I remember Mr. *Dryden*, in the Preface to one of his *Miscellanies*, thinks to be necessary toward the gaining of Fineness of Stile; this being a Qualification I want, it cannot be suppos'd I should understand the Delicacies of Language, the Niceties of good writing; those things I leave to happier, more accurate Pens: My whole Design is to recommend Virtue, to perswade my Sex to improve their Understandings, to prefer Wisdom before Beauty, good Sense before Wealth, and the Sovereignty of their Passions before the Empire of the World: I beg them to do me the Favour to believe one that speaks it from a long Experience, That a greater Delight, a more transporting Satisfaction, results from a pure well-regulated Soul, from a Consciousness of having done Things agreeable to Reason, suitable to the Dignity of ones Nature, than from the highest Gratifications of Sense, the most entertaining Gayeties of an unthinking Life.

4.3 [Mary] Delarivière Manley, from *The Adventures of Rivella; or, the History of the Writer of Atalantis*, 1714

'Introduction'

On one of those fine Evenings that are so rarely to be found in *England*, the Young *Chevalier D'Aumont*, related to the Duke of that Name, was taking the Air in *Somerset-House-Garden*, and enjoying the cool Breeze from the River; which after the hottest Day that had been known that Summer, prov'd very refreshing. He had made an Intimacy with Sir *Charles Lovemore*, a Person of admirable good Sense and Knowledge, and who was now walking in the Garden with him, when *D'Aumont* leaning over the Wall, pleas'd with observing the Rays of the Setting Sun upon the *Thames*, chang'd the Discourse; Dear *Lovemore*, says the *Chevalier*, now the Ambassador is engag'd elsewhere, what hinders me to have the entire Command of this Garden? If you think it a proper Time to perform your Promise, I will command the Door-keepers, that they suffer none to disturb our Conversation. Sir *Charles* having agreed to the Proposal, and Orders being accordingly given, Young *D'Aumont* re-assumed the Discourse: Condemn not my Curiosity, said he, when it puts me upon enquiring after the ingenious Women of your Nation: Wit and Sense is so powerful a Charm, that I am not ashamed to tell you my Heart was insensible to all the fine Ladies of the Court of *France*, and had perhaps still remain'd so, if I had not been softned by the Charms of Madam *Dacier's*[1] Conversation; a Woman without either Youth or Beauty, yet who makes a Thousand Conquests, and preserves them too. I have often admir'd her Learning, answer'd *Lovemore*, and to such a Degree, that if the War had not prevented me, I had doubtless gone to *France* to have seen amongst other Curiosities, a Lady who has made her self admired by all the World: But I do not imagine my Heart would have been in any Danger by that Visit, her Qualifications are of the Sort that strike the Mind, in which the Sense of Love can have but little Part: Talking to Her is conversing with an admirable Scholar, a judicious Critick, but what had That to do with the Heart? If she be as *unhandsom* as Fame reports her, and as *learned*, I should never raise my Thoughts higher than if I were discoursing with some *Person* of my own Sex, great and extraordinary in his Way. You are, I find, a Novice, answer'd *D'Aumont* in what relates to Women; there is no being pleas'd in their Conversation without a Mixture of the Sex which will still be mingling it self in all we say. Some other Time I will give you a Proof of this, and do my self the Honour to entertain you with certain Memoirs relating to Madam *Dacier*, of the Admiration and Applause she has gain'd, and the Conquests she has made; by which you will find, that the *Royal Academy* are not the only Persons that have done her Justice; for whereas they bestow'd but the Prize of Eloquence, others have bestow'd their Heart: I must agree with you, that her Perfections are not of the Sort that inspire immediate Delight, and warm the Blood with Pleasure, as those do who treat well of Love: I have not known any of the Moderns in that Point come up to your famous Author of the *Atalantis*. She has carried the Passion further than could be readily conceiv'd: Her *Germanicus on the Embroider'd Bugle Bed, naked out of the Bath:* - Her *Young and innocent Charlot*, transported with the powerful *Emotion of a just kindling Flame, sinking with Delight and Shame upon the Bosom of her Lover in the Gallery of Books:* Chevalier Tomaso *dying at the Feet of Madam* de Bedamore, *and afterwards possessing Her in that* Sylvan *Scene of Pleasure in the Garden;* are such Representatives of Nature, that must warm the coldest Reader; it raises high Ideas of the Dignity of Human

Kind, and informs us that we have in our Composition, where-with to taste sublime and transporting Joys: After perusing her Inchanting Descriptions, which of us have not gone in Search of Raptures which she every where tells us, as happy Mortals, we are capable of tasting. But have we found them, *Chevalier*, answer'd his Friend? For my Part, I believe that they are to be met with no where else but in her own Embraces. That is what I would experience, reply'd *D'Aumont*, if she have but half so much of the Practice, as the Theory, in the Way of Love, she must certainly be a most accomplish'd Person: You have promised to tell me what you know of her Life and Conduct; I would have her Mind, her Person, her Manner describ'd to me; I would have you paint her with as masterly an Hand, as she has painted others, that I may know her perfectly before I see her.

... By this time, the two *Cavaliers* were near one of the Benches; upon which reposing themselves, Sir *Charles Lovemore*, who perceiv'd young *D'Aumont* was prepar'd with the utmost Atten-tion to hearken to what he should speak, began his Discourse in this manner.

'The History of Rivella'

There are so many Things Praise, and yet Blame-worthy, in *Rivella's* Conduct, that as Her Friend, I know not well how with a good Grace, to repeat, or as yours, to conceal, because you seem to expect from me an Impartial History. Her Vertues are her own, her Vices occasion'd by her Misfortunes; and yet as I have often heard her say, *If she had been a Man, she had been without Fault:* But the Charter of that Sex being much more confin'd than ours, what is not a Crime in Men is scandalous and unpardonable in Woman, as she her self has very well observ'd in divers Places, throughout her own Writings.

Her Person is neither tall nor short; from her Youth she was inclin'd to Fat; whence I have often heard her Flatterers liken her to the *Grecian Venus*. It is certain, considering that Disadvantage, she has the most easy Air that one can have; her Hair is of a pale Ash-colour, fine, and in a large Quantity. I have heard her Friends lament the Disaster of her having had the Small-pox in such an injurious manner, being a beautiful Child before that Distemper; but as that Disease has now left her Face, she has scarce any Pretence to it. Few, who have only beheld her in Publick, could be brought to like her; whereas none that became acquainted with her, could refrain from loving her. I have heard several Wives and Mistresses accuse her of Fascination: They would neither trust their Husbands, Lovers, Sons, nor Brothers with her Acquaintance upon Terms of the greatest Advantage. Speak to me of her Eyes, interrupted the *Chevalier*, you seem to have forgot that Index of her Mind; Is there to be found in them, Store of those animating Fires with which Her Writings are fill'd? Do Her Eyes love as well as her Pen? You reprove me very justly, answer'd the Baronet, *Rivella* would have a good deal of Reason to complain of me, if I should silently pass over the best Feature in her Face. In a Word, you have your self described them: Nothing can be more tender, ingenious, and brilliant with a Mixture so languishing and sweet, when Love is the Subject of the Discourse, that without being severe, we may very well conclude, the softer Passions have their Predominancy in Her Soul.

How are Her Teeth and Lips, spoke the *Chevalier*? Forgive me, dear *Lovemore*, for breaking in so often upon your Discourse; but Kissing being the sweetest leading Pleasure, 'tis impossible a Woman can charm without a good Mouth. Yet, answer'd *Lovemore*, I have seen very great Beauties please, as the common Witticism speaks, *in spight of their Teeth:* I do not find but Love in the general is well natur'd and civil, willing to compound for some Defects, since he knows that 'tis very difficult and rare to find true Symmetry and all Perfections in one Person: Red Hair, Out-Mouth, thin and livid Lips, black broken Teeth, course ugly Hands, long Thumbs, ill form'd dirty Nails, flat, or very large Breasts, splay Feet; which together makes a frightful Composition, yet divided amongst several, prove no Allay to the strongest Passions: But to do *Rivella* Justice, till she grew fat, there was not I believe any Defect to be found in her Body: Her Lips admirably colour'd; Her Teeth small and even, a Breath always sweet; Her Complexion fair and fresh; yet with all this you must be us'd to her before she can be thought thoroughly agreeable. Her Hands and Arms have been publickly celebrated; it is certain, that I never saw any so well turned: Her Neck and Breasts have an establish'd Reputation for Beauty and Colour: Her Feet small and pretty. Thus I have run thro' whatever Custom suffers to be visible to us; and upon my Word, *Chevalier*, I never saw any of *Rivella's* hidden Charms.

Pardon me this once, said *D'Aumont*, and I assure you, dear Sir *Charles*, I will not hastily interrupt you again, What Humour is she of? Is her Manner Gay or Serious? Has she Wit in her Conversation as well as Her Pen? What do you call Wit, answer'd *Lovemore*. If by that Word, you mean a Succession of such Things as can bear Repetition, even down to Posterity? How few are there of such Persons, or rather none indeed, that can be always witty? *Rivella* speaks Things pleasantly; her Company is entertaining to the last; no Woman except one's Mistress wearies one so little as her self: Her Knowledge is universal; she discourses well, and agreeably upon all Subjects, bating a little Affectation, which nevertheless becomes her admirably well; yet this thing is to be commended in her, that she rarely speaks of her own Writings, unless she wou'd expressly ask the Judgment of her Friends, insomuch that I was well pleas'd at the Character a certain Person gave her (who did not mean it much to her Advantage) that one might discourse Seven Years together with *Rivella*, and never find out from her self, that she was a *Wit*, or an *Author*.

I have one Pardon more to ask you, cry'd the *Chevalier* (in a Manner that fully accus'd himself for Breach of Promise) Is she genteel? She is easy, answer'd his Friend, which is as much as can be expected from the *en bonne Point:* Her Person is always nicely clean, and Her Garb fashionable.

What we say in respect of the fair Sex, I find goes for little, persu'd the *Chevalier*, I'll change my Promise of Silence with your Leave, Sir *Charles*, into Conditions of interrupting you when ever I am more than ordinarily pleas'd with what you say, and therefore do now begin with telling you, that I find my self resolved to be in Love with *Rivella*. I easily forgive Want of Beauty in her Face, to the Charms you tell me are in her Person: I hope there are no hideous Vices in her Mind, to deform the fair Idea you have given me of fine Hands and Arms, a beautiful Neck and Breast, pretty Feet, and, I take it for granted, Limbs that make up the Symmetry of the whole.

Rivella is certainly much indebted, continu'd *Lovemore*, to a Liberal Education, and those early Precepts of Vertue taught her and practis'd in her Father's House. There was then such a Foundation laid, that tho' Youth, Misfortunes, and Love, for several Years have interrupted so fair a Building, yet some Time since, she is returned with the greatest Application to repair that Loss and Defect; if not with relation to this World (where Women have found it impossible to be reinstated) yet of the next, which has mercifully told us, *Mankind can commit no Crimes but what upon Conversion may be forgiven.*

Note

1 Anne Dacier (1654–1720), editor and translator of classical texts. Frequently cited as a type of the learned woman (cf. 4.9, 4.11(a), 5.1).

4.4 Eliza Haywood, from *Lasselia: or, the Self-Abandon'd. A Novel*, 1724

'To the Right Honourable the Earl of Suffolk and Bindon.'

My Lord,

When I presume to entreat your Protection of a Trifle such as this, I do more to express my Sense of your unbounded Goodness, than if I were to publish Folio's in your Praise. A great and learned Work honours the Patron who accepts it, but little Performances stand in need of all that Sweetness of Disposition so conspicuous in the Behaviour and Character of your Lordship, to engage a Pardon. 'Tis something to be of a piece with Heaven, to regard the Will more than the merit of the Offering; and my Knowledge how zealous an Imitator you are in all Things else of that, gives me an almost assur'd Hope you will not swerve in *this*, only to punish my Presumption.

My Design in writing this little *Novel* (as well as those I have formerly publish'd) being only to remind the unthinking Part of the World, how dangerous it is to give way to Passion, will, I hope, excuse the too great Warmth, which may perhaps, appear in some particular Pages; for without the *Expression* being invigorated in some measure proportionate to the Subject, 'twou'd be impossible for a Reader to be sensible how far it touches him, or how probable it is that he is falling into those Inadvertencies which the Examples I relate wou'd caution him to avoid.

I take the liberty of mentioning this to your Lordship, to clear my self of that Aspersion which some of my own Sex have been unkind enough to throw upon me, that 'I seem to endeavour to *divert* more than *improve* the Minds of my Readers'. Now, as I take it, the Aim of every Person who pretends to write (tho' in the most insignificant and ludicrous way) ought to tend at least to a good *Moral* Use; I shou'd be sorry to have my Intentions judg'd to be the very reverse of what they are in Reality. How far I have been able to *succeed* in my Desires of infusing those Cautions, too necessary to a Number, I will not pretend to determine: but where I have had the misfortune to *fail*, must impute it either to the *Obstinacy* of those I wou'd persuade, or to my own Deficiency in that very Thing which They are pleased to say I too much abound in – a true Description of Nature.

4.5   Mary Collier, from *The Woman's Labour: an Epistle to Mr. Stephen Duck in Answer to his late Poem, called The Thresher's Labour*,[1] 1739

> No Learning ever was bestow'd on me;
> My Life was always spent in Drudgery:
> And not alone; alas! with Grief I find,
> 10 It is the portion of poor Woman-kind.
> Oft have I thought as on my Bed I lay,
> Eas'd from the tiresome Labours of the Day,
> Our first Extraction from a Mass refin'd,
> Could never be for Slavery design'd;
> Till Time and Custom by degrees destroy'd
> That happy State our Sex at first enjoy'd.
> When Men had us'd their utmost Care and Toil,
> Their Recompence was but a Female Smile;
> When they by Arts or Arms were render'd Great,
> 20 They laid their Trophies at a Woman's Feet;
> They, in those Days, unto our Sex did bring
> Their Hearts, their All, a Free-will Offering;
> And as from us their Being they derive,
> They back again should all due Homage give.
>
>   . . .
>
> When Harvest comes, into the Field we go,
> And help to reap the Wheat as well as you;
> Or else we go the Ears of Corn to glean;

90   No Labour scorning, be it e'er so mean;
But in the Work we freely bear a Part,
And what we can, perform with all our Heart.
To get a Living we so willing are,
Our tender Babes into the Field we bear,
And wrap them in our Cloaths to keep them warm,
While round about we gather up the Corn;
And often unto them our Course do bend,
To keep them safe, that nothing them offend:
Our Children that are able, bear a Share

100   In gleaning Corn, such is our frugal Care.
When Night comes on, unto our Home we go,
Our Corn we carry, and our Infant too;
Weary, alas! but 'tis not worth our while
Once to complain, or *rest at ev'ry Stile;*
We must make haste, for when we Home are come,
Alas! we find our Work but just begun;
So many Things for our Attendance call,
Had we ten Hands, we could employ them all.
Our Children put to Bed, with greatest Care

110   We all Things for your coming Home prepare:
You sup, and go to Bed without delay,
And rest yourselves till the ensuing Day;
While we, alas! but little Sleep can have,
Because our froward Children cry and rave;
Yet, without fail, soon as Day-light doth spring,
We in the Field again our Work begin,
And there, with all our Strength, our Toil renew,
Till *Titan's* golden Rays have dry'd the Dew;
Then home we go unto our Children dear,

120   Dress, feed, and bring them to the Field with care.
Were this your Case, you justly might complain
That Day nor Night you are secure from Pain;
Those mighty Troubles which perplex your Mind,
(*Thistles* before, and *Females* come behind)
Would vanish soon, and quickly disappear,
Were you, like us, encumber'd thus with Care.

. . .

The Harvest ended, Respite none we find;

The hardest of our Toil is still behind:
Hard Labour we most chearfully pursue,
And out, abroad, a Charing often go:
Of which I now will briefly tell in part,
140   What fully to declare is past my Art;
So many Hardships daily we go through,
I boldly say, the like *you* never knew.
When bright *Orion* glitters in the Skies
In *Winter* Nights, then early we must rise;
The Weather ne'er so bad, Wind, Rain, or Snow,
Our Work appointed, we must rise and go;
While you on easy Beds may lie and sleep,
Till Light does thro' your Chamber-windows peep.
When to the House we come where we should go,
150   How to get in, alas! we do not know:
The Maid quite tir'd with Work the Day before,
O'ercome with Sleep; we standing at the Door
Oppress'd with Cold, and often call in vain,
E're to our Work we can Admittance gain:
But when from Wind and Weather we get in,
Briskly with Courage we our Work begin;
Heaps of fine Linen we before us view,
Whereon to lay our Strength and Patience too;
Cambricks and Muslins, which our Ladies wear,
160   Laces and Edgings, costly, fine, and rare,
Which must be wash'd with utmost Skill and Care;
With Holland Shirts, Ruffles and Fringes too,
Fashions which our Fore-fathers never knew.
For several Hours here we work and slave,
Before we can one Glimpse of Day-light have;
We labour hard before the Morning's past,
Because we fear the Time runs on too fast.
    At length bright *Sol* illuminates the Skies,
And summons drowsy Mortals to arise;
170   Then comes our Mistress to us without fail,
And in her Hand, *perhaps*, a Mug of Ale
To cheer our Hearts, and also to inform
Herself, what Work is done that very Morn;
Lays her Commands upon us, that we mind
Her Linen well, nor *leave the Dirt behind*:

Not this alone, but also to take care
We don't her Cambricks nor her Ruffles tear;
And *these* most strictly does of us require,
To save her Soap, and sparing be of Fire;
180   Tells us her Charge is great, nay furthermore,
Her Cloaths are fewer than the Time before.
Now we drive on, resolv'd our Strength to try,
And what we can, we do most willingly;
Until with Heat and Work, 'tis often known,
Not only Sweat, but Blood runs trickling down
Our Wrists and Fingers; still our Work demands
The constant Action of our lab'ring Hands.

    Now Night comes on, from whence you have Relief,
But that, alas! does but increase our Grief;
190   With heavy Hearts we often view the Sun,
Fearing he'll set before our Work is done;
For either in the Morning, or at Night,
We piece the *Summer's* Day with Candle-light.
Tho' we all Day with Care our Work attend,
Such is our Fate, we know not when 'twill end:
When Ev'ning's come, you Homeward take your Way,
We, till our Work is done, are forc'd to stay;
And after all our Toil and Labour past,
Six-pence or Eight-pence pays us off at last;
200   For all our Pains, no Prospect can we see
Attend us, but *Old Age* and *Poverty.*

. . .

    But to rehearse all Labour is in vain,
Of which we very justly might complain:
For us, you see, but little Rest is found;
Our Toil increases as the Year runs round.
While you to *Sisiphus*[2] yourselves compare,
240   With *Danaus' Daughters*[3] we may claim a Share;
For while he labours hard against the Hill,
Bottomless Tubs of Water *they* must fill.
    So the industrious Bees do hourly strive
To bring their Loads of Honey to the Hive;
Their sordid Owners always reap the Gains,
And poorly recompense their Toil and Pains.

Notes

1 In which he had claimed that women gossiped rather than doing their share of hay-making.
2 Condemned in Hades eternally to push up a hill a large stone, which immediately rolled down again.
3 Condemned in Hades eternally to try to fill, with water, jars with holes in the bottom.

4.6 'A.D.' [Anne Dutton], from *A Letter To such of the Servants of Christ, who May have any Scruple about the Lawfulness of PRINTING any Thing written by a Woman*, 1743

Honour'd Brethren,
Having heard that some of you have objected against my appearing in *Print;* as if it was contrary to the revealed *Will* of God: I thought it my Duty, meekly and humbly to offer to your Consideration, what is satisfactory to my own Soul in this regard: And,

First, I beg Leave to assure you, that my Design in publishing what I have written; was only the Glory of God, and the Good of Souls. This *End* I know you approve of. And that the *Means* I have made use of to attain it, is Lawful and Right, will be evident, if you consider,

Secondly, That my appearing in Print, is not *against* any of the Laws of Christ in the sacred Records. These I highly value, and desire ever to obey with the greatest Delight. It is not against *that*, I Tim. ii. 12. *But I suffer not a Woman to Teach, nor to usurp Authority over the Man, but to be in Silence.* . . . it is a Publick Authoritative Teaching in the Church, that is here forbidden unto *Women:* And that it is in this regard only, they are commanded to be in Silence. And *Printing* is a Thing of a very different Consideration.

For tho' what is printed is published to the *World*, and the Instruction thereby given, is in this regard *Publick*, in that it is presented to every ones View: Yet it is *Private* with respect to the *Church*. *Books* are not Read, and the Instruction by them given in the *public Assemblies* of the Saints: But visit every one, and converse with them in their own *private Houses*. And therefore the Teaching, or Instruction thereby given is *private:* and of no other Consideration than that of Writing a private Letter to a Friend, or of having private *Conference* with him for his Edification. And this is not only permitted to all the Saints, of whatever Sex they be, But,

Thirdly, It is *commanded*, Rom. xiv. 19. *Let us therefore follow after the Things which make for Peace, and Things wherewith one* (any one, Male or Female) *may edify another.* If it is the Duty of *Women* to seek the *Edification* of their Brethren and Sisters; then it is their Duty to use the *Means* of it, whether it be in speaking, writing, or printing: Since all these are *private*, and proper to the *Sphere* which the Lord has allotted them. Thus any Believer, Male or Female, that is gifted for, and inclin'd to publish their Thoughts in Print, about any Truth of Christ, for the private Instruction and Edification of the Saints; it is *permitted*, yea, *commanded* so to do. And unless *Women* were excluded from being *Members* of Christ's mystical Body, *their Usefulness*, in all due Means, ought not to be hindred. Since it is declar'd, that *from Christ the Head, the whole Body, fitly joined together, and compacted by that which every Joint supplieth, according to the effectual Working in the Measure of every Part, maketh Increase of the Body, to the edifying of it self in Love*, Eph. iv. 16. If the *whole Body*, from Christ the Head, has Nourishment ministred to it, by that which *every Joint* supplieth, even those weak ones, of the *Female* Sex; then they must have some *Way* of communicating what they receive from Christ, to the rest of their Fellow-members. And if it should be said, *this ought to be in private Converse:* I must beg Leave to add, and in *Printing* too. For this is one *Way* of private Converse with the Saints: Only it is a more *extensive one*, of talking with *Thousands*, which otherwise could not have been spoke with, nor can ever be seen *Face to Face in the Flesh. . . .*

Fourthly . . . *this* of communicating ones Mind in *Print*, is as *private*, with respect to particular *Persons*, as if one did it particularly unto every one by *himself* in ones *own House*. There is only this *Difference:* The one is communicating ones Mind by *Speech*, in ones *own* private House: The other is doing it by *Writing*, in the private House of *another* Person. Both are still *private*. And to this *last*, there still needs not the *publick* Authority of Christ in his Church; (as there does for Preaching) because this is not *publick*, but *private* Teaching. That which is exhibited in *Books*, can never be prov'd to be *publick* Teaching, unless the Books were *design'd* for the Instruction of *Publick* Assemblies, and are accordingly *read* in them.

Once more, since *Women* are *allow'd* the Liberty of the *Press*, and some have us'd it about *Trifles*, and it is to be fear'd under the Dictates of Satan, to the Propagation of his Kingdom: Shall none of that *Sex* be suffer'd to appear on *Christ's Side*, to tell of the Wonders of his *Love*, to seek the *Good* of Souls, and the Advancement of the Redeemer's *Interest*? . . .

Imagine then, my dear Friends, when my *Books* come to your *House*, that I am come to give you a *Visit;* (for indeed by *them* I do) and patiently attend to the Lispings of a *Babe:* Who knows but the Lord may ordain *Strength* out of the Babe's Mouth? And give you a Visit *Himself*, by so weak a *Worm*, to your strong Consolation? It is all one to Omnipotence, to work by Worms, as by Angels. And remember, that the more contemptible and weak the *Instrument* is that the Lord *works* by, the more it commands the Glory of his *Grace*, and the Excellency of his *Power*.

4.7   Teresia Constantia Phillips, from *An Apology for the Conduct of Mrs. Teresia Constantia Phillips more Particularly That Part of it which relates to her Marraige with an eminent Dutch Merchant . . ., 1748*

from *Volume I*

Thus you find a young Creature (for she was then but just turn'd of thirteen Years) launched at once into the wide World, naked, destitute and friendless, without any other means of Living than what she could earn by her Needle; to which she applied herself with Assiduity and Prudence far surpassing her Years. While she employ'd her Time in this Manner, she was encouraged to make frequent Visits to the Widow of General *Douglas*, formerly an Acquaintance of her Mother's; and the Kindness with which that good Lady always received her, prompted her to repeat the Visits as often as Opportunity would permit; and *Sunday* especially, she used to pass at her Lodgings in *Killigrew-Court, Scotland-Yard*.

Amongst the many unfortunate People who were ruin'd in that fatal Year 1720,[1] was the Son of a Nobleman;[2] who, to shelter himself in that Time of public Calamity, had taken Refuge in the Verge of the Court, and lodg'd in the same House with Mrs. *Douglas*, and on the same Floor; the Doors of their Apartments exactly facing each other.

A young Creature, with all the Charms and Accomplishments that confessedly adorned Miss *Phillips*, could not escape the Eyes of a Gentleman, whose Reason (as all who have the Honour of knowing him will admit) was absolutely subordinate to his Passions in Matters of Amour; and whose peculiar Taste was for Girls of that Age.

He observed that Miss came frequently there, and took all Opportunities to watch her himself, giving also his Servant *James* (now handsomely provided for in the King's Stables) Directions to observe when she repeated her Visits.

This Fellow, a most faithful Pimp to his Master's Pleasures, at last watched Miss *Phillips* home: She then lodged in *Hedge-Lane*, at the House of an Embroiderer, who had been a Servant to her Mother, and was very tender of and kind to her. As soon as he had made this Discovery, he followed her perpetually with Letters from his Master; the Meaning of which, she (poor Creature) was at that Age too innocent to understand.

At other Times Mr. *Grimes* (for that was the Name the Gentleman assum'd) would wait himself, on the Stairs, her coming; and, as often as he could find a convenient Opportunity, force Letters down her Back or Breast; for she was then in what the Ladies call a strait-bodied Coat: There were no Promises, no Allurements, unemploy'd to persuade her to a *tête a tête* Conversation in his Room; but that she absolutely refused: And tho', like most Girls, she was extremely pleas'd with the Thoughts of being so much a Woman as to have a Lover; yet she never dreamt there was any thing criminal in his Intentions, and was only amused with the Expectations of being, as he told her she would be, made a great Lady, and have the World at her Command. All which, and a thousand more such delusive Promises, it is become fashionable in a *pretty Fellow* to swear to, without Hesitation, on such Occasions.

[Mrs. Douglas discovers the intrigue and tells Teresia's father who brings her home. Her step-mother, whose ill-treatment was the reason for her originally leaving home, again becomes jealous. Teresia resents this more than ever now she is 'ador'd by a fine young Gentleman'.]

The next unfortunate Thing that befel her, was the making a Confident in her Distress of an old Woman, a Hoop-Petticoat-Maker, who used to work for her Mother-in-Law; and, by this

Means, had Access to the Family. This was a Woman of the most corrupt Morals, thoroughly acquainted with the vicious Part of the World, and had made it her constant Practice to live by betraying such unhappy young Women as she could get acquainted with.

To this Confident our young Miss made her Complaints; and, at the same Time, acquainted her with the Offers that were made her by Mr. *Grimes*, if she would leave her Father. The old Woman, improving the Hint, told her, That she could see no Crime in withdrawing herself from her Father, since, at the same Time, it would free her from the Tyranny of her Mother-in-Law, which was absolutely insupportable. In short, the poor simple Girl, thus unhappily, and, I think, hardly circumstanced, was easily persuaded (and no Wonder) to break her Chain.

The old Woman instantly prepar'd every thing for her Escape, and took a Lodging for her at the House of Mr. *Gregg*, a Bookseller, at the Corner of *Northumberland Rails* in the *Strand*, and accompanied her thither: As soon as this was done, she informed Mr. *Grimes* of it. What happened between them on this Occasion, the Reader will not be at a Loss to imagine: But the main Difficulty was still to contrive their meeting; for Mr. *Grimes* could not come to her, nor she to him, without being seen; which might have given her Father an Opportunity of once more bringing her back to her Prison. But Things did not long continue in this State of Uncertainty; her Lover continued to write her the most passionate Letters that Man could invent, some of which are now in her Possession; where, among other Things, he promises to make a handsome Provision for her; which Promise, however, the Reader will see, he intended as much to perform, as that of his making her a great Lady, *&c.*

But to give the Reader a better Idea of the Pains he took to accomplish his dishonourable Ends, we refer them to the following Letters, which, after this Length of Time, by meer Accident, have been preserved.

Nov. 1, 1721

My lovely Girl,
I am in Raptures to think you have at last resolved to come away; *James* tells me you propose To-morrow: I beg you will order the Lodging to be taken as near this Place as possible. My Angel must

be very careful how she comes, for Fear of being dog'd; for, if they can find you out, you may be sure your Father will force you back, and then I shall again be miserable, and my Girl once more be exposed to the Abuses of that cruel Woman. Take Courage, my adorable Girl! and be assured, while I have Life, I will protect you from her and all the World: I shall be distracted 'till I know you are safe out of their Hands. Never mind Cloaths; for, if they perceive you are making any Preparations, they will be more upon their Guard. I have ordered *James* to be upon the Watch at your Door To-night, between Eleven and Twelve, when your Father is a-bed: I wish you would contrive to speak one Word to him, that I may know you continue your Resolution: Then I shall go to Bed the happiest of all Men; if not, the most miserable; yet always, my adorable Girl!

Your most passionate Admirer   T.G.

Nov. 2, 1721

My lovely Angel,
James tells me, you have made a Confident of a Gentlewoman who comes to your House: I tremble for Fear this Woman, whoever she is, should betray you! Who knows, but she is set in your Way as a Spy? I hope the best, but the Man who adores you like me must necessarily fear the worst. I am distracted to think I am so circumstanced I cannot wait upon you myself, nor shall I have an easy Moment 'till you are come away. I think the Place you propose, a very good one; if she cannot go and take it, I will, if you please, send *James*. O Heaven! how shall I long for Eight o'Clock, that I think is the Hour fixed: The God of Love shall guard you, my adorable Girl! I am sure his Mother had never half your Charms. *James* shall be near to watch your coming out: What Transports will the News bring, my lovely Girl! to the Love-sick

T. GRIMES

Nov. 2, Ten o'Clock

My lovely Charmer,
James brings me this Moment the joyful News of your being safely arrived at your Lodgings: My Joys are inexpressible! I have stolen from Table a Moment, to congratulate my Angel upon her Deliverance, and have only Time to assure her, that I am, unalterably,

Her most passionate Adorer,   T.G.

. . .

He took Care to send the old Lady Money, to supply Miss with every thing that she might want. At last the fatal Moment came: One Day, that the King returned from *Hanover*, there were great Rejoicings and Fireworks, which Miss was invited, by her Lover, to see from his Window that fronted the Street: She accordingly went, tho' (as I have heard her say) not without inconceivable Reluctance and Horror. At her coming in, he received her with all possible Marks of Respect, Tenderness, and Affection; and assured her, that the Business of his Life should be to protect and make her happy; that she had nothing henceforward to fear, either from Fortune, or the Cruelties of a Mother-in-Law, from whose Power she should be for ever freed: In fine, nothing could be more passionate in all his Declarations of Love and Fondness for her. When the Illuminations were over, there was set on the Table some Sweetmeats, Wine, &c. he prevailed on her to sit down, and, during the whole Evening, offered nothing that might alarm her with his Intentions: *He press'd her extremely to drink a Glass or two of Wine*, and when she consented, *he deceived her, by giving her Barbados Water.* She had been so little accustomed to Wine, that it was easy to put such an Imposition upon her: and, no Doubt, the Liquor had the desired Effect upon her tender Head: However, when she express'd a Desire to go Home, he began, by little and little, to discover his Design; and, at last, gave pretty Miss to understand, that she must sleep there that Night. What Effect soever the Liquor had upon her, it was not sufficient to lull her into a quiet Submission to such a Proposal; and, upon his absolutely refusing to let her go, it put her into the most terrible Agonies: Tears and Prayers were all in vain; she was then in his Power, and he resolved to make Use of it. However, he tried first what could be done by fair Means, protesting to her, that tho' no *Ceremony* had pass'd between them, he should always look upon her as his *Wife*, and would instantly make such a *Provision* for her, as should put her out of the *Power of Fortune;* but, at last, finding nothing, that he could invent or say, could reconcile her to the Thoughts of staying there, as he walk'd backwards and forwards in the Room, he took an Opportunity of *coming behind her*, while she sat upon an old-fashion'd high-back'd Cane Chair, and, *catching hold of her Arms, drew her Hands behind the Chair*, which he held fast with his Feet. In *this* Position, it was an easy Matter for him with one Hand to secure both her's, and to take the

Advantage, he had previously meditated, of ripping up the Lacing of her Coat with a Penknife; which he performed with such Precipitation, as even to cut her. When her Coat was off, he tore away, with very little Difficulty, what else she had on.

I believe the Reader will not be offended, if I pass over in Silence what followed from this base Procedure; for all honest Minds will be sufficiently shock'd with the Ideas, which they may naturally form to themselves of the succeeding Scene, without the Help of Description: Let it suffice, that her Ruin takes it's Date from that fatal Night; tho' not effected without the greatest Treachery, Force, and Cruelty, on the Part of her Lover. For my Part, I am affected to the last Degree, even at the Thoughts of such a Complication of Misfortunes on one hand, and Villainy on the other.

from *Volume II*

But, alas! Ladies! even you, whose spotless Virtues may not always prove your Security, when irritated by a matrimonial Falshood, remember, you will find there is less Repentance apt to follow the passive Pain, than generally attends an inconsiderate Resentment of the Injury: And tho' hard may be the Task to go thro' with, yet how easily is the Truth of it conceivable? Nature, 'tis true, may say, How much easier is it to admire Instruction, than to follow it? In vain would preaching Philosophers, or pathetic Poets endeavour to charm you into milder Measures, unless they themselves could feel the Pain: For the Provocation, and Impatience of such pungent Injuries, are insupportable.

But happy is she, on whom Heaven has bestow'd this necessary Blessing of Patience! tho', to give those laudible Teachers their due, our Apologist confesses, even in her lively Days of Liberty and Pleasure, with what conscious Emotion (at a Play) she has seen the meek, and passive Virtue of a neglected Wife, triumph over the Trespass of a careless Husband; and, with inexpressible Pleasure, beheld the endearing Reward of his returning Tenderness.

But here perhaps we may seem to talk a little out of Character, tho' strictly following the Sentiments of our Apologist; that she thinks contrary to what she has practis'd, she consciously confesses: But will the Severity of what she has suffered for her Faults and Follies, recommend them to others? No surely! they must rather frighten the Innocent, by the Calamities which follow them, from any Levities that may subject them to such Scenes of Misery.

If therefore these serious Sentiments are just, shall they be less valuable, because they are those of a Woman who had not the Prudence to put them in Practice? Oh, no! remember, Fair Ones, 'tis *Experience, a sorely punished Experience*, that speaks to you; and however unfavourable an Opinion you may have of the Preacher, the Doctrine can do you no Harm, should your Virtue incline you to follow it.

Could she have over-look'd the Ramblings of Mr. *B--*, how much more to be commended had been her Conduct and Discretion? for at this Time, as she had all the Appearances of being his Wife, she ought, we confess, to have kept up the Dignity of her Station, *by only scorning the Injuries she never deserved*. But so it will be, while *the Lords of the Creation usurp* the Power of making Laws to themselves. No Wonder, then, if Infidelity in the Men is softened into *Gallantry;* but in the Ladies, hardened into *Infamy:* And yet what mighty Advantage do these partial Tyrants reap by their vast Superiority? Have not they found that *Nature* has *ballanced Accounts* with them? Pardon her, Ladies; if the Complaint be reasonable, it is just we make it.

Notes

1 A reference to the South Sea Bubble crisis.
2 'Mr. Grimes' is usually assumed to be Philip Dormer Stanhope, 4th Earl of Chesterfield, whose mother was Elizabeth, the daughter to whom Halifax addressed his *Advice* (1.1) He wrote *Letters Written to his Son* (1774), in which women are described as 'only children of a larger growth'.

4.8   Charlotte Charke, from *A Narrative of the Life of Mrs. Charlotte Charke*, 1755

'The Author to Herself'

Madam,

Tho' Flattery is universally known to be the Spring from which Dedications frequently flow, I hope I shall escape that Odium so justly thrown on poetical Petitioners, notwithstanding my Attempt to illustrate those WONDERFUL QUALIFICATIONS by which you have so EMINENTLY DISTINGUISH'D YOUR-SELF, and gives you a just Claim to the Title of a NONPAREIL OF THE AGE.

That thoughtless Ease (so peculiar to yourself) with which you have run thro' many strange and unaccountable Vicissitudes of Fortune, is an undeniable Proof of the native indolent Sweetness of your Temper. With what Fortitude of Mind have you vanquish'd Sorrow, with the fond Imagination and promissary Hopes (ONLY FROM YOURSELF) of a Succession of Happiness, neither WITHIN YOUR POWER OR VIEW?

Your exquisite Taste in Building must not be omitted; The magnificent airy Castles, for which you daily drew out Plans without Foundation, must, could they have been distinguishable to Sight, long ere this have darken'd all the lower World; nor can you be match'd, in Oddity of Fame, by any but that celebrated Knight-Errant of the Moon, G---E A---R ST---S;[1] whose Memoirs, and yours conjoin'd, would make *great Figures in History*, and might justly claim a Right to be transmitted to Posterity; as you are, without Exception, two of *the greatest Curiosities* that ever were the Incentives to the most *profound Astonishment*.

My Choice of you, Madam, to patronize my Works, is an evidential Proof that I am not disinterested in that Point; as the World will easily be convinc'd, from your natural Partiality to all I have hitherto produc'd, that you will tenderly overlook *their Errors*, and, to the utmost of your Power, endeavour *to magnify their Merits*. If, by your Approbation, the World may be perswaded into a tolerable Opinion of my Labours, I shall, for the Novelty-sake, venture for once to call you, FRIEND; a Name, I own, I never *as yet have known you by*.

Your two Friends, PRUDENCE and REFLECTION, I am inform'd, have lately ventur'd to pay you a Visit; for which I heartily congratulate you, as nothing can possibly be more joyous to the Heart than the Return of absent Friends, after a long and painful Peregrination.

Permit me, Madam, to subscribe myself for the future, what I ought to have been some Years ago,

> *Your real Friend,*
> *And humble Servant,*
> Charlotte Charke.

Note

1 George Alexander Stevens (1710-84), would-be actor and wit who was enjoying some popularity in the 1750s.

4.9 Susanna Centlivre, from *Works*, 1761

'To the World'

Be it known that the Person with Pen in Hand is no other than a Woman, not a little piqued to find that neither the Nobility nor Commonalty of the Year 1722, had Spirit enough to erect in *Westminster-Abbey*, a Monument justly due to the Manes of the never to be forgotten Mrs. *Centlivre*, whose Works are full of lively Incidents, genteel Language, and humorous Descriptions of real Life, and deserved to have been recorded by a Pen equal to that which celebrated the [a]Life of *Pythagoras*. Some Authors have had a *Shandeian* Knack of ushering in their own Praises, sounding their own Trumpet, calling Absurdity Wit, and boasting when they ought to blush; but our Poetess had Modesty, the general Attendant of Merit. She was even asham'd to proclaim her own great Genius, probably because the Custom of the Times discountenanced poetical Excellence in a Female. The Gentlemen of the Quill published it not, perhaps envying her superior Talents; and her Bookseller, complying with national Prejudices, put a fictitious Name to her *Love's Contrivance*, thro' Fear that the Work shou'd be condemned, if known to be Feminine. With modest Diffidence she sent her Performances, like Orphans, into the World, without so much as a Nobleman to protect them; but they did not need to be supported by her Interest, they were admired as soon as known, their real Standard, Merit, brought crowding Spectators to the Play-houses, and the female Author, tho' unknown, heard Applauses, such as have since been heaped on that great Author and Actor *Colley Cibber*.

Her Play of the *Busy Body*, when known to be the Work of a Woman, scarce defray'd the Expences of the First Night. The thin

Audience were pleased, and caused a full House the Second; the Third was crowded, and so on to the Thirteenth, when it stopt, on Account of the advanced Season; but the following Winter it appear'd again with Applause, and for Six Nights successively, was acted by rival Players, both at *Drury-Lane*, and at the *Hay-Market* Houses.

See here the effects of Prejudice, a Woman who did Honour to the Nation, suffer'd because she was a Woman. Are these Things fit and becoming a free-born People, who call themselves polite and civilized! Hold! let my Pen stop, and not reproach the present Age for the Sins of their Fathers. . . .

This Justice I must do the present Race of Mankind, their Eyes now seem open to Conviction, they acknowlege the real Merit of our Poetess, and of some other female Writers. . . .

Our Employment is chiefly in Retirement, and private Life, where our Actions, not being conspicuous, are little regarded; but the *present Days* have seen a Genius employed in translating, and illustrating, *Epictetus*,[1] and the Empress of *Germany* convinces the World that she is a Politician fearless even of the Horrors of War.

A pleasing Prospect I've lately had, *viz.* the Work of the ingenious Lord *Corke*, and the not less ingenious Mr. *Samuel Johnson*, who have took Pains to translate a large Part of Father *Brumoy's Greek* Theatre, and were not ashamed that their Labours should be joined to those of Mrs. *Lennox*.[2] This convinces me that not only that barbarous Custom of denying Women to have Souls, begins to be rejected as foolish and absurd, but also that bold Assertion, that Female Minds are not capable of producing literary Works, equal even to those of *Pope*, now loses Ground, and probably the next Age may be taught by our Pens that our Geniuses have been hitherto cramped and smothered, but not extinguished, and that the Sovereignty which the male Part of the Creation have, until now, usurped over us, is unreasonably arbitrary: And further, that our natural Abilities entitle us to a larger Share, not only in Literary Decisions, but that, with the present Directors, we are equally intitled to Power both in Church and State.

(a) Madam *Dacier* [see 4.3, note 1].

1 Elizabeth Carter (see 4.11).
2 Charlotte Lennox (1729?–1804), novelist and translator, author of *The Female Quixote* (1752).

II Public Images

4.10   John Duncombe, from *The Feminiad. A Poem*, 1754

> Shall lordly man, the theme of ev'ry lay,
> Usurp the muse's tributary bay;
> In kingly state on *Pindus'* summit sit,
> Tyrant of verse, and arbiter of wit?
> By *Salic* law the female right deny,
> And view their genius with regardless eye?
> Justice forbid! and every muse inspire
> To sing the glories of a sister-quire!
> Rise, rise bold swain; and to the list'ning grove
> 10   Resound the praises of the sex you love;
> Tell how, adorn'd with every charm, they shine,
> In mind and person equally divine,
> Till man, no more to female merit blind,
> *Admire* the person, but *adore* the mind.
>   To these weak strains, O thou! the sex's friend
> And constant patron, RICHARDSON! attend!
> Thou, who so oft with pleas'd, but anxious care,
> Hast watch'd the dawning genius of the fair,
> With wonted smiles wilt hear thy friend display
> 20   The various graces of the female lay;
> Studious from folly's yoke their minds to free,
> And aid the gen'rous cause espous'd by thee.
>   Long o'er the world did *Prejudice* maintain,
> By sounds like these, her undisputed reign:
> 'Woman! she cry'd, to thee, indulgent heav'n
> Has all the charms of outward beauty giv'n:
> Be thine the boast, unrival'd, to enslave
> The great, the wise, the witty, and the brave;
> Deck'd with the *Paphian*[1] rose's damask glow,

30 And the vale-lilly's vegetable snow,
  Be thine, to move majestic in the dance,
  To roll the eye, and aim the tender glance,
  Or touch the strings, and breathe in melting song,
  Content to emulate that airy throng,
  Who to the sun their painted plumes display,
  And gaily glitter on the hawthorn spray,
  Or wildly warble in the beechen grove,
  Careless of ought but music, joy, and love.'
   Heav'ns! could such artful, slavish sounds beguile
40 The freeborn sons of *Britain's* polish'd isle?
  Could they, like fam'd *Ulysses'* dastard crew,
  Attentive listen, and enamour'd view,
  Nor drive the *Syren* to that dreary plain,
  In loathsome pomp, where eastern tyrants reign,
  Where each fair neck the yoke of slav'ry galls,
  Clos'd in a proud seraglio's gloomy walls,
  And taught, that level'd with the brutal kind,
  Nor sense, nor souls to women are assign'd.
   Our *British* nymphs with happier omens rove,
50 At Freedom's call, thro' Wisdom's sacred grove,
  And, as with lavish hand each sister Grace
  Shapes the fair form and regulates the face,
  Each sister Muse, in blissful union join'd,
  Adorns, improves, and beautifies the mind.
  Ev'n now fond fancy in our polish'd land
  Assembled shows a blooming, studious band:
  With various arts our rev'rence they engage,
  Some turn the tuneful, some the moral page,
  These, led by Contemplation, soar on high,
60 And range the heav'ns with philosophic eye;
  While those, surrounded by a vocal choir,
  The canvas tinge, or touch the warbling lyre.
  Here, like the stars' mixt radiance, they unite
  To dazzle and perplex our wand'ring sight:
  The Muse each charmer singly shall survey;
  Thus may she best their vary'd charms display,
  And tune to each her tributary lay.

      . . .

  First let the Muse with gen'rous ardor try

To chase the mist from dark Opinion's eye:
Nor mean we here to blame that father's care,
Who guards from learned wives his booby heir,
80   Since oft that heir with prudence has been known,
To dread the genius that transcends his own:
The wise themselves should with discretion chuse,
Since letter'd nymphs their knowledge may abuse,
And husbands oft experience to their cost
The prudent housewife in the scholar lost:
But those incur deserv'd contempt, who prize
Their own high talents, and their sex despise,
With haughty mien each social bliss defeat,
And sully all their learning with conceit:
90   Of such the parent justly warns his son,
And such the Muse herself will bid him shun.
But lives there one, whose unassuming mind,
Tho' grac'd by nature, and by art refin'd,
Pleas'd with domestic excellence, can spare
Some hours from studious ease to social care,
And with her pen that time alone employs
Which others waste in visits, cards and noise;
From affectation free, tho' deeply read,
'With wit well natur'd, and with books well bred?'
100   With such (and such there are) each happy day
Must fly improving, and improv'd away;
Inconstancy might fix and settle there,
And Wisdom's voice approve the chosen fair.
Nor need we now from our own Britain rove
In search of genius, to the Lesbian grove,
Tho' Sappho there her tuneful lyre has strung,
And amorous griefs in sweetest accents sung,
Since here, in Charles's days, amidst a train
Of shameless bards, licentious and profane,
110   The chaste [a]ORINDA rose; with purer light,
Like modest Cynthia, beaming thro' the night:
Fair Friendship's lustre, undisguis'd by art,
Glows in her lines, and animates her heart;
Friendship, that jewel, which, tho' all confess
Its peerless value, yet how few possess!
For her the never-dying myrtle weaves

172

A verdant chaplet of her odorous leaves,
Her praise, re-echo'd by the Muse's throng,
Will reach far distant times, and live as long
120   As Cowley's wit, or fam'd Roscommon's song.
Who can unmov'd hear [b]WINCHELSEA reveal
Thy horrors, Spleen! which all, who paint, must feel?
My praises would but wrong her sterling wit,
Since Pope himself applauds what she has writ.

    . . .

    The modest Muse a veil with pity throws
140   O'er Vice's friends and Virtue's female foes;
Abash'd she views the bold unblushing mien
Of modern [c]Manley, Centlivre, and Behn;
And grieves to see One nobly born disgrace
Her modest sex, and her illustrious race.
Tho' harmony thro' all their numbers flow'd,
And genuine wit its ev'ry grace bestow'd,
Nor genuine wit nor harmony excuse
The dang'rous sallies of a wanton Muse:
Nor can such tuneful, but immoral lays,
150   Expect the tribute of impartial praise:
As soon might [d] Phillips, Pilkington and V---
Deserv'd applause for spotless virtue gain.
    But hark! what Nymph[e], in Frome's embroider'd
        vale,
With strains seraphic swells the vernal gale?
With what sweet sounds the bord'ring forest rings?
For sportive Echo catches, as she sings,
Each falling accent, studious to prolong
The warbled notes of ROWE'S ecstatic song.
Old Avon pleas'd his reedy forehead rears,
160   And polish'd Orrery delighted hears.
See with what transport she resigns her breath,
Snatch'd by a sudden, but a wish'd for, death!
Releas'd from earth, with smiles she soars on high
Amidst her kindred spirits of the sky,
Where Faith and Love those endless joys bestow,
That warm'd her lays, and fill'd her hopes below.

Notes

(a) Mrs. Catherine Phillips, the celebrated Orinda, was distinguish'd by most of the wits of King Charles's reign, and died young; lamented by many of them in commendatory verses prefix'd to her poems. Her pieces on Friendship are particularly admir'd. [See 4.1, note 3.]

(b) Anne, Countess of Winchelsea, a lady of great wit and genius, wrote (among others) a poem, much admir'd, on the Spleen, and is prais'd by Mr. Pope, &c. under the poetical name of Ardelia.

(c) The first of these wrote the scandalous memoirs call'd Atalantis, and the other two are notorious for the indecency of their plays. [See 4.3, 4.9, 4.1, note 3.]

(d) These three ladies have endeavour'd to immortalize their shame, by writing and publishing their own memoirs. [Phillips: see 4.7. Laetitia Pilkington (1712–50): her *Memoirs* (1748) are a mixture of self-justification and anecdotes about well-known literary men, especially Swift. Frances Anne Vane, Viscountess (1713–88): her *Memoirs of a Lady of Quality* are included in Smollett's *Peregrine Pickle*.]

(e) The character of Mrs. Rowe and her writings is too well known to be dwelt on here. It may be sufficient to say, that without any previous illness she met at last with that sudden death for which she had always wished. [See 1.2, 4.1.]

1 A reference to Aphrodite, Greek goddess of love, associated with Paphos in Cyprus.

4.11(a)   from *Monthly Review*, 18, 1758

All the Works of Epictetus, which are now extant . . . Translated from the original Greek by Elizabeth Carter.

The Work before us, will be no small mortification to the vanity of those men, who presume that the fair sex are unequal to the laborious pursuit of philosophic speculations.

Those assumers have been ready to acknowledge the Ladies preheminence with respect to light and ornamental talents; but, the more solid and noble faculties, they have reserved as their own prerogative. They have arrogated this superior excellence, as a distinction they derive from Nature, for which they are solely indebted to the advantages of education.

If women had the benefit of liberal instructions, if they were inured to study, and accustomed to learned conversation - in short, if they had the same opportunity of improvement with the men, there can be no doubt but that they would be equally capable of reaching any intellectual attainment.

Many Ladies have been very witty; some few have been very learned; but we have never, till now, seen these accomplishments united with an acute understanding and solid judgment, sufficient to unravel the intricacies of Philosophy. France now can no longer boast her *Dacier*,[1] but must be compelled to own that our women excel theirs in Sense and Genius, as far as they surpass them in Modesty and Beauty.

Note

1 Dacier: see 4.3, note 1.

4.11(b)   from *Critical Review*, 13, 1762

Elizabeth Carter, *Poems on Several Occasions*

There never was perhaps an age wherein the fair sex made so conspicuous a figure with regard to literary accomplishments as in our own. We may all remember the time, when a woman who could *spell* was looked on as an extraordinary phenomenon, and a *reading* and *writing* wife was considered as a *miracle;* but the case at present is quite otherwise. Learning is now grown so fashionable amongst the ladies, that it becomes every gentleman to carry his Latin and Greek with him whenever he ventures into female company. Many of our young officers complain of the *pedantry* of their mistresses, and of being talked to by them in languages which they don't understand; whilst our scholars from the university, when they come to their father's houses, are foiled at their own weapons, and vexed to the heart to find their sisters as wise as themselves: but all this is the natural consequence of the present system of education, as practised by the two sexes. The men *retreat*, and the women *advance*. The men prate and dress; the women read and write: it is no wonder, therefore, that they should get the upper hand of us; nor should we be at all surprised, if, in the next age, women should give lectures in the classics, and men employ themselves in knotting and needlework.

We were naturally led into this train of thought (which we hope our readers will not construe into mis-timed *raillery*) by considering the extraordinary merit of the little volume now before us, which contains some of the prettiest poems that have been published for a long time. Mrs. Carter's character, as a scholar, is already sufficiently established; her learning can only be excelled by the fertility of her genius, the warmth of her imagination, and the harmony of her numbers. . . .

It has often been remarked, with what degree of truth we will not pretend to determine, that the female muse is seldom altogether so chaste as could be wished, and that most of our lady-writers are rather deficient in point of morality. To the honour of Mrs. Carter it may be said, that there is scarce a line in this volume which does not breathe the purest sentiments, and tend in some measure to the advancement of religion and virtue, which is, in our opinion, their strongest recommendation.

4.12   from *Monthly Review*, 20, 1759

The Bracelet, or the Fortunate Discovery

The most we can do, with respect to those numerous novels, that issue continually from the press, is to give rather a character than an account of each. To do even this, however, we find no easy task; since we might say of them, as Pope, with less justice, says of the *ladies*,[1]

Most *novels* have no character at all.

Note

1 Pope, 'Epistle to a Lady' (1735), l. 2.

4.13   James Fordyce, from *Sermons to Young Women*, 1766[1]

Sermon IV: *'On Female Virtue'*

Beside the beautiful productions of that incomparable pen [that of Richardson], there seem to me to be very few, in the style of Novel, that you can read with advantage. – What shall we say of certain books, which we are assured (for we have not read them) are in their nature so shameful, in their tendency so pestiferous, and contain such rank treason against the royalty of Virtue, such horrible violation of all decorum, that she who can bear to peruse them must in her soul be a prostitute, let her reputation in life be what it will. But can it be true – say, ye chaste stars, that with innumerable eyes inspect the midnight behaviour of mortals – can it be true, that any young woman, pretending to decency, should endure for a moment to look on this infernal brood of futility and lewdness?

Nor do we condemn those writings only, that, with an effrontery which defies the laws of God and men, carry on their very forehead the mark of the beast. We consider the general run of Novels as utterly unfit for you. Instruction they convey none. They paint scenes of pleasure and passion altogether improper for you to behold, even with the mind's eye. Their descriptions are often loose and luscious in a high degree; their representations of love between the sexes are almost universally overstrained. All is dotage, or despair; or else ranting swelled into burlesque. In short, the majority of their lovers are either mere lunatics, or mock-heroes. A sweet sensibility, a charming tenderness, a delightful anguish, exalted generosity, heroic worth, and refinement of thought; how seldom are these best ingredients of virtuous love mixed with any judgment or care in the composition of their principal characters!

In the Old Romance the passion appeared with all its enthusiasm. But then it was the enthusiasm of honour; for love and honour were there the same. The men were sincere, magnanimous, and noble; the women were patterns of chastity, dignity, and affection. They were only to be won by real heroes; and this title was founded in protecting, not in betraying, the sex. The proper merit with them consisted in the display of disinterested goodness, undaunted fortitude, and unalterable fidelity. The turn of those books was influenced by the genius of the times in which they were composed; as that, on the other hand, was nourished by them. The characters they drew were, no doubt, often heightened beyond nature; and the incidents they related, it is certain, were commonly blended with the most ridiculous extravagance. At present, however, I believe they may be read with perfect safety, if indeed there be any who choose to look into them.

The times in which we live are in no danger of adopting a system of romantic virtue. The parents of the present generation, what with selling their sons and daughters in marriage, and what with teaching them by every possible means the glorious principles of Avarice, have contrived pretty effectually to bring down from its former flights that idle, youthful, unprofitable passion, which has for its object personal attractions, in preference to all the wealth of the world. With the successful endeavours of those profoundly politic parents, the levity of dissipation, the vanity of parade, and the fury of gaming, now so prevalent, have concurred to cure completely in the fashionable of both sexes any tendency to mutual fondness.

. . .

To come back to the species of writing which so many young women are apt to doat upon, the offspring of our present Novelists, I mean the greater part; with whom we may join the common herd of Play-writers. Beside the remarks already made on the former, is it not manifest with respect to both, that such books lead to a false taste of life and happiness; that they represent vices as frailties, and frailties as virtues; that they engender notions of love unspeakably perverting and inflammatory; that they overlook in a great measure the finest part of the passion, which one would suspect the authors had never experienced; that they turn it most commonly into an affair of wicked or of frivolous gallantry; that on many occasions they take off from the worst crimes committed in the prosecution of it, the horror which ought ever to follow them; on some occasions actually reward those very crimes, and almost on all leave the female readers with this persuasion at best, that it is their business to get husbands at any rate, and by whatever means? Add to the account, that repentance for the foulest injuries which can be done the sex, is generally represented as the pang, or rather the start, of a moment; and holy wedlock converted into a sponge, to wipe out at a single stroke every stain of guilt and dishonour, which it was possible for the hero of the piece to contract. – Is this a kind of reading calculated to improve the principles, or preserve the Sobriety, of female minds? How much are those young women to be pitied, that have no wise parents or faithful tutors to direct them in relation to the books which are, or which are not, fit for them to read! How much are those parents and tutors to be commended, who with particular solicitude watch over them in so important a concern!

I conclude with saying, that the subject of this discourse has unavoidably suggested some ideas, which, had we not undertaken to address young women at large, we should have certainly suppressed for the sake of more modest natures, whom we would not willingly pain, no not for a moment. But such we hope will be candid enough to excuse us, if, by throwing out to others what to them would have been unnecessary, we may be happily instrumental in rescuing were it but one of their sex from the slavery of vice, or defending a single innocent from its snares.

Note

1 In Jane Austen's *Pride and Prejudice*, chapter 14, Mr Collins chooses Fordyce's *Sermons* to read to his cousins.

4.14 from *Critical Review*, 27, 1769

The History of Miss Eliza Musgrove

Few Novels of the modern manufacture are calculated to stand the test of a strict examination; and as this under our inspection seems to have been written by a female hand, it would be as unfair as unpolite to *review* it with the severity of Criticism. – It seldom happens that ladies equal in genius to *Lennox*, *Brookes*, and *Scott*,[1] figure in this walk of literature: though some, much inferior to *them* in strength and spirit, have discovered talents, of which they have no reason to be ashamed. Among these the authoress of this little history, carried on in the epistolary way, which is upon the whole interesting and affecting, may, we apprehend, be ranked.

Note

1 Lennox: see 4.9, note 2. Frances Brooke (1724–89): novelist, dramatist, and essayist. Her most acclaimed work was *The History of Lady Julia Mandeville* (1763); Sarah Scott (1723–95): novelist and historian, sister of Elizabeth Montagu (see 4.17, note 1), and author of *Millenium Hall*, a female utopian fantasy.

4.15 from *Monthly Review*, 48, 1773

Woodbury; or the Memoirs of William Marchmont Esq. and Miss Walbrook

Surely the youthful part of the fair sex have as keen a relish for novels, as they have for green apples, green gooseberries, or other such kind of crude trash, otherwise it would not be found worth while to cultivate these literary weeds, which spring up, so plenteously, every month, even under the scythe of criticism! If such is the case, the ladies must be gratified; but we would advise them to be least free with those that are of a pernicious tendency. As to the above-mentioned performance, though somewhat insipid, it is, at least, innocent.

4.16   from *Monthly Review*, 48, 1773

The History of Pamela Howard. By the Author of Indiana Danby

Comedy and Tragedy have here joined to finish an entertainment with which the Ladies in general will be pleased; and even the Gentlemen, (the *sentimental* Gentlemen, we mean) may make tolerable shift to *while away* a vacant hour on the perusal of a story, the beginning of which will divert them: but the conclusion is pregnant with that kind of horrible distress which humanity will think *too much*. – It is not a finished piece; but there are touches in it which prove the Writer possessed of abilities for this kind of writing. It seems to be the product of a female pen. This branch of the literary *trade* appears, now, to be almost entirely engrossed by the Ladies.

4.17   Mary Scott, from *The Female Advocate; A Poem. Occasioned by Reading Mr. Duncombe's Feminead*, 1774

'*To a Lady*'

Mr. DUNCOMBE'S Feminead you and I have often read with the most grateful pleasure; and undoubtedly you remember, that we have also regretted that it was only on a small number of Female Geniuses that Gentleman bestowed the wreath of Fame; and have wished to see those celebrated whom he omitted, as well as those who have obliged the world with their literary productions, since the publication of his elegant Poem.

Being too well acquainted with the illiberal sentiments of men in general in regard to our sex, and prompted by the most fervent zeal for their privileges, I took up the pen with an intention of becoming their advocate; but thinking myself unequal to the task, it was quickly laid aside, and probably never would have been resumed, had not your partiality to the Author led you to have been pleased with the specimen which you saw.

It may perhaps be objected that it was unnecessary to write on this subject, as the sentiments of all men of sense relative to female education are now more enlarged than they formerly were. I allow that they are so; but yet those of the generality (of men of sense and learning I mean, for it would be absurd to regard the opinions of those who are not such) are still very contracted. How much has been said, even by writers of distinguished reputation, of the distinction of sexes in souls, of the studies, and even of the virtues proper for women? If they have allowed us to study the imitative arts, have they not prohibited us from cultivating an acquaintance with the sciences? Do they not regard the woman who suffers her faculties to rust in a state of listless indolence, with a more favourable eye, than her who engages in a dispassionate search after truth? And is not an implicit acquiescence in the dictates of their understandings, esteemed by them as the sole criterion of good sense in a woman? I believe I am expressing myself with warmth, but I cannot help it; for when I speak, or write, on this subject, I feel an indignation which I cannot, and which indeed I do not wish to suppress: It has folly and cruelty for its objects, and therefore must be laudable; folly, because if there really are those advantages resulting from a liberal education which it is insinuated they have derived from thence, the wider those advantages are diffused, the more will the happiness of society be promoted: And if the pleasures that flow from knowledge are of all others the most refined and permanent, it surely is extreme barbarity to endeavour to preclude us from enjoying them, when they allow our sensations to be far more exquisite than their own. But I flatter myself a time may come, when men will be as much ashamed to avow their narrow prejudices in regard to the abilities of our sex, as they are now fond to glory in them. A few such changes I have already seen; for facts have a powerful tendency to convince the understanding; and of late, Female Authors have appeared with honour, in almost every walk of literature.

The Female Advocate

. . .

     Say MONTAGU[1] can this unartful verse
     Thy Genius, Learning, or thy Worth rehearse?
     To paint thy talents justly should conspire
360   Thy taste, thy judgment, and thy SHAKESPEARE'S fire.
     Well hath thy Pen with nice discernment trac'd
     What various pow'rs the Matchless Poet grac'd;
     Well hath thy Pen his various beauties shown,
     And prov'd thy soul congenial to his own.
     Charm'd with those splendid honours of thy Name,
     Fain would the Muse relate thy nobler Fame;
     Dear to Religion, as to Learning dear,
     Candid, obliging, modest, mild, sincere,
     Still prone to soften at another's woe,
370   Still fond to bless, still ready to bestow.

. . .

     TALBOT,[a] did e'er mortality enshrine
     A mind more gen'rous, meek, or kind, than thine?
     Delightful moralist! thy well-wrote page
     Shall please, correct, and mend the rising age;
     Point out the road the thoughtless many miss,
     That leads through virtue to the realms of bliss.
     Fain would my soul thy sentiments imbibe,
400   And fain thy manners in my own transcribe:
     Genius and Wit were but thy second praise,
     Thou knew'st to win by still sublimer ways;
     Thy Angel-goodness, all who knew approv'd,
     Honour'd, admir'd, applauded too, and lov'd!
     Fair shall thy fame to latest ages bloom,
     And ev'ry Muse with tears bedew thy tomb.

. . .

     Man, seated high on Learning's awful throne,
     Thinks the fair realms of knowledge his alone;
     But you, ye fair, his Salic Law disclaim:
440   Supreme in Science shall the Tyrant reign!
     When every talent all-indulgent Heav'n

In lavish bounty to your share hath giv'n?
   With joy ineffable the Muse surveys
The orient beams of more resplendent days:
As on she raptur'd looks to future years,
What a bright throng to Fancy's view appears!
To them see Genius her best gifts impart,
And Science raise a throne in ev'ry heart!
One turns the moral, one th'historic page;
450   Another glows with all a SHAKESPEARE'S rage!
With matchless NEWTON now one soars on high,
Lost in the boundless wonders of the sky;
Another now, of curious mind, reveals
What treasures in her bowels Earth conceals;
Nature's minuter works attract her eyes;
Their laws, their pow'rs, her deep research descries.
From sense abstracted, some, with arduous flight,
Explore the realms of intellectual light;
With unremitting study seek to find,
460   How mind on matter, matter acts on mind:
Alike in nature, arts, and manners read,
In ev'ry path of knowledge, see they tread!
Whilst men, convinc'd of Female Talents, pay
To Female Worth the tributary lay.
   Yet now there sure are some of nobler kind,
From all their sex's narrow views refin'd,
Who, truly wise, attempt not to controul
The generous ardor of th'aspiring soul:
Such, tuneful DUNCOMBE, thou, whose Attic lays
470   Demand the warmest strains of grateful praise:
Fearless of censure, boldly thou stood'st forth
An able Advocate for Female Worth!
For that! may the far-sounding Voice of Fame,
To latest Ages bear thy honour'd Name;
For that! may Fancy still her aid impart,
And still the Muse's smile dilate thy heart;
For that! may Hope still strew thy path with flow'rs,
And ev'ry blessing crown thy circling hours!

Notes

(a) Mrs. Catherine Talbot . . . . This truly excellent Lady was blest with the happiest natural talents: her understanding was vigorous, her imagination lively, and her taste refined. Her virtues were equal to her genius, and rendered her at once the object of universal love and admiration. She was the Author of 'Reflections on the Seven Days of the Week;' and of 'Essays on various Subjects,' 2 volumes. Her writings breathe the noblest spirit of Christian benevolence; and discover a more than common acquaintance with human nature.

1 Elizabeth Montagu (1720–1800): essayist, letter-writer, and literary hostess, known as the 'Queen of the Bluestockings', the group of wealthy, well-educated women which included Elizabeth Carter (see 4.11) and Catherine Talbot (1721–70), above.

4.18 Clara Reeve, from *The Progress of Romance*, 1785

'Evening VII'

Euphrasia. . . . Among our early Novel-writers we must reckon Mrs. *Behn*.[1] – There are strong marks of Genius in all this lady's works, but unhappily, there are some parts of them, very improper to be read by, or recommended to virtuous minds, and especially to youth. – She wrote in an age, and to a court of licentious manners, and perhaps we ought to ascribe to these causes the loose turn of her stories. – Let us do justice to her merits, and cast the veil of compassion over her faults. – She died in the year 1689, and lies buried in the cloisters of Westminster Abbey. – The inscription will shew how high she stood in estimation at that time.

Hortensius. Are you not partial to the sex of this Genius? – when you excuse in her, what you would not to a man?

Euph. Perhaps, I may, and you must excuse me if I am so, especially as this lady had many fine and admirable qualities, besides her genius for writing.

Sophronia. Pray let her rest in peace, – you were speaking of the inscription on her monument, I do not remember it.

Euph. It is as follows:

Mrs. APHRA BEHN, 1689
Here lies proof that wit can never be
Defence enough against mortality.

Let me add that Mrs. *Behn* will not be forgotten, so long as the Tragedy of *Oronooko* is acted . . . .

Hort. Peace be to her *manes!* – I shall not disturb her, or her works.

Euph. I shall not recommend them to your perusal *Hortensius*. The next female writer of this class is Mrs. *Manley*,[2] whose works are still more exceptionable than Mrs. *Behn*'s, and as much inferior to them in point of merit. – She hoarded up all the public and private scandal within her reach, and poured it forth, in a work too well known in the last age, though almost forgotten in the present; a work that partakes of the style of the Romance, and the Novel. I forbear the name, and further observations on it, as Mrs. *Manley*'s works are sinking gradually into oblivion. I am sorry to say they were once the fashion, which obliges me to mention them, otherwise I had rather be spared the pain of disgracing an Author of my own sex.

Soph. It must be confessed that these books of the last age, were of worse tendency than any of those of the present.

Euph. My dear friend, there were bad books at all times, for those who sought for them. – Let us pass over them in silence.

Hort. No not yet. – Let me help your memory to one more Lady-Author of the same class. – Mrs. *Heywood* [sic].[3] – She has the same claim upon you as those you have last mentioned.

Euph. I had intended to have mentioned Mrs. *Heywood* though in a different way, but I find you will not suffer any part of her character to escape you.

Hort. Why should she be spared any more than the others?

Euph. Because she repented of her faults, and employed the latter part of her life in expiating the offences of the former. – There is reason to believe that the examples of the two ladies we have spoken of, seduced Mrs. *Heywood* into the same track; she certainly wrote some amorous novels in her youth, and also two books of the same kind as Mrs. *Manley*'s capital work, all of which I hope are forgotten.

Hort. I fear they will not be so fortunate, they will be known to posterity by the infamous immortality, conferred upon them by *Pope* in his Dunciad.

Euph. Mr. *Pope* was severe in his castigations, but let us be just to merit of every kind. Mrs. *Heywood* had the singular good fortune to recover a lost reputation, and the yet greater honour to atone for her errors. – She devoted the remainder of her life and labours to the service of virtue. Mrs. *Heywood* was one of the most voluminous female writers that England ever produced, none of her latter works are destitute of merit, though they do not rise to the highest pitch of excellence. – *Betsey Thoughtless* is reckoned her best Novel; but those works by which she is most likely to be known to posterity, are the *Female Spectator*, and the *Invisible Spy*. – this lady died so lately as the year 1758.

Soph. I have heard it often said that Mr. *Pope* was too severe in his treatment of this lady, it was supposed that she had given some private offence, which he resented publicly as was too much his way.

Hort. That is very likely, for he was not of a forgiving disposition. – If I have been too severe also, you ladies must forgive me in behalf of your sex.

Euph. Truth is sometimes severe. – Mrs. *Heywood*'s wit and ingenuity were never denied. I would be the last to vindicate her faults, but the first to celebrate her return to virtue, and her atonement for them.

Soph. May her first writings be forgotten, and the last survive to do her honour!

Notes

1 Aphra Behn: see 4.1, note 3.
2 See 4.3.
3 See 4.4.

4.19   Richard Polwhele, from *The Unsex'd Females: A Poem*, 1798

       Survey with me, what ne'er our fathers saw,
       A female band despising NATURE'S law,[a]
       As 'proud defiance' flashes from their arms,
       And vengeance smothers all their softer charms.
       I shudder at the new unpictur'd scene,
       Where unsex'd woman vaunts her imperious mien;
       Where girls, affecting to dismiss the heart,
       Invoke the Proteus of petrific art;
       With equal ease, in body or in mind,
20   To Gallic freaks or Gallic faith resign'd,

The crane-like neck, as Fashion bids, lay bare,
Or frizzle, bold in front, their borrow'd hair;
Scarce by a gossamery film carest,
Sport, in full view, the meretricious breast;
Loose the chaste cincture, where the graces shone,
And languish'd all the Loves, the ambrosial zone;
As lordly domes inspire dramatic rage,
Court prurient Fancy to the private stage;
With bliss botanic[b] as their bosoms heave,
30   Still pluck forbidden fruit, with mother Eve,
For puberty in sighing florets pant,
Or point the prostitution of a plant;
Dissect[c] its organ of unhallow'd lust,
And fondly gaze the titillating dust;
With liberty's sublimer views expand,
And o'er the wreck of kingdoms[d] sternly stand;
And, frantic, midst the democratic storm,
Pursue, Philosophy! thy phantom-form.
Far other is the female shape and mind,
40   By modest luxury heighten'd and refin'd;
Those limbs, that figure, tho' by Fashion grac'd,
By Beauty polish'd, and adorn'd by Taste;
That soul, whose harmony perennial flows,
In Music trembles, and in Color glows;
Which bids sweet Poesy reclaim the praise
With faery light to gild fastidious days,
From sullen clouds relieve domestic care,
And melt in smiles the withering frown of war.
Ah! once the female Muse, to NATURE true,
50   The unvalued store from FANCY, FEELING drew;
Won, from the grasp of woe, the roseate hours,
Cheer'd life's dim vale, and strew'd the grave with
      flowers.
But lo! where, pale amidst the wild, she draws
Each precept cold from sceptic Reason's vase;
Pours with rash arm the turbid stream along,
And in the foaming torrent whelms the throng.

. . .

63   See Wollstonecraft, whom no decorum checks,

Arise, the intrepid champion of her sex;
O'er humbled man assert the sovereign claim,
And slight the timid blush[e] of virgin fame.
'Go, go (she cries) ye tribes of melting maids,
Go, screen your softness in sequester'd shades;
With plaintive whispers woo the unconscious grove,
70   And feebly perish, as despis'd ye love.
What tho' the fine Romances of Rousseau[1]
Bid the frame flutter, and the bosom glow;
Tho' the rapt Bard, your empire fond to own,
Fall prostrate and adore your living throne,
The living throne his hands presum'd to rear,
Its seat a simper, and its base a tear;
Soon shall the sex disdain the illusive sway,
And wield the sceptre in yon blaze of day;[f]
Ere long, each little artifice discard,
80   No more by weakness[g] winning fond regard;

. . .

To the bold heights where glory beams, aspire,
Blend mental energy with Passion's fire,
Surpass their rivals in the powers of mind
90   And vindicate *the Rights of womankind*.'
She spoke: and veteran BARBAULD[2] caught the strain,
And deem'd her songs of Love, her Lyrics vain;
And ROBINSON[3] to Gaul her Fancy gave,
And trac'd the picture of a Deist's grave!
And charming SMITH[4] resign'd her power to please,
Poetic feeling and poetic ease;
And HELEN,[5] fir'd by Freedom, bade adieu
To all the broken visions of Peru;
And YEARSELEY,[6] who had warbled, Nature's child,
100   Midst twilight dews, her minstrel ditties wild,
(Tho' soon a wanderer from her meads and milk,
She long'd to rustle, like her sex, in silk)
Now stole the modish grin, the sapient sneer,
And flippant HAYS[7] assum'd a cynic leer.

. . .

'O come (a voice seraphic seems to say)
170   Fly that pale form – come sisters! come away.

188

Come, from those livid limbs withdraw your gaze,
Those limbs which Virtue views in mute amaze;
Nor deem, that Genius lends a veil, to hide
The dire apostate, the fell suicide.[h] –
Come, join, with wonted smiles, a kindred train,
Who court, like you, the Muse; nor court in vain.
Mark, where the sex have oft, in ancient days,
To modest Virtue, claim'd a nation's praise;
Chas'd from the public scene the fiend of strife,
180   And shed a radiance o'er luxurious life;
In silken fetters bound the obedient throng
And soften'd despots by the power of song.
'Yet woman owns a more extensive sway
Where Heaven's own graces pour the living ray:
And vast its influence o'er the social ties,
By Heaven inform'd, if female genius rise –
Its power how vast, in critic wisdom sage,
If MONTAGUE[8] refine a letter'd age;
And CARTER,[9] with a milder air, diffuse
190   The moral precepts of the Grecian Muse;
And listening girls perceive a charm unknown
In grave advice, as utter'd by CHAPONE[10]; . . .'.
203   She ceas'd; and round their MORE[i] the sisters sigh'd!
Soft on each tongue repentant murmurs died;
And sweetly scatter'd (as they glanc'd away)
Their conscious 'blushes spoke a brighter day.'

Notes

(a) Nature is the grand basis of all laws human and divine: and the woman, who has no regard to nature, either in the decoration of her person, or the culture of her mind, will soon 'walk after the flesh, in the lust of uncleanness, and despise government'.

(b) Botany has lately become a fashionable amusement with the ladies. But how the study of the sexual system of plants can accord with female modesty, I am not able to comprehend. . . . I have, several times, seen boys and girls botanizing together. [Polwhele is indirectly attacking Erasmus Darwin's poem *Loves of the Plants* (1789) which describes sexual reproduction in plants in anthropomorphic terms.]

(c) Miss Wollstonecraft does not blush to say, in an introduction to a book designed for the use of young ladies, that, 'in order to lay the axe at the root of corruption, it would be proper to familiarize the sexes to an unreserved discussion of those topics, which are generally avoided in conversation from a principle of false delicacy; and that it would be right to speak of the organs of generation as freely as we mention our eyes or our hands.' To such language our botanizing girls are doubtless familiarized: and, they are in a fair way of becoming worthy disciples of Miss W. If they do not take heed to their ways, they will soon exchange the blush of modesty for the bronze of independence.

[Polwhele refers to Wollstonecraft's 'Introductory Address to Parents' in her *Elements of Morality for the Use of Children* (1790), a translation of a German work by C. G. Salzmann: 'I would willingly have said something of chastity and impurity; for impurity is now spread so far, that even children are infected; and by it the seeds of every virtue, as well as the germe of their posterity, which the Creator has implanted in them for wise purposes, are weakened or destroyed. I am thoroughly persuaded that the most efficacious method to root out this dreadful evil, which poisons the source of human happiness, would be to speak to children of the organs of generation as freely as we speak of the other parts of the body, and explain to them the noble use which they were designed for, and how they may be injured' (pp.xiv–xv).]

(d) The female advocates of Democracy in this country, though they have had no opportunity of imitating the French ladies, in their atrocious acts of cruelty; have yet assumed a stern serenity in the contemplation of those savage excesses.

(e) That Miss Wollstonecraft was a sworn enemy to blushes, I need not remark. But many of my readers, perhaps, will be astonished to hear, that at several of our boarding-schools for young ladies, a blush incurs a penalty.

(f) Her visual nerve was purged with euphrasy: she could see the illumination fast approaching, unperceived as it was by common mortals.

(g) 'Like monarchs, we have been flattered into imbecillity, by those who wish to take advantage of our weakness;' says Mary Hays . . . [in her *Letters and Essays, Moral and Miscellaneous*, 1793]. But, whether flattered or not, women were always weak: and female weakness hath accomplished, what the force of arms could not effect. . . .

(h) I know nothing of Miss Wollstonecraft's character or conduct, but from the Memoirs of Godwin, with whom this lady was afterwards connected. 'We did not marry,' says Godwin: but during her pregnancy by G. they married. She died in consequence of child-birth, in 1797. A woman who has broken through all religious restraints, will commonly be found ripe for every species of licentiousness. . . . I cannot but think, that the Hand of Providence is visible, in her life, her death, and in the Memoirs themselves. As she was given up to her 'heart's lusts,' and let 'to follow her own imaginations,' that the fallacy of her doctrines and the effects of an irreligious conduct, might be manifested to the world; and as she died a death that strongly marked the distinction of the sexes, by pointing out the destiny of women, and the diseases to which they are liable; so her husband was permitted, in writing her Memoirs, to labour under a temporary infatuation, that every incident might be seen without a gloss - every fact exposed without an apology. [On Godwin's *Memoir*, see 3.9, note 4.]

(i) Miss Hannah More may justly be esteemed, as a character, in all points, diametrically opposite to Miss Wollstonecraft; exerpting, indeed, her genius and literary attainments. To the great natural talents of Miss W. Miss More has added the learning of Lady Jane Grey without the pedantry, and the Christian graces of Mrs. Rowe, without the enthusiasm. . . . . [See 3.9, 1.2, 4.10.]

1 Rousseau, *Julie ou la Nouvelle Heloïse* (1761), in which the heroine's illicit passion is sympathetically presented.

2 Anna Barbauld (1743–1825), poet, essayist, and defender of various radical causes such as the abolition of slavery.

3 Robinson: see 5.6.

4 Charlotte Smith (1749–1806), best known as a novelist and included here no doubt because of the social criticism in her novels and her admiration for Wollstonecraft.

5 Helen Maria Williams: see 3.7, note 1.

6 Ann Yearsley (1752–1806), the 'Bristol milkmaid', a working-class poet patronized by Hannah More with whom she later quarrelled.

7 Mary Hays: see 5.5.

8 Elizabeth Montagu: see 4.17, note 1.

9 Elizabeth Carter: see 4.11.

10 Hester Chapone: see 3.2.

5

FEMINISMS

'Feminism', a term first used at the end of the nineteenth century, is clearly anachronistic in an eighteenth-century context. It is nevertheless useful in signalling the continuities between its modern political definition and various important eighteenth-century texts where the central concern is similarly to locate and change the cultural practices responsible for women's oppression. The writers represented here share that essential motivation, but beyond that, like modern feminists, their strategies and terms of analysis differ widely – are even, in some cases, antagonistic. The discourses of oppression, like those through which oppression is countered, are historically specific, and the danger of the anachronism comes in the tendency to reduce these earlier defences of women to versions of modern debates, obscuring potentially illuminating, and sometimes uncomfortable, historical differences. Attention to that specificity – then and now – is crucial for our own survival. Feminism is always vulnerable to containment by dominant ideologies of gender: the attempt to identify the alliances, blindnesses, and successes of these earlier feminist texts, as they negotiate other political ideologies and discourses of gender, can only make us more alert to our own discursive context.

One of the most important questions raised by these texts is that of where these women write from. What debates have enabled their critique of sexual power relations? I want to single out four such debates which are recurrently evident in the passages here, though their terms necessarily shift in the course of the century. These are: philosophical rationalism; debates about the nature of political authority; debates about women's education (cf. Section 3); and responses to anti-female satire.

These debates give feminists throughout the period a conceptual base and vocabulary from which to attack 'Custom', the power of received opinion to naturalize a view of women which is a distortion of their actual potential – in modern terms, to analyse the construction of 'women' by ideology. In the eighteenth century, the arguments revolve around definitions of women's 'nature', their God-given role (which is why one recurrent topic of debate is the exact significance of the *Genesis* story – see 5.2, 5.3, 5.4). Rationalism provided a means of arguing against inherent sexual difference. At the beginning of the period, for example, Mary Astell's plan for a women's seminary (5.1) is based on her Christian Platonist belief in the 'desire to advance and perfect its Being . . . planted by GOD in all Rational Natures'. Those 'rational natures' are ungendered: the struggle for perfection is a duty for women as much as for men. 'Sophia' (5.4), in rather less other-worldly terms, bases her daring claim that women are as capable as men of military office on her belief that there is no 'inward or outward' sexual difference 'excepting what merely tends to giving birth to posterity'. And again, at the end of the century, Mary Robinson (5.6) makes the vital claim that 'in activity of mind', men and women are equals. She and Mary Hays (5.5) were members of radical political groups in the period following the French Revolution, and follow Catherine Macaulay (3.5) and Mary Wollstonecraft in applying the politicized ideals of Enlightenment rationalism to the position of women.[1] For Mary Hays, it is 'rational *liberty*' (my emphasis) which 'the God of nature seems manifestly to have intended, for every living creature' (cf. 4.19 for a virulent anti-Jacobin attack on 1790s feminists).

The adaptation of the language of political libertarianism for a feminist position is a recurrent strategy in these texts, and it is no coincidence that the main feminist debates take place at the beginning and end of the period, after the 'Glorious Revolution' of 1688 and the French Revolution of 1789. Hays, for example, is particularly far-seeing in her argument that successful political revolution is impossible without equality for women. Carefully dissociating herself, through the language of gradualism, from the violence which followed the French Revolution, she nevertheless endorses the perfectibilist ideals of 1790s radicals like

Godwin (with whom she was closely associated). At the beginning of the century, the language of the Glorious Revolution similarly informs the *Essay in Defence of the Female Sex* (5.2). Locke's political rationalism from the *Two Treatises of Government* (1690) is applied to the 'unreasonable Authority' which men exercise over women: tyranny, whether national or domestic, justifies rebellion. And the Whig demands of 1688 for the constitutional right of representation are claimed for women in *Hardships of the English Laws* (5.4). Using a recurrent analogy with anti-slavery arguments (cf. 5.2), the writer points out the hypocrisy of a legal system based on rights of liberty and property which are denied to half the population.

All these texts are written within the rationalist tradition of Locke, Hobbes, and, later, Enlightenment philosophy, and see authority, whether political or domestic, as an arbitrary power, open to reasonable question. In this context, Mary Astell's is an isolated voice. Her contempt for 'vain, insignificant men' is absolute, but so is her reverence for a hierarchical order ordained by God within which women are required only to 'understand our own duty'. The contrast between Astell, the High Church Jacobite, and the dissenting Whig politics of the exactly contemporary *Essay in Defence* (which was at one time, incredibly, thought to be by Astell) is striking as an example of feminisms aligning themselves with very different contemporary images of femininity as they negotiate the demands of other political allegiances. The two texts have nothing in common beyond a recognition of the systematic educational disadvantages suffered by women: Astell endorses a religious vocation based on a rejection of the secular pleasures celebrated in the *Essay;* her strategy is to transcend the worldly order rather than reverse the subordination of private to public, feminine to masculine values, as the *Essay* (like 'Sophia' (5.4)) suggests.

The *Essay*'s outspoken practicality seems more approachable to a modern reader than Astell's religious separatism, but, in spite of its identification of women with spiritual values, it is Astell's position which is arguably more resistant to containment. The *Essay* puts the case forcefully for women's invisible cultural power, arguing that conventional evaluations of men and women's social importance should be reversed because 'conversation' (meaning all kinds of social relationship) with women is a civilizing influence. But, in failing to dislodge the separation of public and private spheres, the *Essay* dangerously coincides with the repressive discourses of conduct literature in which women are seduced into subordination through just such promises of influence (see 1.1, 1.3, 3.1, 3.9). 'Sophia's' claim for women's right to public office, together with her stress on the arbitrariness of terms like 'effeminate' and 'manly', carefully avoids any such implicit endorsement of separate spheres and thus of inherent sexual difference, and both Astell and Hays give devastating analyses of the social construction of femininity, and of women's internalization of conduct values. For Hays, at the end of the period, the object of attack is the impossibly contradictory image created by the discourse of sensibility – 'What a mixture of strength and weakness, – of greatness and littleness, – of sense and folly' – the pervasiveness of which is evident as it intrudes into Robinson's text, making her basic appeal to an undifferentiated human nature look less secure: 'the passions of men originate in sensuality; those of women, in sentiment: man loves corporeally, woman mentally', and again, 'Man is a despot by nature'. Arguments for an essential 'nature' very easily collapse back into conventional, repressive definitions of sexual difference.

In their treatment of women's sexuality, all these texts inevitably reinforce conventional morality, the most radical claim being for a change in male sexual behaviour. In Manley or Phillips (4.3, 4.7), the articulation of female sexuality was the equivocal result of self-defence, but writing on behalf of women in general, and within the discourse of rationalism, it is impossible for these texts to go further than advocating a distanced sympathy for the 'fallen' woman (see 5.5, 3.5) – though, in a different genre, the novel, Mary Hays was able to explore in detail the relationship between sensibility and female desire.[2] In Astell, sexuality is sublimated into religious satisfactions, the language of physical pleasure transferred to the 'Acme of delight which the devout Seraphic Soul enjoys', and in various ways the other writers dissociate themselves from 'those Women, whose Vices and ill Conduct expose them deservedly to the Censure of the other Sex' (5.2). This defensive reaction against the identification of women's writing with sexuality (cf. Section 4) brings us back to the question of where these women write from, and whether their oppositional strategies can ever escape the categories already provided by the dominant ideology.

The point can be made slightly differently by focusing on genre and looking at the role of satiric discourse in some of these texts. Defences of women written in answer to anti-female satire were one of the major sources of early 'feminist' writing, and the *Essay* and 'Sophia', particularly, are still working within this tradition: both texts, for example, have a tendency to digress into witty portraits of male types, like the Beau, or the judge besotted by his maid. More seriously, their central strategy also derives from the highly formalized interchanges of satiric discourse (cf. 2.1, 2.4, 1.2). This is the trick of evaluative reversal – whereby the 'feminine' categories and qualities attacked by the anti-female satirists are defended and valorized. Not surprisingly, as I have already suggested, it is at exactly these points that these texts are most vulnerable theoretically – underwriting rather than rewriting patriarchal categories.

This point-scoring – the constant hazard of a defensive position – survives to some extent in Robinson ('Which is the nobler creature?'). But Robinson also turns disadvantage resoundingly to women's account in her final argument that imposed public silence has resulted in the writings which 'will be the monuments from which the genius of British women will rise to immortal celebrity': a fitting conclusion for an anthology of this kind.

Notes

1 Both Hays and Robinson, elsewhere in their texts, pay tribute to Mary Wollstonecraft, the writer most obviously missing from this section. Her *Vindication of the Rights of Woman* must clearly be central to any view of eighteenth-century feminism, but, because it is easily available, I have chosen to represent Wollstonecraft in this anthology by her earlier and less widely known *Thoughts on the Education of Daughters* (1.7, 3.4), a text which, like Wollstonecraft's novels and Robinson here, demonstrates the difficult negotiations in 1790s feminism between rationalism and sensibility.

2 See Mary Hays, *Memoirs of Emma Courtney* (1796; rpt. London: Pandora Press, 1987).

5.1 Mary Astell, from *A Serious Proposal to the Ladies, for the Advancement of their True and Greatest Interest*, 1694; 3rd edn 1696

LADIES,

. . . What a pity it is, that whilst your Beauty casts a lustre all around you, your Souls which are infinitely more bright and radiant (of which if you had but a clear Idea, as lovely as it is, and as much as you now value it, you wou'd then despise and neglect the mean *Case* that encloses it) shou'd be suffer'd to over-run with Weeds, lie fallow and neglected, unadorn'd with any Grace! Altho' the Beauty of the mind is necessary to secure those Conquests which your Eyes have gain'd, and Time that mortal Enemy to handsome Faces, has no influence on a lovely Soul, but to better and improve it. For shame let's abandon that *Old*, and therefore one wou'd think, unfashionable employment of pursuing Butterflies and Trifles! No longer drudge on in the dull beaten road of Vanity and Folly, which so many have gone before us, but dare to break the enchanted Circle that custom has plac'd us in, and scorn the vulgar way of imitating all the Impertinences of our Neighbours. Let us learn to pride our selves in something more excellent than the invention of a Fashion; And not entertain such a degrading thought of our own *worth*, as to imagine that our Souls were given us only for the service of our Bodies, and that the best improvement we can make of these, is to attract the Eyes of Men. We value *them* too much, and our *selves* too little, if we place any part of our desert in their Opinion; and don't think our selves capable of Nobler Things than the pitiful Conquest of some worthless heart. She who has opportunities of making an interest in Heaven, of obtaining the love and admiration of GOD and Angels, is too prodigal of her Time, and injurious to her Charms, to throw them away on vain insignificant men. She need not make her self so cheap, as to descend to court their Applauses; for at the greater distance she keeps, and the more she is above them, the more effectually she secures their esteem and wonder. Be so generous then, Ladies, as to do nothing unworthy of you; so true to your Interest, as not to lessen your Empire and depreciate your Charms. Let not your Thoughts be wholly busied in observing what respect is paid you, but a part of them at least, in studying to deserve it. And after all, remember that Goodness is the truest

Greatness; to be wise for your selves the greatest Wit; and *that* Beauty the most desirable which will endure to Eternity.

Pardon me the seeming rudeness of this Proposal, which goes upon a supposition that there's something amiss in you, which it is intended to amend. My design is not to expose, but to rectifie your Failures. To be exempt from mistake, is a privilege few can pretend to, the greatest is to be past Conviction and too obstinate to reform. Even the *Men*, as exact as they wou'd seem, and as much as they divert themselves with our Miscarriages, are very often guilty of greater faults, and such, as considering the advantages they enjoy, are much more inexcusable. But I will not pretend to correct their Errors, who either are, or at least *think* them selves too wise to receive Instruction from a Womans Pen. My earnest desire is, That you Ladies, would be as perfect and happy as 'tis possible to be in this imperfect state; for I love you too well to endure a spot upon your Beauties, if I can by any means remove and wipe it off. I would have you live up to the dignity of your Nature, and express your thankfulness to GOD for the benefits you enjoy by a due improvement of them: As I know very many of you do, who countenance that Piety which the Men decry, and are the brightest Patterns of Religion that the Age affords; 'tis my grief that all the rest of our Sex do not imitate such Illustrious Examples, and therefore I would have them encreas'd and render'd more conspicuous, that Vice being put out of countenance, (because Vertue is the only thing in fashion) may sneak out of the World, and its darkness be dispell'd by the confluence of so many shining Graces. The Men perhaps will cry out that I teach you false Doctrine, for because by their seductions some amongst us are become very mean and contemptible, they would fain persuade the rest to be as despicable and forlorn as they. We're indeed oblig'd to them for their management, in endeavouring to make us so, who use all the artifice they can to spoil, and deny us the means of improvement. So that instead of inquiring why all Women are not wise and good, we have reason to wonder that there are any so. Were the Men as much neglected, and as little care taken to cultivate and improve them, perhaps they wou'd be so far from surpassing those whom they now dispise, that they themselves wou'd sink into the greatest stupidity and brutality. The preposterous returns that the most of them make, to all the care and pains that is bestow'd on them, renders this no uncharitable, nor improbable Conjecture. One wou'd therefore almost think, that the wise disposer of all things, foreseeing how unjustly Women are denied opportunities of improvement from *without* has therefore by way of compensation endow'd them with greater propensions to Vertue and a natural goodness of Temper *within*, which if duly manag'd, would raise them to the most eminent pitch of heroick Vertue. Hither, Ladies, I desire you wou'd aspire, 'tis a noble and becoming Ambition, and to remove such Obstacles as lie in your way is the design of this Paper. We will therefore enquire what it is that stops your flight, that keeps you groveling here below, like *Domitian* catching Flies[1] when you should be busied in obtaining Empires.

Altho' it has been said by Men of more Wit than Wisdom, and perhaps of more malice than either, that Women are naturally incapable of acting Prudently, or that they are necessarily determined to folly, I must by no means grant it; that Hypothesis would render my endeavours impertinent, for then it would be in vain to advise the one, or endeavour the Reformation of the other. Besides, there are Examples in all Ages, which sufficiently confute the Ignorance and Malice of this Assertion.

The Incapacity, if there be any, is acquired not natural; and none of their Follies are so necessary, but that they might avoid them if they pleas'd themselves. Some disadvantages indeed they labour under, and what these are we shall see by and by and endeavour to surmount; but Women need not take up with mean things, since (if they are not wanting to themselves) they are capable of the best. Neither God nor Nature have excluded them from being Ornaments to their Families and useful in their Generation; there is therefore no reason they should be content to be Cyphers in the World, useless at the best, and in a little time a burden and nuisance to all about them. And 'tis very great pity that they who are so apt to over-rate themselves in smaller Matters, shou'd, where it most concerns them to know and stand upon their Value, be so insensible of their own worth. The Cause therefore of the defects we labour under is, if not wholly, yet at least in the first place, to be ascribed to the mistakes of our Education, which like an Error in the first Concoction, spreads its ill Influence through all our Lives.

The Soil is rich and would if well cultivated produce a noble Harvest, if then the Unskilful Managers, not only permit, but incourage noxious Weeds, tho' we shall suffer by the Neglect, yet they ought not in justice to blame any but themselves, if they reap the Fruit of this their foolish Conduct. Women are from their very Infancy debar'd those Advantages, with the want of which they are afterwards reproached, and nursed up in those Vices which will hereafter be upbraided to them. So partial are Men as to expect Brick where they afford no Straw; and so abundantly civil as to take care we shou'd make good that obliging Epithet of *Ignorant*, which out of an excess of good Manners, they are pleas'd to bestow on us! . . .

For that Ignorance is the cause of most Feminine Vices, may be instanc'd in that Pride and Vanity which is usually imputed to us, and which I suppose if throughly sifted, will appear to be some way or other, the rise and Original of all the rest. These, tho' very bad Weeds, are the product of a good Soil, they are nothing else but Generosity degenerated and corrupted. A desire to advance and perfect its Being, is planted by GOD in all Rational Natures, to excite them hereby to every worthy and becoming Action; for certainly next to the Grace of GOD, nothing does so powerfully restrain people from Evil and stir them up to Good, as a generous Temper. And therefore to be ambitious of perfections is no fault, tho' to assume the Glory of our Excellencies to our selves, or to Glory in such as we really have not, are. And were Womens haughtiness express'd in disdaining to do a mean and evil thing, wou'd they pride themselves in somewhat truly perfective of a Rational nature, there were no hurt in it. But then they ought not to be denied the means of examining and judging what is so; they should not be impos'd on with tinsel ware. If by reason of a false Light, or undue Medium, they chuse amiss, theirs is the loss, but the Crime is the Deceivers. She who rightly understands wherein the perfection of her Nature consists, will lay out her Thoughts and Industry in the acquisition of such Perfections: But she who is kept ignorant of the matter, will take up with such Objects as first offer themselves, and bear any plausible resemblance to what she desires; a shew of advantage being sufficient to render them agreeable baits to her who wants Judgment and Skill to discern between reality and pretence. From whence it easily follows, that she who has nothing else to value her self upon, will be proud of her Beauty, or Money and what that can purchase; and think her self mightily oblig'd to him, who tells her she has those Perfections which she naturally longs for. Her inbred self-esteem and desire of good, which are degenerated into Pride and mistaken Self-love, will easily open her Ears to whatever goes about to nourish and delight them; and when a cunning designing Enemy from without, has drawn over to his Party these Traytors within, he has the Poor unhappy Person, at his Mercy, who now very glibly swallows down his Poyson, because 'tis presented in a Golden Cup, and credulously hearkens to the most disadvantageous Proposals, because they come attended with a seeming esteem. She whose Vanity makes her swallow praises by the whole sale, without examining whether she deserves them, or from what hand they come, will reckon it but gratitude to think well of him who values her so much, and think she must needs be merciful to the poor despairing Lover whom her Charms have reduc'd to die at her feet. . . .

When a poor Young Lady is taught to value her self on nothing but her Cloaths, and to think she's very fine when well accoutred; When she hears say, that 'tis Wisdom enough for her to know how to dress her self, that she may be amiable in his eyes, to whom it appertains to be knowing and learned; who can blame her if she lay out her Industry and Money on such Accomplishments, and sometimes extends it farther than her misinformer desires she should? When she sees the vain and the gay, making Parade in the World and attended with the Courtship and admiration of the gazing herd, no wonder that her tender Eyes are dazled with the Pageantry, and wanting Judgment to pass a due Estimate on them and their Admirers, longs to be such a fine and celebrated thing as they? What tho' she be sometimes told of another World, she has however a more lively perception of this, and may well think, that if her Instructors were in earnest when they tell her of *hereafter*, they would not be so busied and concerned about what happens *here*. She is it may be, taught the Principles and Duties of Religion, but not Acquainted with the Reasons and Grounds of them; being told 'tis enough for her to believe, to examine why, and wherefore, belongs not to her.

. . .

Now as to the Proposal, it is to erect a *Monastery*, or if you will (to avoid giving offence to the scrupulous and injudicious, by names which tho' innocent in themselves, have been abus'd by super-stitious Practices,) we will call it a *Religious Retirement*, and such as shall have a double aspect, being not only a Retreat from the World for those who desire that advantage, but likewise, an Institution and pre[c]ious discipline, to fit us to do the greatest good in it; such an Institution as this (if I do not mightily deceive my self) would be the most probable method to amend the present and improve the future Age. For here those who are convinc'd of the emptiness of earthly Enjoyments, who are sick of the vanity of the world and its impertinencies, may find more substantial and satisfying entertainments, and need not be confin'd to what they justly loath. Those who are desirous to know and fortify their weak side, first do good to themselves, that hereafter they may be capable of doing more good to others; or for their greater security are willing to avoid *temptation*, may get out of that danger which a continual stay in view of the Enemy, and the familiarity and unwearied application of the Temptation may expose them to; and gain an opportunity to look into themselves to be acquainted at home and no longer the greatest strangers to their own hearts. Such as are willing in a more peculiar and undisturb'd manner, to attend the great business they came into the world about, the service of GOD and improvement of their own Minds, may find a convenient and blissful recess from the noise and hurry of the world. A world so cumbersom, so infectious, that altho' thro' the grace of GOD and their own strict watchfulness, they are kept from sinking down into its corruptions, 'twill however damp their flight to heav'n, hinder them from attaining any eminent pitch of Vertue.

You are therefore Ladies, invited into a place, where you shall suffer no other confinement, but to be kept out of the road of sin: You shall not be depriv'd of your grandeur, but only exchange the vain Pomps and Pageantry of the world, empty Titles and Forms of State, for the true and solid Greatness of being able to despise them. You will only quit the Chat of insignificant people for an ingenious Conversation; the froth of flashy Wit for real Wisdom; idle tales for instructive discourses. . . . Here are no Serpents to deceive you, whilst you entertain your selves in these delicious Gardens. No Provocations will be given in this Amicable

Society, but to Love and to good Works, which will afford such an entertaining employment, that you'll have as little inclination as leisure to pursue those Follies, which in the time of your ignorance pass'd with you under the name of love, altho' there is not in nature two more different things, than *true Love* and that *brutish Passion* which pretends to ape it. Here will be no Rivalling but for the Love of GOD, no Ambition but to procure his Favour, to which nothing will more effectually recommend you, than a great and dear affection to each other. Envy that Canker, will not here disturb your Breasts; for how can she repine at anothers well-fare, who reckons it the greatest part of her own? No Covetousness will gain admittance in this blest abode, but to amass huge Treasures of good Works, and to procure one of the brightest Crowns of Glory. You will not be solicitous to encrease you[r] Minds, esteeming no Grandeur like being conformable to the meek and humble JESUS. So that you only withdraw from the noise and trouble, the folly and temptation of the world, that you may more peaceably enjoy your selves, and all the innocent Pleasures it is able to afford you, and particularly that which is worth all the rest, a Noble, Vertuous and Disinteress'd Friendship. And to compleat all, that *Acme* of delight which the devout Seraphic Soul enjoys, when dead to the World, she devotes her self entirely to the Contemplation and fruition of her Beloved; when having disengag'd her self from all those Lets which hindred her from without, she moves in a direct and vigorous motion towards her true and only Good, whom now she embraces and acquiesces in with such an unspeakable pleasure, as is only intelligible to those who have tried and felt it, which we can no more describe to the dark and sensual part of Mankind, than we can the beauty of Colours and harmony of Sounds to the Blind and Deaf. In fine, the place to which you are invited is a Type and Antepast of Heav'n, where your Employment will be as there, to magnify GOD, to love one another, and to communicate that useful *knowledge*, which by the due improvement of your time in Study and Contemplation you will obtain, and which when obtain'd, will afford you a much sweeter and more durable delight, than all those pitiful diversions, those revellings and amusements, which now thro your ignorance of better, appear the only grateful and relishing Entertainments.

. . . one great end of this Institution shall be, to expel that cloud of Ignorance which Custom has involv'd us in, to furnish our minds with a stock of solid and useful Knowledge, that the Souls of Women may no longer be the only unadorn'd and neglected things. It is not intended that our *Religious* should waste their time, and trouble their heads about such unconcerning matters, as the vogue of the world has turn'd up for Learning, . . . but busy themselves in a serious enquiry after *necessary* and *perfective* truths, something which it *concerns* them to know, and which tends to their real interest and perfection . . . . Such a course of Study will be neither too troublesome nor out of the reach of a Female Virtuoso; for it is not intended she shou'd spend her hours in learning *words* but *things*, and therefore no more Languages than are necessary to acquaint her with useful Authors. Nor need she trouble her self in turning over a great number of Books, but take care to understand and digest a few well-chosen and good ones. Let her but obtain right Ideas, and be truly acquainted with the nature of those Objects that present themselves to her mind, and then no matter whether or no she be able to tell what fanciful people have said about them: And throughly to understand Christianity as profess'd by the *Church* of *England*, will be sufficient to confirm her in the truth, tho' she have not a Catalogue of those particular errors which oppose it. . . .

We pretend not that Women shou'd teach in the Church, nor usurp Authority where it is not allow'd them; permit us only to understand our *own* duty, and not be forc'd to take it upon trust from others; to be at least so far learned, as to be able to form in our minds a true Idea of Christianity, it being so very necessary to fence us against the danger of these *last* and *perilous days*, in which Deceivers a part of whose Character is to *lead captive silly Women*, need not *creep into Houses* since they have Authority to proclaim their Errors on the *House top*.[2] And let us also acquire a true Practical Knowledge such as will convince us of the absolute necessity of *Holy Living* as well as of *Right Believing*, and that no Heresy is more dangerous than that of an ungodly and wicked Life. And since the *French Tongue* is understood by most Ladies, methinks they may much better improve it by the study of Philosophy (as I hear the *French Ladies* do) *Des Cartes, Malebranche*[3] and others, than by reading idle *Novels* and *Romances*. 'Tis strange we shou'd be so forward to imitate their Fashions and Fopperies, and have no regard to what really deserves our Imitation! And why shall it not be thought as genteel to understand *French Philosophy*, as to be accoutred in a *French Mode?* Let therefore the famous Madam *D'acier, Scudery*, &c.[4] and our own incomparable *Orinda*,[5] excite the Emulation of the English Ladies.

The Ladies, I'm sure, have no reason to dislike this Proposal, but I know not how the Men will resent it to have their enclosure broke down, and Women invited to tast of that Tree of Knowledge they have so long unjustly *Monopoliz'd*. But they must excuse me, if I be as partial to my own Sex as they are to theirs, and think Women as capable of Learning as Men are, and that it becomes them as well.

. . .

And if after so many Spiritual Advantages, it be convenient to mention Temporals, here Heiresses and Persons of Fortune may be kept secure from the rude attempts of designing Men; And she who has more Money than Discretion, need not curse her Stars for being expos'd a prey to bold importunate and rapacious Vultures. She will not here be inveigled and impos'd on, will neither be bought nor sold, nor be forc'd to marry for her own quiet, when she has no inclination to it, but what the being tir'd out with a restless importunity occasions. Or if she be dispos'd to marry, here she may remain in safety till a convenient Match be offer'd by her Friends, and be freed from the danger of a dishonourable one. Modesty requiring that a Woman should not love before Marriage, but only make choice of one whom she can love hereafter; She who has none but innocent affections, being easily able to fix them where Duty requires.

And though at first I propos'd to my self to speak nothing in particular of the employment of the *Religious*, yet to give a Specimen how useful they will be to the World, I am now inclin'd to declare, that it is design'd a part of their business shall be to give the best Education to the Children of Persons of Quality, who shall be attended and instructed in lesser matters by meaner Persons deputed to that Office, but the forming of their minds shall be the particular care of those of their own Rank, who cannot have a more pleasant and useful employment than to exercise and encrease their own knowledge, by instilling it into these young ones, who are most like to profit under such Tutors. For how can their little Pupils forbear to credit them, since they do not decry the World (as others may be thought to do) because they cou'd not enjoy it, but when they had it in their power, were courted and caress'd by it, for very good Reasons and on mature deliberation, thought fit to relinquish and despise its offers for a better choice? Nor are mercenary people on other accounts capable of doing so much good to young Persons; because having often but short views of things themselves, sordid and low Spirits, they are not like to form a generous temper in the minds of the Educated. Doubtless 'twas well consider'd of him, who wou'd not trust the breeding of his Son to a Slave, because nothing great or excellent could be expected from a person of that condition.

And when by the increase of their Revenue, the *Religious* are enabled to do such a work of Charity, the Education they design to bestow on the Daughters of Gentlemen who are fallen into decay will be no inconsiderable advantage to the Nation. For hereby many Souls will be preserv'd from great Dishonours and put in a comfortable way of subsisting, being either receiv'd into the House if they incline to it, or otherwise dispos'd of. It being suppos'd that prudent Men will reckon the endowments they here acquire a sufficient *Dowry*, and that a discreet and vertuous Gentlewoman will make a better Wife than she whose mind is empty tho' her Purse be full.

Notes

1 From Suetonius's life of the Roman Emperor Domitian, in which it is claimed he spent an hour each day alone just catching flies.
2 An example of Astell's conservative political position. The allusion is to the practice of 'occasional conformity' by which Dissenters qualified technically for public office by now and again taking communion in the Church of England. Astell later campaigned for this to be outlawed.
3 Descartes (1596–1650): French dualist philosopher whose stress on the power of individual reason to prove the existence of God liberated philosophy from scholasticism and was the basis of subsequent sceptical philosophy. Malebranche (1638–1715): Astell was much influenced by his re-reading of Descartes in idealist terms, arguing that the function of reason was to love God, not to prove his existence.
4 Dacier: see 4.3, note 1. Madeleine de Scudéry (1607–1701): French novelist and literary hostess, author of long, complex and impeccably

moral romances, the most famous of which are *Artamène ou Le Grand Cyrus* (1649–53; cf. 1.2, note 4) and *Clélie* (1656–60).
5 Orinda: see 4.1, note 3.

5.2   from *An Essay in Defence of the Female Sex*, 1696

The Question I shall at present handle is, whether the time an ingenious Gentleman spends in the Company of Women, may justly be said to be misemploy'd, or not? I put the question in general terms; because whoever holds the affirmative must maintain it so, or the Sex is no way concern'd to oppose him. On the other side I shall not maintain the Negative, but with some Restrictions and Limitations; because I will not be bound to justifie those Women, whose Vices and ill Conduct expose them deservedly to the Censure of the other Sex, as well as of their own. . . .

Our Company is generally by our Adversaries represented as unprofitable and irksome to Men of Sense, and by some of the more vehement Sticklers against us, as Criminal. These Imputations as they are unjust, especially the latter, so they favour strongly of the Malice, Arrogance and Sottishness of those, that most frequently urge 'em; who are commonly either conceited Fops, whose success in their Pretences to the favour of our Sex has been no greater than their Merit, and fallen very far short of their Vanity and Presumption, or a sort of morose, ill-bred, unthinking Fellows, who appear to be Men only by their Habit and Beards, and are scarce distinguishable from Brutes but by their Figure and Risibility. But I shall wave these Reflections at present, however just, and come closer to our Argument. If Women are not quallified for the Conversation of ingenious Men, or, to get yet further, their friendship, it must be because they want some one condition, or more, necessarily requisite to either. The necessary Conditions of these are Sense, and good nature, to which must be added, for Friendship, Fidelity and Integrity. Now if any of these be wanting to our Sex, it must be either because Nature has not been so liberal as to bestow 'em upon us; or because due care has not been taken to cultivate those Gifts to a competent measure in us.

The first of these Causes is that, which is most generally urg'd against us, whether it be in Raillery, or Spight. I might easily cut this part of the Controversy short by an irrefragable Argument, which is, that the express intent, and reason for which Women was created, was to be a Companion and help meet to Man; and that consequently those, that deny 'em to be so, must argue a Mistake in Providence, and think themselves wiser than their Creator. But these Gentlemen are generally such passionate Admirers of themselves, and have such a profound value and reverence for their own Parts, that they are ready at any time to sacrifice their Religion to the Reputation of their Wit, and rather than lose their point, deny the truth of the History. There are others, that though they allow the Story yet affirm, that the propagation, and continuance of Mankind, was the only Reason for which we were made; as if the Wisdom that first made Man, cou'd not without trouble have continu'd that Species by the same or any other Method, had not this been most conducive to his happiness, which was the gracious and only end of his Creation. But these superficial Gentlemen wear their Understandings like their Clothes, always set and formal, and wou'd no more Talk than Dress out of Fashion; Beau's that, rather than any part of their outward Figure shou'd be damag'd, wou'd wipe the dirt off their shoes with their Handkercher, and that value themselves infinitely more upon modish Nonsense, than upon the best Sense against the Fashion. . . .

. . . I shall desire those, that hold against us to observe the Country People, I mean the inferiour sort of them, such as not having Stocks to follow Husbandry upon their own Score, subsist upon their daily Labour. For amongst these, though not so equal as that of Brutes, yet the Condition of the two Sexes is more level, than amongst Gentlemen, City Traders, or rich Yeomen. Examine them in their several Businesses, and their Capacities will appear equal; but talk to them of things indifferent, and out of the Road of their constant Employment, and the Ballance will fall on our side, the Women will be found the more ready and polite. Let us look a little further, and view our Sex in a state of more improvement, amongst our Neighbours the *Dutch*. There we shall find them managing not only the Domestick Affairs of the Family, but making and receiving all Payments as well great as small, keeping the Books, ballancing the Accounts, and doing all the Business, even the nicest of Merchants, with as much Dexterity and Exactness as their, or our Men can do. And I have often hear'd some of our considerable Merchants blame the conduct of our Country-Men in this point; that they breed our Women so ignorant of Business; whereas were they taught Arithmetick, and other Arts which require not much bodily strength, they might supply the places of abundance of lusty Men now employ'd in sedentary Business; which would be a mighty profit to the Nation by sending those Men to Employments, where hands and Strength are more requir'd, especially at this time when we are in such want of People. Beside that it might prevent the ruine of many Families, which is often occasion'd by the Death of Merchants in full Business, and leaving their Accounts perplex'd, and embroil'd to a Widdow and Orphans, who understanding nothing of the Husband or Father's Business, occasions the Rending, and oftentimes the utter Confounding a fair Estate; which might be prevented, did the Wife but understand Merchants Accounts, and were made acquainted with the Books.

. . .

It remains then for us to enquire, whether the Bounty of Nature be wholly neglected, or stifled by us, or so far as to make us unworthy the Company of Men? Or whether our Education (as bad as it is) be not sufficient to make us a useful, nay, a necessary part of Society for the greatest part of Mankind. This cause is seldom indeed urg'd against us by the Men, though it be the only one, that gives 'em any advantage over us in understanding. But it does not serve their Pride there is no Honour to be gain'd by it: For a Man ought no more to value himself upon being Wiser than a Woman, if he owe his Advantage to a better Education, and greater means of Information, then he ought to boast of his Courage, for beating a Man, when his Hands were bound. Nay, it would be so far from Honourable to contend for preference upon this Score, that they would thereby at once argue themselves guilty both of Tyranny, and of Fear: I think I need not have mention'd the latter; for none can be Tyrants but Cowards. For nothing makes one Party slavishly depress another, but their fear that they may at one time or other become Strong and Couragious enough to make themselves equal to, if not superiour to their Masters. This is our Case; for Men being sensible as well of the Abilities of Mind in our Sex, as of the strength of Body in their own, began to grow Jealous, that we, who in the Infancy of the

World were their Equals and Partners in Dominion, might in process of Time, by Subtlety and Stratagem, become their Superiours; and therefore began in good time to make use of Force (the Origine of Power) to compel us to a Subjection, Nature never meant; and made use of Natures liberality to them to take the benefit of her kindness from us. From that time they have endeavour'd to train us up altogether to Ease and Ignorance; as Conquerors use to do to those, they reduce by Force, that so they may disarm 'em, both of Courage and Wit; and consequently make them tamely give up their Liberty, and abjectly submit their Necks to a slavish Yoke. As the World grew more Populous, and Mens Necessities whetted their Inventions, so it increas'd their Jealousy, and sharpen'd their Tyranny over us, till by degrees, it came to that height of Severity, I may say Cruelty, it is now at in all the Eastern parts of the World, where the Women, like our Negroes in our Western Plantations, are born slaves, and live Prisoners all their Lives. Nay, so far has this barbarous Humour prevail'd, and spread it self, that in some parts of *Europe*, which pretend to be most refin'd and civiliz'd, in spite of Christianity, and the Zeal for Religion which they so much affect, our Condition is not very much better. And even in *France*, a Country that treats our Sex with more Respect than most do, We are by the *Salique Law* excluded from Soveraign Power. The *French* are an ingenious People, and the Contrivers of that Law knew well enough, that We were no less capable of Reigning, and Governing well, than themselves; but they were suspicious, that if the Regal Power shou'd fall often into the hands of Women, they would favour their own Sex, and might in time restore 'em to their Primitive Liberty and Equality with the Men, and so break the neck of that unreasonable Authority they so much affect over us; and therefore made this Law to prevent it. The Historians indeed tell us other Reasons, but they can't agree among themselves, and as Men are Parties against us, and therefore their Evidence may justly be rejected. To say the truth Madam, I can't tell how to prove all this from Ancient Records; for if any Histories were anciently written by Women, Time, and the Malice of Men have effectually conspir'd to suppress 'em; and it is not reasonable to think that Men shou'd transmit, or suffer to be transmitted to Posterity, any thing that might shew the weakness and illegallity of their Title to a Power they still exercise so arbitrarily, and are so fond of. . . . But since our Sex can hardly boast of so great Privileges, and so easie a Servitude any where as in *England*, I cut this ungrateful Digression short in acknowledgment; tho' Fetters of Gold are still Fetters, and the softest Lining can never make 'em so easy, as Liberty.

. . .

Let us look into the manner of our Education, and see wherein it falls short of the Mens, and how the defects of it may be, and are generally supply'd. In our tender years they are the same, for after Children can Talk, they are promiscuously taught to Read and Write by the same Persons, and at the same time both Boys and Girls. When these are acquir'd, which is generally about the Age of Six or Seven Years, they begin to be separated, and the Boys are sent to the *Grammer-School*, and the Girls to *Boarding Schools*, or other places, to learn Needle Work, Dancing, Singing, Musick, Drawing, Painting, and other Accomplishments, according to the Humour and Ability of the Parents, or Inclination of the Children. Of all these, Reading, and Writing are the main Instruments of Conversation; though Musick and Painting may be allow'd to contribute something towards it, as they give us an insight into two Arts, that makes up a great part of the Pleasures and Diversions of Mankind. Here then lies the main Defect, that we are taught only our Mother Tongue, or perhaps *French*, which is now very fashionable, and almost as Familiar amongst Women of Quality as Men; whereas the other Sex by means of a more extensive Education to the knowledge of the *Roman* and *Greek* Languages, have a vaster Feild for their Imaginations to rove in, and their Capacities thereby enlarg'd. To see whether this be strictly true or not, I mean in what relates to our debate, I will for once suppose, that we are instructed only in our own Tongue, and then enquire whether the Disadvantage be so great as it is commonly imagin'd. You know very well, *Madam*, that for Conversation, it is not requisite we should be Philologers, Rhetoricians, Philosophers, Historians, or Poets; but only that we should think pertinently, and express our thoughts properly, on such matters as are the proper Subjects for a mixt Conversation. The *Italians*, a People as delicate in their Conversation as any in the World, have a Maxim, That our selves, our Neighbours, Religion, or Business, ought never to be the Subject. . . . Nor need any one to fear, that by these limitations Conversation shou'd be restrain'd to too narrow a compass, there are subjects enough that are in themselves neither insipid, nor offensive such as Love, Honour, Gallantry, Morality, News, Raillery, and a numberless train of other Things copious and diverting. Now I can't see the necessity of any other Tongue beside our own, to enable us to talk plausibly, or judiciously, upon any of these Topicks: Nay, I am very confident, that 'tis possible for an ingenious Person to make a very considerable progress in most parts of learning, by the help of *English* only. For the only reason I can conceive of learning Languages, is to arrive at the Sense, Wit, or Arts, that have been communicated to the World in 'em. Now of those that have taken the pains to make themselves Masters of those Treasures, many have been so generous as to impart a share of 'em to the Publick, by Translations for the use of the Unlearned; and I flatter my self sometimes, that several of these were more particularly undertaken by Ingenious, good Natur'd Men in Kindness and Compassion to our Sex. . . . Nor can I imagine for what good Reason a Man skill'd in Latin, and Greek, and vers'd in the Authors of Ancient Times shall be call'd Learned; yet another who perfectly understands *Italian, French, Spanish, High Dutch*, and the rest of the *European* Languages, is acquainted with the Modern History of all those Countries, knows their Policies, has div'd into all the Intrigues of the several Courts, and can tell their mutual Dispositions, Obligations, and Ties of Interest one to another, shall after all this be thought Unlearned for want of those two Languages. Nay, though he be never so well vers'd in the Modern Philosophy, Astronomy, Geometry and Algebra, he shall notwithstanding never be allow'd that honourable Title. I can see but one apparent Reason for this unfair procedure; which is, that when about an Age and an half ago, all the poor remains of Learning then in Being, were in the hands of the Schoolmen; they would suffer none to pass Muster, that were not deeply engag'd in those intricate, vexatious and unintelligible Trifles, for which themselves contended with so much Noise and Heat; or at least were not acquainted with *Plato* and *Aristotle*, and their Commentators; from whence the Sophistry and Subtleties of the Schools at that time were drawn. This Usurpation was maintain'd by their Successors, the Divines, who to this day pretend almost to the Monopoly of Learning; and though some generous Spirits have broke the neck of this Arbitrary, Tyrannical Authority; yet can't they prevail to extend the name of Learning beyond their Studies, in which the Divines are more particularly conversant. Thus you shall have 'em allow a Man to be a wise Man, a good Naturalist, a good Mathematician, Politician, or Poet, but not a Scholar, a learned Man, that is no Philologer. For my part I think these Gentlemen have just inverted the use of the Term, and given that to the knowledge of words, which belongs more properly to Things. I take Nature to be the great Book of Universal Learning, which he that reads best in all, or any of its Parts, is the greatest Scholar, the most learned Man; and 'tis as ridiculous for a Man to count himself more learned than another, if he have no greater extent of knowledge of things, because he is more vers'd in Languages; as it would be for an Old Fellow to tell a Young One, his own Eyes were better than the other's because he Reads with Spectacles, the other without.

... I have often thought that the not teaching Women Latin and Greek, was an advantage to them, if it were rightly consider'd, and might be improv'd to a great heigth. For Girles after they can Read and Write (if they be of any Fashion) are taught such things as take not up their whole time, and not being suffer'd to run about at liberty as Boys, are furnish'd among other toys with Books, such as *Romances, Novels, Plays* and *Poems;* which though they read carelessly only for Diversion, yet unawares to them, give 'em very early a considerable Command both of Words and Sense; which are further improv'd by their making and receiving Visits with their Mothers, which gives them betimes the opportunity of imitating, conversing with, and knowing the manner, and address of elder Persons. These I take to be the true Reasons why a Girl of Fifteen is reckon'd as ripe as a Boy of One and Twenty, and not any natural forwardness of Maturity, as some People would have it. These advantages the Education of Boys deprives them of, who drudge away the Vigour of their Memories at Words, useless ever after to most of them, and at Seventeen or Eighteen are to begin their Alphabet of Sense, and are but where the Girls were at Nine or Ten. Yet because they have learnt Latin and Greek, reject with Scorn all *English* Books their best helps, and lay aside their Latin ones, as if they were already Masters of all that Learning, and so hoist Sail for the wide World without a Compass to Steer by. Thus I have fairly stated the

difference between us, and can find no such disparity in Nature
or Education as they contend for; but we have a sort of
ungenerous Adversaries, that deal more in Scandal than Argument, and when they can't hurt us with their Weapons, endeavour to annoy us with stink Pots. Let us see therefore, *Madam*,
whether we can't beat them from their Ammunition, and turn
their own Artillery upon them; for I firmly believe there is
nothing, which they charge upon us, but may with more Justice be
retorted upon themselves.

. . .

Impertinence comes next under Consideration . . . . *Impertinence*
is a humour of busying our selves about things trivial, and of no
Moment in themselves, or unseasonably in things of no concern
to us, or wherein we are able to do nothing to any Purpose. Here
our Adversaries insult over us, as if they had gain'd an intire
Victory, and the *Field* were indisputable; but they shall have no
cause for *Triumph*, this is no Post of such mighty advantage as they
fondly persuade themselves. This *Presumption* arises from an
Erroneous Conceit, that all those things in which they are little
concern'd, or consulted, are triffles below their care or notice,
which indeed they are not by Nature so well able to manage.
Thus, when they hear us talking to, and advising one another
about the Order, Distribution and Contrivance of *Houshold
Affairs*, about the *Regulation* of the *Family*, and *Government* of
Children and *Servants*, the provident management of a *Kitchin*, and
the decent ordering of a *Table*, the suitable *Matching* and
convenient disposition of *Furniture*, and the like, they presently
condemn us for impertinence. Yet they may be pleased to
consider, that as the affairs of the World are now divided betwixt
us, the *Domestick* are our share, and out of which we are rarely
suffer'd to interpose our Sense. They may be pleased to consider
likewise, that as light and inconsiderable as these things seem,
they are capable of no Pleasures of Sense higher, or more refin'd
than others of *Brutes* without our care of 'em. For were it not for
that, their Houses wou'd be meer *Bedlams*, their most luxurious
Treats, but a rude confusion of ill Digested, ill mixt Scents and
Relishes, and the fine Furniture, they bestow so much cost on, but
an expensive heap of glittering *Rubbish*. Thus they are beholding
to us for the comfortable enjoyment of what their labour, or good

Fortune hath acquir'd or bestow'd, and think meanly of our care only, because they understand not the value of it. But if we shall be thought impertinent for Discourses of this Nature, as I deny not but we sometimes justly may, when they are unseasonable; what censure must those Men bear, who are perpetually talking of *Politicks*, *State Affairs* and *Grievances* to us, in which perhaps neither they nor We are much concern'd, or if we be, are not able to propose, much less to apply any Remedy to 'em?

. . .

There remains nothing more, but to shew that there are some necessary Qualifications to be acquir'd, some good Improvements to be made by Ingenious *Gentlemen* in the Company of our Sex.

Of this number are *Complacence*, *Gallantry*, *Good Humour*, *Invention*, and *an Art*, which (tho' frequently abus'd) is of admirable use to those that are Masters of it, the *Art* of *Insinuation*, and many others. 'Tis true, a Man may be an Honest and Understanding Man, without any of these Qualifications; but he can hardly be a Polite, a Well Bred, and Agreable, Taking Man, without all, or most of these. Without 'em, *Honesty*, *Courage*, or *Wit*, are like Rough *Diamonds*, or *Gold* in the *Ore*, they have their intrinsick Value, and Worth before, but they are doubtful and obscure, till they are polish'd, refin'd and receive *Lustre*, and *Esteem* from these.

The Principal of these is *Complacence*, a good Quality, without which in competent Measure no Man is fitted for Society. This is best learnt in our Company, where all Men affect Gaiety, and endeavour to be agreable. *State News*, *Politicks*, *Religion*, or private *Business* take up the greatest Part of their Conversation, when they are among themselves only. These are Subjects that employ their Passions too much, to leave any room for *Complacence;* they raise too much heat to suffer Men to be easie and pleasant, and Men are too serious when they talk of 'em, to suppress their natural Temper, which are apt to break out upon any Opposition. Men are as apt to defend their Opinions, as their Property, and wou'd take it as well to have their Titles to their Estates question'd, as their Sense; and perhaps in that they imitate the Conduct of our Sex, and do, like indulgent Mothers, that are most tender of those Children that are weakest. But however it be, I have observ'd when such Arguments have been introduc'd even in our Company, and by Men that affect Indifference, and abundance of Temper, that very few have been able to shew so much Mastery, but that something appear'd either in their Air, or Expression, or in the Tone of their Voices, which argued a greater Warmth, and Concern, than is proper for the Conversation of *Gentlemen*, or the Company of *Ladies*. These Uneasinesses happen not so often among us, because the Men look upon us to have very little Interest in the Publick Affairs of the World, and therefore trouble us very seldom with their grave, serious Trifles, which they debate with so much earnestness among one another. They look upon us as Things design'd and contriv'd only for their Pleasure, and therefore use us tenderly, as Children do their Favourite Bawbles. They talk gayly, and pleasantly to us, they do, or say, nothing that may give us any Disgust, or *Chagrin*, they put on their chearfullest Looks, and their Best Humour, that they may excite the like in us; They never oppose us but with a great deal of Ceremony, or in Raillery, not out of a Spirit of Opposition, (as they frequently do one another) but to maintain a pleasant Argument, or heigthen by variety of Opinions an agreable Entertainment. Mirth, and Good Humour reign generally in our Society, Good Manners always; For with us Men shew in a manner, the Reverse of what they are one to another: They let their thoughts play at Liberty, and are very careful of the Expression, that nothing harsh, or obscene escape 'em, that may shock a tender Mind, or offend a modest Ear. This Caution it is, which is the Root of *Complacence*, which is nothing but a Desire to oblige People, by complying with their Humours. 'Tis true some Tempers are too Obstinate, and froward, ever to arrive at any great Heigth of this good Quality, yet there is nothing so stubborn, but it may be bent. Assiduity and constant Practice will contract such Habits, as will make any thing easie and familiar, even to the worst contriv'd Disposition; but where Nature concurs, Men are soon Perfect. This is one great advantage Men reap by our Society, nor is it to be despis'd by the Wisest of 'em, who know the use of this Accomplishment, and are sensible, that it is hardly, if at all, to be acquir'd, but by conversing with us, For tho' Men may have Wit and Judgment, yet the Liberty they take of thwarting, and opposing one another makes 'em Eager and

Disputative, Impatient, Sowre, and Moross; till by conversing with us they grow insensibly asham'd of such Rustick Freedom.

5.3 from *The Hardships of the English Laws in relation to Wives*, 1735

In a late Address made to his Majesty by a very ingenious Writer, he presumes upon the Privilege of the Free-born Subjects of *England* to approach their Sovereign, represent their Grievances, and humbly implore Redress.

We hope that this inestimable Privilege is not wholly confined to the *Male* Line, but that we his Majesty's faithful *Female* Subjects, may also shelter ourselves under his most gracious Protection, our Condition being of all others in his Dominions the most deplorable, we being the least able to help ourselves, and the most exposed to Oppression.

This is certainly true, in every State of Life, but in none so notoriously, and without all Redress, as when we put ourselves in a Condition of adding to his Majesty's Subjects by becoming *Wives*, under which Character we humbly address his most sacred Majesty, and the honourable Houses of Parliament, for an Alteration or a Repeal of some Laws, which, as we conceive, put us in a worse Condition than *Slavery* itself.[1]

We are now apprehensive of more frequent Oppression from these Laws, as this is an Age in which the Foundation of all the noble Principles of Christianity (which are our only Protection) are broken up, and *Deism*,[2] that Underminer of all that is truly laudable, with its Legions of Immorality, Prophaneness, and consummate Impudence are let in upon us.

All religious Truths may, and ought to be the Subject of an humble and modest Enquiry; but are by no Means, the proper Objects of Ridicule and Contempt. But since some Men by their extraordinary Flights of Conceit have thought fit to assail the Almighty, and are endeavouring to bring over the rest of their Sex, as fast as they can, 'tis Time for Us to look about us, and to use all justifiable Methods to provide against the impending Danger: For since we seem to be hastening into a *State* of *Nature*, in which there can be no Appeal but to the Laws of our Country, and the Authority of Scripture is going down, which directs a Man to erect a private *Court* of *Equity* in his own Breast, what shall restrain the

Strong from oppressing the *Weak*, if the Laws of our Country do not, they being in such a State the only established Rules of Society?

I humbly hope therefore, that this will not be thought an unseasonable Representation of our Condition, since supposing a Man no Christian, he may be as *Despotick* (excepting the Power over Life itself) as the Grand Seignior in his Seraglio, with this Difference only, that the *English* Husband has but *one Vassal* to treat according to his variable Humour, whereas the Grand Seignior having *many*, it may be supposed, that some of them, at some Times may be suffered to be at quiet.

What our Fate will be God only knows, if the present Wits of the Age should be attended with Success, and strengthened by Numbers. As for Arguments, they are out of the Question with them, their Weapons being *Points* of *Wit, smart Jests*, and *all-confounding Laughter*. These they brandish about against Heaven or Earth, as they happen to oppose their Wills and Inclinations, which stand with them for Reason and Religion.

If therefore we may claim the Privilege of *English* Subjects to speak our Grievances, and be indulged with a gracious Attention, the following Particulars, contain the chief Articles of our Complaint.

I. That the Estate of Wives is more disadvantagious than *Slavery* itself.

II. That Wives may be made Prisoners for Life at the Discretion of their *Domestick Governors*, whose Power, as we at present apprehend, bears no Manner of Proportion to that Degree of Authority, which is vested in any other Set of Men in *England*. For though the Legislature, acting collectively, may dispose of Life and Fortune; no individual, not even the Sovereign himself, can *imprison* any Person for *Life*, at *Will* and *Pleasure;* the *Habeas Corpus* Act,[3] providing for the Condemnation or Enlargement of the Prisoner.

III. That Wives have no Property, neither in their *own Persons, Children*, or *Fortunes*.

I grant the Laws I presume to complain of, gratify some Mens *Pride*, fall in with their *Interest*, and oblige their *Humours;* that they will be very loath to part with them, and that they can plead

Prescription for them. But I deny that they are reasonable or just. All which I shall endeavour to prove,

By Facts, and
By Observations upon them.

Case I. The first Case I cite, was lately determined in the Court of Delegates in Doctor's Commons, relating to the Will of one Mrs. *Lewis* a Widow. While she was in that State she made a Will; soon after she married again; and in some time her second Husband died, and she again became a Widow, without any Children by either Husband. The Will which she made in her first Widowhood remaining, and being found after her Death, the Question was, whether it was a good Will or not? The Council for the Will cited many Authorities from the civil Law, and shewed, that among the *Romans*, if a Man had made his Will, and was afterwards taken *Captive*, such Will *revived* and became again in Force, by the Testator's repossessing his *Liberty:* And thence inferred, that as Marriage was a *State* of *Captivity*, Wills made by Women who became *Free* by Survivorship ought to *revive* with their Freedom.

But the Court finding one Distinction, *viz.* that Marriage was a *voluntary* Act and Captivity the Effect of *Compulsion*, the Judges determined the Will to be void.

Observation, The Arguments of the Council make the Estate of Wives *equal* to, the Distinction of the Court *worse* than, Slavery itself.

. . .

Case IV. The next Instance I shall produce, is the Case of Mr. *Veezey*, tryed at the *Old Bailey*, where it was proved that he confined his Wife for some Years in a Garret, without Fire, proper Cloathing, or any of the Comforts of Life; that he had frequently Horse-whipt her; that her Sufferings were so great and intolerable, that she destroyed her wretched Life by flinging herself out at the Window.

But as there was Bread found in the Room, which, though hard and mouldy, was supposed sufficient to sustain Life; and as it was not thought that he pushed her out at the Window himself, he was acquitted, and that Complaint of her Sufferings served only to instruct Husbands in the full Extent of their despotick Power.

Observation, . . . it appears that Husbands have a more *Afflictive* Power than that of *Life* and *Death*.

About five Years ago, a modest agreeable Gentlewoman, well educated, married a young Tradesman, he set up with a good Fortune of his and hers, and in three Years Time, by his Vices, Extravagancies, and Follies, ran it out every farthing. Upon which he flung himself into the Army, in the Condition of a common foot Soldier.

She then desired his Permission to serve a Lady of Quality, by which means she hoped to be able to provide for their two Children. But he refused it, unless he might have leave to visit her, when he pleased;[4] and the Wages which she should earn, being his not hers, unless it was paid to him, he might have sued the Person, who should entertain her. This effectually barred the Doors against her as a Servant. If by the Kindness of Friends she should be enabled to take an House, and set up in any Way of Business to maintain herself and helpless Infants, it would be only giving him an Opportunity to *Plunder* her at *Discretion*.

The last Resource in such a Case is, to transact her Business in another's Name. But it is very difficult to find a Friend generous enough to involve himself in the intricate Affairs of an helpless undone Woman, who may be commanded from the Place and Employment, at the Pleasure of her Lord and Master, against whose Injunctions she can make no Appeal. The most that her Friends can do, is to afford her a small Pittance by Stealth in the Nature of an Alms, by which she may be sometimes relieved, but never provided for, unless they were in Condition to settle an Estate in Trustee Hands for her Use, which (considering the Power her Husband has over her Person) he may soon convert to his own.

Observation, Hence it appears, that Wives have no Property neither in their intellectual, or personal Abilities, nor in their Fortunes.[5]

. . .

Obj[ection] X. All these are rare Cases, and for the generality Wives have no Reason to complain.

But no Thanks to the Laws of our Country for that Exemption; let every particular Woman who is well treated, thank God and her Husband for the Blessing. At the same Time, she may reflect, that she is in the Condition of a Slave, tho' she is not treated as such, according to the Opinion of a late eminent Member of the House of Commons, who declared in that honourable Assembly, that he thought 'that Nation in a State of Slavery, where any Man had it in his Power to make them so, tho' perhaps the Rod might not always be held over their Backs'.

Tho' I have taken the Liberty to speak my sense of these Laws, and the Consequences of them, which are the Causes of our Complaint; and also to answer some Objections, which I suppos'd might be made, yet I don't presume to address my self to the Legislature to argue, but to refer it to them to decide, and shall humbly and readily acquiesce in their Determinations, upon this and all other Occasions.

But till I am better informed, I hope I may be pardoned, if I confess that I hardly believe it possible to reconcile these Laws, with the Rights and Privileges of a free People. That there should be so great a Part of the Community, who have never been notorious Offenders against it, entirely deprived of their Liberty, or even of making Use of their Ingenuity and Industry to procure them a Subsistance, when those who should provide it for them, refuse it, or are incapable of it.

I suppose the prime Design, and ultimate End of all equitable Governments, is so to proportion Authority and Subjection, that they may in some sort Counter-poise each other; by investing *Governing* with such *Prerogatives*, and allowing the *Governed* such *Privileges*, that each Part may be provided for, according to their several just Pretensions; and that no one Set of People might be exposed to Oppression, either from their publick or private Governors; that Order and Equity may run through all Ranks, and compose one uniform collective Body.

'Tis from these Considerations (I apprehend) that our Laws forbid the buying and selling Men, there being such an absolute Inconsistency in the Conditions of a Free-born *English* Man and a Slave, that they will by no Means comport in the same Community.[6]

From hence also, one Part of domestick Authority is relaxed from what it was amongst the *Romans*. With them a Son was esteemed so much at the Father's Disposition, that by an obsolete Law, the Father was invested with the Power of Life and Death; but afterwards with that of moderate Correction only; yet the Son was still his Father's Property, and could be freed from his Jurisdiction only by being advanced to some dignified Office in the State, or by Emancipation.

The Father's Power over the Son's Property also was very correspondent to that over his Person: But this domestick Authority, being thought inconsistent with the Nature of our free Constitution, which admits not of arbitrary Proceedings, at the Age that a Child is supposed to be able to judge for himself, he is at his own Disposal, as is also his Property.

What I would observe from hence is, that tho' domestick Authority is lessened as to Children, that it is augmented as to Wives, as I have shewn in the foregoing Instances, and that Wives have not a Degree of Liberty and Property, correspondent to that Degree of Liberty and Property, which is allowed all other subordinate Persons in the whole Community.

Omnipotence itself disclaims the Power of doing Evil, the exact Rectitude of the Will of the Almighty is an everlasting Restriction.

Our King, his happiest and greatest Viceregent upon Earth, lays no Claim to the Power of Oppression: and it is no more to the Diminution of his Honour, than it is to the Restraint of his Actions, that our Laws guard us from suffering by his Authority.

Since then, the God of Heaven and Earth, in and from himself, acts always by the Rules of Justice and Mercy; and our Sovereign knows it to be his most distinguishing Honour to be under Obligations to govern his People, by the same unerring Rules; shall I be accused of Confidence or Presumption, for humbly beseeching that our domestick Lords, may be under the same happy Obligations in their private Capacities, which are so true an Honour to our King, in his most illustrious Station?

I hope the Justice and Integrity of my own Heart which acquits me before God, will also plead my Excuse before Men, for making these Representations; especially since I apprehend, that I am justified by the Laws of the Land, which allow every *English* Subject, the Privilege to speak his own Grievances.

. . .

I come now to consider one Objection, which still remains against all I can say, and which I am sensible no Art or Eloquence, can ever obviate, namely, *my Sex.* Custom and Education has dwindled us into very Trifles! such meer Insignificants! that it

may be thought Presumption and Folly in one of us, to presume
to plead our own Cause, even tho' it should appear to be upon the
most justifiable Pretensions.

Notwithstanding this discouraging Reflection, I shall . . .
explain the original Curse of Subjection passed upon the Woman,
and shew that the Laws of *England* go far beyond it.

. . . after the nicest Search Mr. *Wollaston* and Mr. *Hobbs*[7] could
make into Nature, they could find no Foundation in Nature for
that very great Superiority which is ascribed to the Man.

How comes it to pass then, that the Opinions and Customs of all
Nations should give them that Superiority, even when 'tis
supposed they could have had no Information of the Curse of
Subjection passed upon the Woman? I say all Nations, the
Exceptions being too few to destroy a general Rule, tho' enough
to establish Mr. *Hobbs*'s Assertion that the Superiority is not
founded in Nature.

In answer to the foregoing Question, I reply that all Nations are
the Progeny of *Adam* and *Eve*, and that for some Ages after their
Children branched out into Families, they must have had a
Tradition of the Curse of Subjection passed upon the Woman,
and formed the Government of their Families accordingly: When
Men became more numerous upon the Earth, and united
themselves into greater Communities, that Authority was kept
up, even where 'tis possible the Tradition might be lost upon
which it was first founded. And when Men had the Authority, tho'
they might not all know that it was by divine Appointment, it is not
to be imagined that they would voluntarily give it up, but would
rather transmit it from Generation to Generation. And thus it
must be from the very Words of the Curse, which not only
implied a Command to the Wife to obey her Husband, but
contained also a positive Declaration that she should be in that
Subjection, to which God then commanded her Acquiescence.

It is somewhat beside my present Purpose, yet I would observe
here, that as this universal Subjection of the Sex must arise from
this Origin, it is one good Evidence of the Truth of Revelation, for
since it is not a Law of Nature, how should such a Custom spread,
itself through all Nations in all Ages, it if did not take its Rise from
Revelation at first.

. . .

As the Woman's Sin was in the undue Gratification of her *Will*, in her *Will* shall she be punished: She shall depend upon her Husband in all Matters of Pleasure, Diversion, and Delight: Her *Desires* should be circumscribed by his, whom she should reverence in Acquiescence to divine Authority: He should have the supreme command in his Family, and she should act in Subordination to him.

This I humbly apprehend to be the Scripture Extent and Meaning of the Curse. And not that God precluded himself from any farther Authority over the Woman; by delivering her so far into the Power of her Husband, as that she might rob and murder at his Command.

Neither did he preclude the Woman from doing any Good, except she had her Husband's Command or Permission. . . .

I beg to know whether we have not a right by Nature, to be permitted to do all that Good, which God has given us Abilities to do?

And whether it can be supposed that God gave Man an Authority in Opposition to his own?

And whether by the Nature of Societies, and established Rules of Government, all Parts of a Community have not a Right to a Degree of Liberty and Property correspondent to the Constitution under which they live?

'Tis nothing to the Purpose to say, we should make an ill Use of this Liberty, for if the Law of God, and the Rules of Equity allow it us, we have a Right to it, and must answer for the Misapplication of our Liberty (as Husbands do for theirs) to God alone.

Notes

1 By marriage the husband and wife are one person in law: that is the very being or legal existence of the woman is suspended during the marriage, or at least incorporated and consolidated into that of the husband'. (William Blackstone, *Commentaries on the Laws of England*, 1765, (5th edn) I, 442.)
2 Natural religion', belief in the existence of a god without accepting revelation.
3 Writ protecting a prisoner by requiring them to be physically presented in court. (Temporarily suspended in 1794 and 1798 as part of the repressive reaction of Pitt's government to the French Revolution.)

4 A woman's right to refuse conjugal relations even with her estranged husband was not legally guaranteed until 1891.

5 And continued to have none until the Married Women's Property Act was passed in 1882.

6 The position of black slaves in England was less clear-cut. Until the 'Somersett ruling' of 1772 which guaranteed freedom to a slave when they arrived on English soil, the issue was contentious and slaves were openly bought and sold in this country.

7 William Wollaston, *The Religion of Nature Delineated* (1731), and Thomas Hobbes, *Leviathan* (1651): used here as examples of deism (see note 2). The writer accepts their view that in the state of nature women are not inferior to men, but nevertheless wants to disprove their rejection of the truth of revelation.

5.4 'Sophia', from *Beauty's Triumph: or, The Superiority of the Fair Sex invincibly proved*, 1751, Part One, *Woman not Inferior to Man*, 1739

Section II, *'In what esteem the* Women *are held by the* Men, *and how justly'*

Men seem to conclude, that all other creatures were made for them, because they themselves were not created till all were in readiness for them. How far this reasoning will hold good, I will not take upon me to say. But, if it has any weight at all, I am sure it must rather prove, that the *Men* were made for our use than we for their's, as we were not produc'd till they were form'd to receive us, and till it was judg'd by the Creator himself, that they could not be happy without our Society.

That the province of breeding children belongs solely to us, is as certain, as that the office of getting them is wholly their's. And if the latter entitles them to any degree of public esteem and respect, surely the former entitles us to an equal share; since the immediate concurrence of both is so essentially necessary for the propagation of human nature, that either without the other would be entirely useless. Where then is the reason for under-rating us, or claiming superiority over us, for an office in life, in which they bear so equal a share with us? It is too well known to be dissembled, that the office of nursing children is held by the *Men* in a despicable light, as something low and degrading. Whereas, had they nature for their guide, they would not need to be told, that there is no employment in a common-wealth which deserves more honour, or greater thanks and rewards. Let it be consider'd what are the advantages accruing to mankind from it, and it's merit must stand immediately confest. Nay, I know not whether it may not appear to render *Woman* deserving of the first places in civil society.

Why, or to what end, do the individuals of human species associate together, but for the better preservation of life, and the peaceable enjoyment of every thing conducive to that purpose? Do not such then as contribute the most to these public advantages deserve the greatest share of public esteem? And who are these but the *Women*, in the generous disinterested employ of nursing the *Men* in their infancy?

It is from this principle that princes are consider'd as the chief persons in the state, and in quality of such receive the first honours of it; that is, because they are at least supposed to have the greatest share of toil care and foresight for the prosperity of the public weal: So, in proportion, we pay more or less of that respect to such as are under the Sovereign, at a lesser or greater distance from him, because the nearer or farther off they are from sharing with him in the fatigues of serving the public, the more or less useful to society they must be consider'd. For the same reason, we are apt to prefer soldiers to gowns-men; because they are supposed to stand as a bulwark between us and our enemies. And all mankind give to persons such a degree of respect as they suppose them to merit by being useful. And since this is the case throughout life, are not the *Women*, by the very same rule, entitled to the greatest share of public esteem, who are incomparably the greatest contributors to the public good? *Men* can absolutely dispense with princes, merchants, soldiers, lawyers, &c. as they did in the beginning of time, and as savages do still. But can they in their infancy do without nurses? And since they themselves are too awkward for that important office, are not *Women* indispensably wanted? In a peaceful orderly state, the major part of *Men* are useless in their office, with all their authority; but *Women* will never cease to be useful, while there are *Men*, and those *Men* have children. Of what other use are Judges, Magistrates, and their dependant officers in the execution of justice, any more than to secure their property to persons, who, if the Constitution allowed it, wou'd perhaps be able to do themselves justice in a more exact and expeditious manner? But *Women*, more truly useful, are employ'd in preserving their lives to enjoy that property. Soldiers are esteem'd and rewarded because engaged in defending full-grown *Men*, who are equally, and often more, capable of defending themselves. How much more then is our sex worthy their esteem and gratitude, who watch and labour for their safety, when as yet they know not what they are, are unable to distinguish between friends and foes, and are naked of every defence but that of tears! If princes and statesmen sometimes exert themselves in the service of the public, ambition is their motive, and power, riches, or splendor, the point of view. But our more generous souls are bias'd only by the good we do to the children we breed and nurture: Daily experience reminding us, that all the gratification we can hope for from the unnatural creatures, for the almost infinite pains, anxieties, care, and assiduities to which we subject ourselves on their account, and which cannot be matched in any other state of civil society, is an ungrateful treatment of our persons, and the basest contempt of our sex in general. Such the generous offices we do them: Such the ungenerous returns they make us!

Surely then nothing but a corrupt imagination can make *Men* look upon an office of such high importance to them, as mean and contemptible, or as less valuable than it really is. How largely are they rewarded who succeed in taming a tyger, an elephant, or such like animals; and shall *Women* be neglected for spending years in the taming that *fiercer animal* MAN? If the source of this unjust partiality be inquired into, we shall find, that the only cause why these important services done by US are too little valued, is, their being so frequent and usual.

However, as the pleasure, which the generosity of our sex makes us take in that office, is sufficient to make us discharge ourselves of it with the utmost tenderness, without any view of reward, I do not here mean to complain of our receiving none. I would only beg leave to say, that our being so much more capable than the male kind to execute that office well, no ways proves us unqualified to execute any other. Indeed, the *Men* themselves seem tacitly agreed to acknowledge as much: But then, according to their wonted disinterestedness, they are still for confining all our other Talents to the pleasant limits of obeying and gratifying our masters. . . .

Section III, 'Whether Women *are inferior to* Men *in their intellectual capacity, or not*'

... It is a very great absurdity, to argue that learning is useless to *Women*, because forsooth they have not a share in public offices, which is the end for which *Men* apply themselves to it. *Virtue* and *felicity* are equally requisite in a private as in a public station, and *learning* is a necessary means to both. It is by that we acquire an exactness of thought, a propriety of speech, and a justness of action: Without that we can never have a right knowledge of ourselves: It is that which enables us to distinguish between right and wrong, true and false: And finally, that alone can give us skill to regulate our passions, by teaching us, that true happiness and virtue consist not so much in enlarging our possessions as in contracting our desires.

Besides, let it be observed, what a wretched circle this poor way of reasoning among the *Men* draws them insensibly into. Why is *learning* useless to us? because we have no share in public offices. And why have we no share in public offices? because we have no *learning*. They are sensible of the injustice they do us, and are reduced to the mean shift of cloaking it at the expence of their own reason. But let truth speak for once: Why are they so industrious to debar us that learning, we have an equal right to with themselves, but for fear of our sharing with, and outshining them, those public offices they fill so miserably? The same sordid selfishness which urges them to engross all power and dignity to themselves, prompts them to shut up from us that knowledge which wou'd have made us their competitors.

As nature seems to have design'd the *Men* for our drudges, I cou'd easily forgive them the usurpation by which they first took the trouble of public employments off our hands, if their injustice were content with stopping there. But as one abyss calls on another, and vices seldom go single, they are not satisfied with engrossing all authority into their own hands, but are confident enough to assert that they possess it by right. Their reason for this assertion is what I have already hinted at, *viz.* because we were form'd by nature to be under perpetual subjection to them, for want of abilities to share with them in *government* and *public offices*.

Section V, 'Whether the Women *are fit for public offices, or not*'

... But why do the *Men* persuade themselves that we are less fit for public employments than they are? Can they give any better reason than custom, and prejudice, form'd in them by external appearances, for want of a closer examination? If they did but give themselves the leisure to trace things back to their fountain-head, and judge of the sentiments and practices of *Men* in former ages from what they discover in their own times, they would not be so open as they are to errors and absurdities in all their opinions. And particularly with regard to *Women*, they wou'd be able to see, that if we have been subjected to their authority, it has been by no other law than that of the stronger: And that we have not been excluded from a share in the power and privileges which lift their sex above ours, for want of natural capacity, or merit, but for want of an equal spirit of violence, shameless injustice, and lawless oppression, with theirs.

Nevertheless, so weak are their intellectuals, and so untuned are their organs to the voice of reason, that custom makes more absolute slaves of their senses than they can make of us. They are so inur'd to see things as they now are, that they cannot represent to themselves how they can be otherwise. It wou'd be extremely odd, they think, to see a *Woman* at the head of an army giving battle; or at the helm of a nation giving laws; pleading causes in a court of judicature; preceded in the street with sword, mace, and other ensigns of authority, as magistrates; or teaching rhetoric, medicine, philosophy, and divinity, in quality of university professors.

If by oddity they understand something in its nature opposite to the genuine unbias'd rules of good-sense, I believe the *Men* will find it a difficult task, to prove the oddity in such a sight, or any real inconsistence in it with *rectified reason*. For if *Women* are but considered as rational creatures, abstracted from the disadvantages imposed upon them by the unjust usurpation and tyranny of the *Men*, they will be found, to the full, as capable as the *Men*, of filling these offices. ['Sophia' makes her point by citing examples of individual women's achievements.] ...

I must own, indeed, in this age, to see a *Woman*, however well qualified, exert herself in any of these employments, cou'd not but as greatly surprize us, as to see a man or woman drest in the garb worn in the days of *W*. RUFUS. And yet our wonder in either case wou'd be the sole effect of novelty, or of the revival of an obsolete custom, new to us. If from time immemorial the *Men* had been so little envious, and so very impartial, as to do justice to our abilities, by admitting us to our right of sharing with them in public action, they wou'd have been as accustom'd to see us filling public offices, as we are to see them disgrace them; and to see a lady at a bar, or on a bench, wou'd have been no more strange, than it is now, to see a grave judge whimpering at his maid's knees, or, a lord embroidering his wife's petticoat: A *Schurman*,[1] with a thesis in her hand, displaying nature in it's most innocent useful lights, wou'd have been as familiar a sight, as a physician in his chariot conning *Ovid's* Art of Love: And an *Amazon*, with an helmet on her head, animating her embattled troops, wou'd have been no more a matter of surprize, than a milliner behind a counter with a thimble on her finger, or than a peer of *Great Britain* playing with his *garter*. . . .

Section VII, '*Whether* Women *are naturally qualified for military offices, or not*'

. . . There can be no real difference pointed out between the inward or outward constitution of *Men* and *Women*, excepting what merely tends to giving birth to posterity. And the differences thence arising are no ways sufficient to argue more natural strength in the one than in the other, to qualify them more for military labours. Are not the *Women* of different degrees of strength, like the *Men*? Are there not strong and weak of both sexes? *Men* educated in sloth and softness are weaker than *Women;* and *Women*, become harden'd by necessity, are often more robust than *Men*. . . .

What has greatly helped to confirm the *Men* in the prejudiced notion of *Women's* natural weakness, is the common manner of expression which this very vulgar error gave birth to. When they mean to stigmatise a *Man* with want of courage they call him *effeminate*, and when they would praise a *Woman* for her courage they call her *manly*. But as these, and such like expressions, are merely arbitrary, and but a fulsome compliment which the *Men* pass on themselves, they establish nothing. The real truth is, That humanity and integrity, the characteristics of our sex, make us abhor unjust slaughter, and prefer honourable peace to unjust war. And therefore, to use these expressions with propriety, when a *Man* is possest of our virtues he should be call'd effeminate by way of the highest praise of his good-nature and justice; and a *Woman* who departs from our sex by espousing the injustice and cruelty of the *Men's* nature, should be call'd a *Man: that is*, one whom no sacred ties can bind to the observation of just treaties, and whom no blood-shed can deter from the most cruental violence and rapine.

Note

1 Schurman: see 4.1, note 3.

5.5 Mary Hays, from *Appeal to the Men of Great Britain in behalf of the Women*, 1798

'What Men Would Have Women To Be'

Of all the systems, – if indeed a bundle of contradictions and absurdities may be called a system, – which human nature in its moments of intoxication has produced; that which men have contrived with a view to forming the minds, and regulating the conduct of women, is perhaps the most completely absurd. And, though the consequences are often very serious to both sexes, yet if one could for a moment forget these, and consider it only as a system, it would rather be found a subject of mirth and ridicule than serious anger.

What a chaos! – What a mixture of strength and weakness, – of greatness and littleness, – of sense and folly, – of exquisite feeling and total insensibility, – have they jumbled together in their imaginations, – and then given to their pretty darling the name of woman! How unlike the father of gods and men, the gay, the gallant Jupiter, who on producing wisdom the fruit of his brains, presented it to admiring worlds under the character of a female!

But in the composition of Man's woman, wisdom must not be spoken of, nay nor even hinted at, yet strange to tell! there it must be in full force, and come forth upon all convenient occasions. This is a mystery which, as we are not allowed to be amongst the initiated, we may admire at an awful distance, but can never comprehend.

Again how great in some parts of their conduct, and how insignificant upon the whole, would men have women to be! For one example; – when their love, their pride, their delicacy; in short, when all the finest feelings of humanity are insulted and put to the rack, what is the line of conduct, then expected from them?

I need not explain that the situation I here allude to is, – when a woman finds that the husband of her choice, the object of her most sincere and constant love, abandons himself to other attachments; and not only this, but when, – the natural consequences of these, – estrangement of affection and estrangement of confidence follow, which are infinitely cutting to a woman of sensibility and soul; what I say is the line of conduct then expected from a creature declared to be, – weak by nature, and who is rendered still weaker by education?

Now here is one of those absurdities of which I accuse men in their system of contradictions. They expect that this poor weak creature, setting aside in a moment, love, jealousy, and pride, the most powerful and universal passions interwoven in the human heart, and which even men, clothed in wisdom and fortitude, find so difficult to conquer, that they seldom attempt it – that she shall notwithstanding lay all these aside as easily as she would her gown and petticoat, and plunge at once into the cold bath of prudence, of which though the wife only is to receive the shock, and make daily use of, yet if she does so, it has the virtue of keeping both husband and wife in a most agreeable temperament. Prudence being one of those rare medicines which affect by sympathy, and this being likewise one of those cases, where the husbands have no objections to the wives acting as principals, nor to their receiving all the honor and emoluments of office; even if death should crown their martyrdom, as has been sometimes known to happen.

Dear, generous creatures!

. . . may I be permitted to advise men to consider, whether it would not be better for them to be more consistent, and not quite so unreasonable, with regard to their expectations as to the character and conduct of women? And may I be permitted to add, more guarded and exemplary in their own? For, though men declare themselves superior to women in degree, yet in kind they must acknowledge themselves so closely akin, that their example by the very superiority they claim, is of the greater necessity, because the more likely to be followed. Indeed, if carrying every thing agreed upon by the common sense of mankind to be called good, to its utmost perfection on the one hand; and if on the other, suppressing every baser passion, compose what we call virtue; and if that virtue is not to be reduced to a name, a mere political engine in the hands of the most powerful, – Where is perfection to be expected but in man? – where but in him who declares himself to be - Lord paramount, of the creation? Why will not people consider how much more difficult it is to support, than to assume superiority of character!

Notwithstanding this declaration of their own superiority however, it is a compliment which men are by no means backward in paying to women, that they are better formed by nature than themselves, for the perfection of virtue; and especially of those virtues which are of most difficult attainment, and which occur most commonly in life. Perhaps this may be true; but if so, it is granting all and more than I wish; for the moment that this is admitted, you either degrade virtue and all good morals, by supposing them capable of being perfected by, and best suited to, beings of an inferior order – upon which terms no order of rational beings can be supposed very anxious about the attainment of them – Or, leaving these, I mean virtue and good morals, in their proper places, and supposing them inherent in the soul of man, because planted there by the hand of God; and yet still insisting on the necessity and propriety of women practising them, in a stricter degree than men; you from that moment, I say, tacitly grant to women, that superiority of mind, which you have not generosity enough openly to avow.

But we relinquish willingly this kind of preference which you force upon us, and which we have no title to; and which indeed is an intolerable burthen in the way you contrive to administer it; and instead of this, we only entreat of you to be fair, to be candid, and to admit, that both sexes are upon a footing of equality, when they are permitted to exert in their different spheres of action, the talents their Creator has been pleased to bestow upon them.

. . .

If then the sex in general, agree in thinking themselves injured, and compelled to act a part in society unequal to their abilities, and pretensions; how honourable would it be for men, to turn some degree of their attention to a subject, which viewed in every light is of such consequence to mankind! And if after examining it with the same impartiality, which they would expect and demand, in any case where their own interest were concerned; they should find little to applaud in their old system, and little to fear from a new one properly regulated; – how honourable would it be to restore to woman that freedom, which the God of nature seems manifestly to have intended, for every living creature! Liberty, – rational liberty, – such as is consistent with the good order of every branch of society, and in which sense only I would be thought to use the term, never yet injured, man, woman, or child. For though I cannot perhaps express myself, with philosophical precision and propriety; yet I shall be understood when I say, that I hold liberty to be in the moral world, what the very air which we breathe, is to animal and vegetable life. In each case existence is possible with a small, or a moderate degree. Without any, physical, and moral death must ensue. The air itself indeed, on which our life depends, may be rendered as noxious as salutary; and may be condensed, or rarified, till unfit for the purposes of existence – Or impelled by natural causes, engender storms and tempests, which deform the face of creation.

So Liberty, when she 'oversteps the modesty of nature,' changes her very essence, is transformed from our good to our evil genius, and instead of her who cherishes and renovates the heart of man, 'Aye and of woman too,' and under whose auspices every thing great and good must flourish; she becomes a fiend spreading devastation and death around, and leaving her deluded followers, only a shadow and a name.

The desirable point therefore in all cases surely is that, where, as much freedom is enjoyed as is required, to bring forth every degree of possible perfection. And to this point in morals, should all legislation tend, whatever obstacles or prejudices lie in the way.

Now it is to this degree of liberty, as near as human imperfection can manage the matter, that I wish to see a prospect of women being advanced; for, as I have already said, perhaps it might not be safe to entrust them all at once with freedom in that extent which is their due.

Possibly it is better that the mind, as well as the body, should be prepared by degrees to receive any change, or lasting improvement. Perhaps this holds true even in the grand political scale of life; perhaps even there, prudence and good politics go hand in hand. But surely, and without a doubt, moderation ought always to dictate the more private, yet not less interesting appeals, of the one sex to the other.

It is indeed absurd to suppose, from the reasons already advanced, and from a thousand others, that men will see the propriety or the justice of laying aside all at once, claims which they have been accustomed to consider as founded in nature, and supported by reason; – but it is neither absurd nor chimerical to suppose, that men may by degrees, and by calm representation, be brought to consider the subject as they ought, and are bound in justice and honour to do. And this once done there is no reason to fear, but that retribution will naturally follow.

In opposition to this hope, that the situation of women may by degrees be bettered, it may be answered; that since ages have elapsed without women having been in any country put upon the footing which I contend is their due; it amounts almost to a decisive proof, that they will, and ought to remain, pretty nearly on the footing they have been and are; allowing for little alterations, in compliance with times and circumstances.

Now this reasoning I apprehend to be fully more in favor of women than against them; and it brings one of my strongest arguments home. Since, except the experiment had been fairly made, and they been allowed the same advantages of education as men, and permitted to exert in their fullest extent those talents with which their Creator may have endowed them; who is entitled to say, what might have been the consequences to the world? For my part I am sanguine enough to think, that from such an attention to improving the minds, and forming the characters of women, as I propose; consequences of the highest importance would ensue. – Perhaps it is not too bold to say, that to the erroneous ideas with regard to women which have been allowed from indulgence and want of opposition, to take so deep root among mankind, it may be partly imputed, that society has never been upon so perfect a plan as it might have been. And perhaps it is not too daring to prophesy, that till these prejudices are exterminated and done away as if they had never been; society can never arrive at that state of perfection, of which it is really capable.

. . .

Before I quit this subject [female modesty and 'the licentiousness of men'], I am going to recommend, and that perhaps somewhat at large, a species of humanity not much cultivated; but which I consider as worthy of the serious attention of my own sex – and it is this. That however amiable, and indispensable, modesty – the virtue of which we have been treating – undoubtedly is; yet that those who possess it in the most eminent degree, are not entitled upon that account, to despise or condemn too rigorously, that unfortunate portion of the sex who have fallen victims to vice – Or rather let me say to the arts of men; who, by an absurdity of conduct which no good system of morality can possibly countenance, talk indeed of female virtue, and seem even by their laws, to consider it as the chief bond of society; yet never scruple to break this bond, when instigated by a passion, which so ill deserves the name of love, that hatred itself cannot produce consequences so dreadful to the unhappy objects of it.

Did women of virtue then consider; – had they but opportunities of knowing the insinuating, though base arts used by profligate men, to seduce innocent and unsuspecting females – and what sacrifices of truth and honor it often costs them to succeed even with women, who, afterwards perhaps by a train of unfortunate circumstances, turn out pre-eminent in vice, and disgrace to their sex and to human nature – I repeat it, had a virtuous and humane woman but access to know, and consider all these – she would look inward upon herself and say – If I have more purity of heart and conduct, than these unfortunate sisters, have I not more cause for thankfulness than triumph? Can I lay my hand upon my heart and say, what would have been my conduct, precisely in the same circumstances?

When conscience answers these questions, in the way that she most certainly will do, we shall then find two admirable lessons inculcated upon us; – with regard to others pity to the unfortunate; – with regard to ourselves, the most scrupulous caution to avoid whatever has the most remote tendency, to sully the purity of the mind or manners. Not but that I am perfectly convinced that there are of both sexes, whose virtues are of a nature too exalted, and founded upon principles too sacred, to be moved perhaps by any temptation whatever. To say that those who are virtuous are only so, because they have had no temptation to be otherwise, would be lowering the standard of goodness indeed; and would too, be experimentally false; for many have resisted every temptation that imagination can paint. I only would hint, that it is hard to judge, whether the unhappy class of females we allude to, may not be generally, more objects of pity than blame. And indeed I cannot help considering it as a matter of great importance to society, to inculcate; – that compassion and an attention to the circumstances which may have led to the destruction of such, are more likely means of producing reformation among them, and stopping the progress of vice; than that hatred, contempt, and terror, which the modest and virtuous, perhaps, naturally enough feel for such characters, when these are not taken into consideration.

I have heretofore been speaking of those, who, by continuing in the practice of vice, are generally supposed to preclude all sympathy. Yet even in these worst of cases, when we consider among other things, how difficult the return to virtue is made; we must balance well, before we judge rigorously. And if so, how much more compassion is justly due to those, whose quick return to the paths of rectitude, proves, that in some minds nothing can totally extinguish the love of virtue; – not even an acquaintance with its most deadly foe, – not even the blandishments of vice itself. To such penitents every encouragement should undoubtedly be given, that is consistent with delicacy and propriety, and particularly by their own sex; who, are upon every account, much fitter for such a task, than men – feeble advocates, alas! and dangerous patrons, for returning virtue.

Enough has now been said, and it may be supposed by some, too much, upon a topic not the most agreeable. – I have only to urge in my defence, that upon this, as well as upon every other subject on which I have touched; I have the interests of society, and especially of the unfortunate, and unfriended, sincerely at heart.

5.6 'Anne Frances Randall' [Mary Robinson], from *A Letter to the Women of England, on the Injustice of Mental Subordination*, 1799

Supposing that a WOMAN has experienced every insult, every injury, that her vain-boasting, high-bearing associate, man, can inflict: imagine her, driven from society; deserted by her kindred; scoffed at by the world; exposed to poverty; assailed by malice; and consigned to scorn: with no companion but sorrow, no prospect but disgrace; she has no remedy. She appeals to the feeling and reflecting part of mankind; they pity, but they do not seek to redress her: she flies to her own sex, they not only condemn, but they avoid her. She talks of punishing the villain who has destroyed her: he smiles at the menace, and tells her, *she is*, a WOMAN.

Let me ask this plain and rational question, – is not woman a human being, gifted with all the feelings that inhabit the bosom of man? Has not woman affections, susceptibility, fortitude, and an acute sense of injuries received? does she not shrink at the touch of persecution? Does not her bosom melt with sympathy, throb with pity, glow with resentment, ache with sensibility, and burn with indignation? Why then is she denied the exercise of the nobler feelings, an high consciousness of honour, a lively sense of what is due to dignity of character? Why may not woman resent and punish? Because the long established laws of custom, have decreed her *passive!* Because she is by nature organized to feel every wrong more acutely, and yet, by a barbarous policy, denied the power to assert the first of Nature's rights, self-preservation.

How many vices are there that men perpetually indulge in, to which women are rarely addicted. Drinking, in man, is reckoned a proof of good fellowship; and the *bon vivant* is considered as the best and most desirable of companions. Wine, as far as it is pleasant to the sense of tasting, is as agreeable to woman as to man; but its use to excess will render either brutal. Yet man *yields* to its influence, because he is the *stronger-minded* creature; and woman *resists* its power over the senses, because she is the *weaker*. How will the *superiorly* organized sex defend this contradiction? Man will say his passions are stronger than those of women; yet we see women rush not only to ruin, but to death, for objects they love; while men exult in an unmeaning display of caprice, intrigue, and seduction, frequently, without even a zest for the vices they exhibit. The fact is simply this: the passions of men originate in sensuality; those of women, in sentiment: man loves corporeally, woman mentally: which is the nobler creature?

Gaming is termed, in the modern vocabulary, a masculine vice. Has vice then a *sex*? Till the passions of the mind in man and woman are separate and distinct, till the sex of vital animation, denominated soul, be ascertained, on what pretext is woman deprived of those amusements which man is permitted to enjoy? If gaming be a vice (though every species of commerce is nearly allied to it), why not condemn it wholly? why suffer man to persevere in the practice of it; and yet in woman execrate its propensity? Man may enjoy the convivial board, indulge the caprices of his nature; he may desert his home, violate his marriage vows, scoff at the moral laws that unite society, and set even religion at defiance, by oppressing the defenceless; while woman is condemned to bear the drudgery of domestic life, to vegetate in obscurity, to *love* where she abhors, to *honour* where she despises, and to *obey*, while she shudders at subordination. Why? Let the most cunning sophist, answer me, WHY?

. . .

In what is woman inferior to man? In some instances, but not always, in corporeal strength: in activity of mind, she is his equal. Then, by this rule, if she is to endure oppression in proportion as she is deficient in muscular power, *only*, through all the stages of animation the weaker should give precedence to the stronger. Yet we should find a Lord of the Creation with a puny frame, reluctant to confess the superiority of a lusty peasant girl, whom nature had endowed with that bodily strength of which luxury had bereaved him.

The question is simply this: Is woman persecuted and oppressed because she is the *weaker* creature? Supposing that to be the order of Nature; let me ask these human despots, whether a woman, of strong mental and corporeal powers, is born to yield obedience, merely because *she is a woman*, to those shadows of mankind who exhibit the effeminacy of women, united with the mischievous foolery of monkies? I remember once, to have heard one of those modern Hannibals confess, that he had changed his regiments three times, because the regimentals were *unbecoming!*

If woman be the *weaker* creature, why is she employed in laborious avocations? why compelled to endure the fatigue of household drudgery; to scrub, to scower, to labour, both late and early, while the powdered lacquey only waits at the chair, or behind the carriage of his employer? Why are women, in many parts of the kingdom, permitted to follow the plough; to perform the laborious business of the dairy; to work in our manufactories; to wash, to brew, and to bake, while men are employed in measuring lace and ribands; folding gauzes; composing artificial bouquets; fancying feathers, and mixing cosmetics for the preservation of beauty? I have seen, and every inhabitant of the metropolis may, during the summer season, behold strong Welsh girls carrying on their heads strawberries, and other fruits from the vicinity of London to Covent-Garden market, in heavy loads which they repeat three, four, and five times, daily, for a very small pittance; while the *male* domesticks of our nobility are revelling in luxury, to which even their lords are strangers. Are women thus compelled to labour, because they are of the WEAKER SEX?

. . .

Prejudice (or policy) has endeavoured, and indeed too successfully, to cast an odium on what is called a *masculine* woman; or, to explain the meaning of the word, a woman of enlightened understanding. Such a being is too formidable in the circle of society to be endured, much less sanctioned. Man is a despot by nature; he can bear no equal, he dreads the power of woman; because he knows that already half the felicities of life depend on her; and that if she be permitted to demand an equal share in the regulations of social order, she will become omnipotent.

I again recur to the prominent subject of my letter, viz. that woman is denied the first privilege of nature, the power of SELF-DEFENCE. There are lords of the creation, who would not hesitate to rob a credulous woman of fortune, happiness, and reputation, yet they would deem themselves justified in punishing a petty thief, who took from them a watch or a pocket handkerchief. *Man* is not to be deprived of *his* property; *he* is not to be pilfered of the most trifling article, which custom has told him is necessary to *his* ideas of luxury. But WOMAN is to be robbed of that peace of mind which depended on the purity of her character; *she* is to be duped out of all the proud consolations of independence; defrauded of her repose, wounded in the sensibilities of her heart; and, because she is of the *weaker* sex, she is to bear her injuries with *fortitude*.

. . .

Why are women excluded from the auditory part of the British senate? The welfare of their country, cannot fail to interest their feelings; and eloquence both exalts and refines the understanding[a]. Man makes woman a frivolous creature, and then condemns her for the folly he inculcates. He tells her, that beauty is her first and most powerful attraction; her second complacency of temper, and softness of manners. She therefore dedicates half her hours to the embellishment of her person, and the other half to the practice of soft, languishing, sentimental insipidity. She disdains to be strong minded, because she fears being accounted masculine; she trembles at every breeze, faints at every peril, and yields to every assailant, because it would be unwomanly to defend herself. . . .

The embargo upon words, the enforcement of tacit submission, has been productive of consequences highly honourable to the women of the present age. Since the sex have been condemned for exercising the powers of speech, they have successfully taken up the pen and their writings exemplify both energy of mind, and capability of acquiring the most extensive knowledge. The press will be the monuments from which the genius of British women will rise to immortal celebrity: their works will, in proportion as their educations are liberal, from year to year, challenge an equal portion of fame, with the labours of their classical *male* contemporaries!

In proportion as women are acquainted with the languages they will become citizens of the world. The laws, customs and inhabitants of different nations will be their kindred in the propinquity of nature. Prejudice will be palsied, if not receive its death blow, by the expansion of intellect: and woman being permitted to feel her own importance in the scale of society, will be tenacious of maintaining it. She will know that she was created for something beyond the mere amusement of man; that she is capable of mental energies, and worthy of the most unbounded confidence. Such a system of mental equality, would, while it

stigmatized the trifling vain and pernicious race of high fash-
ioned Messalinas, produce such British women, as would equal
the Portias and Arrias of antiquity[b].

Had fortune enabled me, I would build an UNIVERSITY
FOR WOMEN; where they should be politely, and at the same
time classically educated; the depth of their studies, should be
proportioned to their mental powers; and those who were
incompetent to the labours of knowledge, should be dismissed after a
fair trial of their capabilities, and allotted to the more humble
paths of life; such as *domestic and useful occupations*. The wealthy
part of the community who neglected to educate their female
offspring, at this seminary of learning, should pay a fine, which
should be appropriated to the maintenance of the unportioned
scholars. In half a century there would be a sufficient number of
learned women to fill all the departments of the university, and
those who excelled in an eminent degree should receive honorary
medals, which they should wear as an ORDER of LITERARY
MERIT.

O! my unenlightened country-women! read, and profit, by the
admonition of Reason. Shake off the trifling, glittering shackles,
which debase you. Resist those fascinating spells which, like the
petrifying torpedo, fasten on your mental faculties. Be less the
slaves of vanity, and more the converts of Reflection. Nature has
endowed you with personal attractions: she has also given you the
mind capable of expansion. Seek not the visionary triumph of
universal conquest; know yourselves equal to greater, nobler,
acquirements: and by prudence, temperance, firmness, and
reflection, subdue that prejudice which has, for ages past, been
your inveterate enemy. Let your daughters be liberally, classically, philosophically[c], and usefully educated; let them speak
and write their opinions freely; let them read and think like
rational creatures; adapt their studies to their strength of
intellect; expand their minds, and purify their hearts, by teaching
them to feel their mental equality with their imperious rulers. By
such laudable exertions, you will excite the noblest emulation;
you will explode the superstitious tenets of bigotry and fanati-
cism; confirm the intuitive immortality of the soul, and give them
that genuine glow of conscious virtue which will grace them to
posterity.

Notes

(a) Many of the American tribes admit women into their public councils, and allow them the privileges of giving their opinions, *first*, on every subject of deliberation. The ancient Britons allowed the female sex the same right: but in modern Britain women are scarcely allowed to express any opinions at all!

(b) Paetus being commanded by the emperor Nero, to die by his own hands, his wife [Arria], an illustrious Roman woman, was permitted to take leave of him. She felt the impossibility of surviving him, and plunging the poniard into her bosom, exclaimed *'Paetus it is not much,'* and instantly expired. This anecdote I relate for the information of my unlearned readers. [Portia: wife of Marcus Brutus, ardent supporter of the republican cause, said to have wounded herself to prove herself worthy of being told of the conspiracy against Julius Caesar.]

(c) By Philosophy, the writer of this Letter means rational wisdom, neither the flimsy cobwebs of pretended metaphysical and logical mysteries; nor the unbridled liberty which would lead to the boldness of licentious usurpation. A truly enlightened woman never will forget that conscious dignity of character which ennobles and sustains, but never did DEBASE her.

NOTES ON AUTHORS

(See also Janet Todd (ed.), *A Dictionary of British and American Women Writers 1650–1800*, London, 1984.)

Mary Astell (5.1): (1666–1731) feminist and religious polemicist, she gained public respect with *Letters Concerning the Love of God* (1695), her correspondence with John Norris of Bemerton. She was a defender of the High Church Tory position against religious toleration, and in *Some Reflections on Marriage* (1700), she typically combines respect for institutional authority with strong feminist views. Her example as an independent intellectual influenced Mary Chudleigh, Elizabeth Elstob (Anglo-Saxon scholar), and Lady Mary Wortley Montagu.

Elizabeth Carter (4.11): (1717–1806) scholar, poet, translator, and essayist, she was a member of the Bluestocking circle and is best known for her translation of Epictetus which became the standard English version.

Susanna Centlivre (4.9): (d.1723) playwright whose plays were very popular after some initial hostility to her as a woman. She is best known for *The Busy Body* (1709).

Hester Mulso Chapone (3.2): (1727–1801) poet and essayist, she was a friend of Elizabeth Carter and Elizabeth Montagu and a member of Richardson's circle. *Letters on the Improvement of the Mind* is her most important work. She also published *Miscellanies in Prose and Verse* (1775).

Charlotte Charke (4.8): (1713–60) actress, playwright, novelist, and autobiographer, she was the daughter of Colley Cibber, actor-manager of Drury Lane theatre. An itinerant player who at times dressed as a man

244

to avoid creditors, she is best known for her autobiography, which was in part an attempt at reconciliation with her estranged father.

Lady Mary Chudleigh (4.2): (1656–1710) poet and essayist, and admirer of Mary Astell, she is best known for her poem *The Ladies Defence: or, The Bride Woman's Counsellor Answer'd* (1700), an answer to a sermon preached in 1699 by John Sprint arguing that wives owed absolute obedience to their husbands.

Mary Collier (4.5): (fl.1740–60) poet – and 'Washer-Woman', according to her 'Advertisement' to *The Woman's Labour*. She also published *Poems on Several Occasions* (1762) and *The Poems of Mary Collier* (1765?).

Daniel Defoe (2.3): (1660–1731) prolific journalist, polemical writer and novelist, he was one of the major nonconformist ideologues of the new bourgeoisie. His works include instructional manuals, of which *The Family Instructor* (1715), *Religious Courtship* (1722), and *The Complete English Tradesman* (1725) are the most well-known, and novels, including *Moll Flanders* (1722) and *Roxana or, the Fortunate Mistress* (1724).

Joseph Dorman (2.4): known only as the author of *The Female Rake* and of a play, *Sir Roger de Coverly* (1740).

John Duncombe (4.1): (1729–86) poet and writer on archaeology, he was the husband of Susanna Highmore, poet, artist, and member of the Richardson circle.

Anne Dutton (4.6): (1692–1765) a Methodist and prolific religious writer, she corresponded with Wesley on the question of Election.

François de Salignac de la Mothe-Fénélon (3.1): (1651–1715) French religious and educational writer, he was Archbishop of Cambrai and tutor of the Duc de Bourgogne, grandson of Louis XIV.

James Fordyce (4.13): (1720–1796) poet and moderate evangelical presbyterian divine, he was a popular preacher in London during the 1760s.

Robert Gould (2.1): (d.1709?) satirist and playwright. As well as *Love Given O're* he wrote *A Satyr against Man* (1689) and poems in praise of individual women.

Catherine Macaulay Graham (3.5): (1731–91) Whig historian, best known for her *History of England from the Accession of James I to that of the Brunswick Line* (1763–83). This was the first history of the Civil War written by a woman and a republican. She wrote radical Wilkite pamphlets in the 1770s and in 1791 a reply to Burke's *Reflections on the Revolution in France*.

John Gregory (1.6): (1724–73) professor of medicine, University of Edinburgh.

Laetitia Matilda Hawkins (3.7): (1759–1835) novelist and miscellaneous writer, she was strictly educated by her father and claimed to have written many novels which she was 'ashamed' to reveal to her family and publish. An admirer of Hannah More, she similarly combined commitment to women and women's education with a deeply conformist view of their role.

Mary Hays (5.5): (1760–1843) novelist and polemicist, she was a member of radical Dissenting circles in the 1780s and 1790s, influenced by Wollstonecraft's *Vindication of the Rights of Woman*. Her novels, *Memoirs of Emma Courtney* (1796) and *The Victim of Prejudice* (1799), explore the effects on women of restrictive moral conventions. She was attacked by conservatives and became less radical in her later years, admiring Hannah More.

Eliza Haywood (1.5, 4.4): (1693–1756) novelist and periodical writer, her early fiction, influenced by Manley, consisted mainly of seduction narratives (the first of which was the hugely popular *Love in Excess*, 1719) which were extremely popular but criticized for immorality. She cultivated a more acceptable image in later works such as *The Female Spectator*, 1744–6 and *The History of Miss Betsy Thoughtless*, 1751.

Vicesimus Knox (3.3): (1752–1821) scholar, schoolmaster, Whig supporter and prolific writer, his *Letters Moral and Literary* were praised by Samuel Johnson.

Bernard Mandeville (2.2): (1670?–1733) best known as the author of *The Fable of the Bees* (1714–25) which expounds the motto 'private vices, public benefits'.

[Mary] Delarivière Manley (4.3): (1663–1724) novelist, playwright, and political journalist for the Tory interest. She was editor of *The Examiner*, and best known in her lifetime for *The New Atalantis* (1709), a scandal novel attacking pseudonymous contemporary figures and based on a series of seduction narratives.

Martha Mears (2.10): (dates unknown) trained midwife and the last major contributor to the eighteenth-century midwifery dispute.

Hannah More (3.9): (1745–1833) a teacher turned professional writer, a member of the Bluestocking circle, and anti-Jacobin propagandist. Her major works, such as *Cheap Repository Tracts* (1798), are concerned to educate the poor into accepting their station in life. An important member of the evangelical philanthropic movement, she was criticized by other conservatives for teaching the poor to read at all.

Teresia Constantia Phillips (4.16): (1709–65) courtesan and auto-biographer. She was imprisoned for debt several times. Her *Memoirs*, which are mainly about her husband's attempted annulment of their marriage, brought her brief financial independence.

Richard Polwhele (4.19): (1760–1838) miscellaneous writer who contributed to the *Gentleman's Magazine* and wrote frequently for the *Anti-Jacobin Review*.

Clara Reeve (3.6, 4.18): (1729–1807) didactic novelist and critic, she was best known for her Gothic novel *The Old English Baron* (1778).

Samuel Richardson (1.4): (1689–1761) printer and novelist, he was the centre of a group of educated women which included Hester Chapone and Susanna Highmore, and the author of epistolary novels *Pamela* (1740), *Clarissa* (1747–9), and *Sir Charles Grandison* (1753–4) which were influenced by and influential on, women's fiction.

Mary Robinson (5.6): (1758–1800) poet and novelist, she was educated at Hannah More's school in Bristol. She was very popular as an actress in the 1770s and, briefly, mistress of the Prince of Wales. She began to write when ill-health made acting impossible and was attacked for immorality and for her liberal views. Her novels combine sentimental morality with an Enlightenment concern with justice and social criticism.

Elizabeth Singer Rowe (1.2, 4.1): (1674–1737) Dissenting writer on moral and religious subjects and a poet. She was commonly cited in the late eighteenth century as an example of the virtuous literary woman.

George Savile, Marquis of Halifax (1.1): (1633–95) a favourite of Charles II and moderate Whig, he was one of the main instigators of the 'Glorious Revolution' of 1688 which brought William and Mary to the throne.

Mary Scott (4.17): (fl.1744–88) poet. She is known mainly through *The Female Advocate* and her correspondence with Anna Seward. She was a friend of Helen Maria Williams, and an admirer of Catherine Macaulay.

Priscilla Wakefield (3.8): (1751–1832) Quaker philanthropist and prolific writer on education, who began writing to support her family. Her works are mainly textbooks and books of moral instruction for children and parents, in line with her practical educational interests.

Wetenhall Wilkes (1.3): (d.1751) Protestant divine who also wrote *An Essay on the Pleasures and Advantages of Female Literature* (1741).

Mary Wollstonecraft (1.7, 3.4): (1759–97) feminist, writer on education and politics, and novelist, she was a member of radical circles in the early 1790s and a friend of William Godwin whom she later married. She died of puerperal fever following the birth of her daughter Mary (Shelley). She is best known for her *Vindication of the Rights of Woman* (1792), an application of libertarian principles inspired by the French Revolution to the position of women. This followed *A Vindication of the Rights of Men* (1790), a reply to Burke's *Reflections on the Revolution in France*. Her other works include novels – *Mary, A Fiction* (1788) and *Maria, or the Wrongs of Woman* (1797) – and *Letters Written during a Short Residence in Sweden Norway and Denmark* (1796). All her works manifest an interesting tension between the discourses of rationalism and sensibility.

SELECTED BIBLIOGRAPHY

Historical studies

Bridenthal, Renate and Koonz, Claudia (eds), *Becoming Visible: Women in European History* (Boston: Houghton Mifflin, 1977)

Boucé, Paul-Gabriel (ed.), *Sexuality in Eighteenth Century Britain* (Manchester: Manchester University Press, 1982)

Charles, Lindsey and Duffin, Lorna (eds), *Women and Work in Pre-Industrial England* (London: Croom Helm, 1985)

Clark, Alice, *Working Life of Women in the Seventeenth Century* (1919; rpt. London: Cass, 1968)

Dickinson, H. T., *Liberty and Property: Political Ideology in Eighteenth Century Britain* (London: Methuen, 1977)

Foucault, Michel, *The History of Sexuality*, Vol. I (1976; Harmondsworth: Penguin, 1981)

Hill, Bridget (ed.), *Eighteenth-Century Women: An Anthology* (London: Allen & Unwin, 1984)

—— *The First English Feminist: 'Reflections on Marriage' and other writings by Mary Astell* (Aldershot: Gower/Maurice Temple Smith, 1986)

Kelly, Joan, *Women, History, and Theory: The Essays of Joan Kelly* (Chicago and London: University of Chicago Press, 1986)

Pinchbeck, Ivy, *Women Workers and the Industrial Revolution 1750–1850* (1930; rpt. London: Virago, 1981)

Plumb, J. H., *England in the Eighteenth Century* (Harmondsworth: Penguin, 1950)

Porter, Roy, *English Society in the Eighteenth Century* (Harmondsworth: Penguin, 1982)

Reynolds, Myra, *The Learned Lady in England 1650–1760* (Boston and New York: Houghton Mifflin, 1920)

Smith, Hilda L., *Reason's Disciples: Seventeenth Century English Feminists* (Urbana and London: University of Illinois Press, 1982)

Stone, Lawrence, *The Family, Sex and Marriage in England 1500–1800* (1977; abridged edn, Harmondsworth: Penguin, 1979)

Literary studies

Adburgham, Alison, *Women in Print: Writing Women and Women's Magazines from the Restoration to the Accession of Victoria* (London: Allen & Unwin, 1972)

Armstrong, Nancy, *Desire and Domestic Fiction: A Political History of the Novel* (Oxford: Oxford University Press, 1987)

—— and Tennenhouse, Leonard (eds), *The Ideology of Conduct: Essays on Literature and the History of Sexuality* (London and New York: Methuen, 1987)

Brown, Laura and Nussbaum, Felicity (eds), *The New Eighteenth Century: Theory Politics English Literature* (New York and London: Methuen, 1987)

Browne, Alice, *The Eighteenth Century Feminist Mind* (Brighton: Harvester, 1987)

Castle, Terry, *Masquerade and Civilization: The Carnivalesque in Eighteenth Century English Culture and Fiction* (London: Methuen, 1986)

Hagstrum, Jean, *Sex and Sensibility: Ideal and Erotic Love from Milton to Mozart* (Chicago and London: Chicago University Press, 1980)

Lovell, Terry, *Consuming Fiction* (London: Verso, 1987)

Mahl, Mary and Koon, Helen (eds) *The Female Spectator: English Women Writers Before 1800* (Bloomington and London: Indiana University Press, 1977)

Miller, Nancy K., *The Heroine's Text: Readings in the French and English Novel 1722–1782* (New York: Columbia University Press, 1980)

Nussbaum, Felicity, *The Brink of all We Hate: English Satires on Women 1660–1750* (Lexington, Kentucky: University of Kentucky Press, 1984)

Perry, Ruth, *Women, Letters, and the Novel* (New York: AMS Press, 1980)

—— *The Celebrated Mary Astell: An Early English Feminist* (Chicago and London: University of Chicago Press, 1986)

Poovey, Mary, *The Proper Lady and the Woman Writer: Ideology as Style in the Works of Mary Wollstonecraft, Mary Shelley, and Jane Austen* (Chicago: University of Chicago Press, 1984)

Rogers, Katharine, *Feminism in Eighteenth Century England* (Brighton: Harvester, 1982)

Schofield, Mary Anne and Macheski, Cecilia, *Fetter'd or Free? British Women Novelists, 1670–1815* (Athens, Ohio and London: Ohio University Press, 1986)

Shevelow, Kathryn, *Women and Print Culture: The Construction of Femininity in the Early Periodical* (London: Routledge, 1989)

Spacks, Patricia Meyer, *Imagining a Self: Autobiography and the Novel in Eighteenth Century England* (Cambridge, Mass.: Harvard University Press, 1976)

Spencer, Jane, *The Rise of the Woman Novelist* (Oxford: Blackwell, 1986)

Taylor, John Tinnon, *Early Opposition to the English Novel: The Popular Reaction from 1760 to 1830* (New York: King's Crown Press, 1943)

Todd, Janet (ed.), *A Dictionary of British and American Women Writers 1650–1800* (London: Methuen, 1984)
—— *Sensibility: An Introduction* (London and New York: Methuen, 1986)
—— *The Sign of Angellica: Women, Writing and Fiction 1650–1800* (London: Virago, 1989)

INDEX

(Authors whose work is included in the anthology appear in the index only when they are mentioned in other texts.)